CUTTING THE BODY

THE BODY, IN THEORY   Histories of Cultural Materialism

CUTTING THE BODY

Representing Woman in
Baudelaire's Poetry,
Truffaut's Cinema, and
Freud's Psychoanalysis

Eliane DalMolin

Ann Arbor

THE UNIVERSITY OF MICHIGAN PRESS

Copyright © by the University of Michigan 2000
All rights reserved
Published in the United States of America by
The University of Michigan Press
Manufactured in the United States of America
⊚ Printed on acid-free paper

2003   2002   2001   2000   4   3   2   1

*A CIP catalog record for this book is available
from the British Library.*

Library of Congress Cataloging-in-Publication Data

DalMolin, Eliane Francoise.
    Cutting the body : representing woman in Baudelaire's poetry,
Truffaut's cinema, and Freud's psychoanalysis / Eliane DalMolin.
       p.   cm. — (The body, in theory)
    Includes bibliographical references and index.
    ISBN 0-472-11073-X (alk. paper)
    1. Baudelaire, Charles, 1821–1867—Criticism and
interpretation.   2. Truffaut, François—Criticism and
interpretation.   3. Freud, Sigmund, 1856–1939.   4. Body,
Human—Symbolic aspects.   5. Woman (Philosophy)   I. Title.
II. Series.
PQ2191.Z5 D23   2000
841'.8—dc21   99-050860

To Andrew

Preface

"Cut," je tournais mon regard vers lui pour voir s'il était content.
("Cut," I turned around and looked at him to see if he was
happy.)
    —François Truffaut, "En Tournant pour Spielberg," *Le Plaisir des yeux*

Nous pouvons couper où nous voulons, moi ma rêverie, vous le
manuscrit, le lecteur sa lecture.
(We can cut wherever we want, I my reverie, you the manuscript,
the reader his reading.)
    —Charles Baudelaire, "A Arsène Houssaye," *Le Spleen de Paris*

Couper, c'est penser.
(To cut is to think.)
    —Eugénie Lemoine-Luccioni, *La Robe*

A friend remarked that, whenever asked about the topic of this book, I would always begin by saying what it was not. Not about the enormously popular representation of axed bodies, ripped flesh, slashed throats, hacked limbs, and severed heads; not about Jack the Ripper, Norman Bates, Jeffrey Dahmer, Hannibal Lector; not about finding out why they did it, why they are the way they are. If, however, one wishes to start with an aberration, an anecdotal extreme from the broad history of the contemporary representation of bodies, then perhaps it is about why we, as readers and viewers, feast on these freaks of nature's stories and about our inclination and fascination toward the extraordinary example of a very ordinary symbolic gesture, a cultural sign of creation, acumen, and wisdom: cutting.

    This book is about how poets, filmmakers, and psychoanalysts look upon the woman's body, how they examine it in detail as if dissecting it, at times relishing it, at others anguishing over its fragmentation; ultimately it is about how, by *cutting* woman's body they create and think. More specifically, this book is about how Charles Baudelaire, François Truffaut, and Sigmund Freud, based on their inheritance of lyricism, shaped and perpetuated a cultural understanding of women that they continued to represent in what may be called "late romantic" images, despite their respective innovative talents and influence in bringing about decisive cultural moments: modernism, new wave cinema, and psychoanalysis. Beyond traditional representation, it is also about how they began "cutting" the woman's body in new and unpredictable ways, in private and unwitting fantasies underrunning their *texts,* which we can only now read in postmodern terms of difference, disruption, and fragmentation.

Acknowledgments

I want to thank all my "college" friends for inspiring me to write this book: Adlai, Brigitte, Christine, Eva, Frank, Gretchen, Katrina, Luke, Marvin, Nena, Patrick, Patrice, and William. For their intellectual encouragement, their sustained attention, and full support I want to thank Anne, Nelly, Richard, and Phil. I am grateful for my colleagues and friends at the University of Connecticut for sharing their insights and for cheering me along. There is a special place in my heart for Tim and Roger, first of all for being superb individuals and undying friends and also for reading the manuscript, offering incisive comments, reading the manuscript again, and ultimately making it sound and solid. Thanks to my editor, LeAnn Fields, for her total confidence, enthusiasm, and continuous interest in the project. Thanks to Raymonde for strength and love. Thanks to Sophie and Paul for the laughter. And thanks to Andrew, absolutely.

Contents

Introduction

> The first act is always already a cut: one must cut into the magma
> to beget form. Before the cut, there is nothing, after there is only
> a shape, a line, and an unassimilable remnant.
> —Eugénie Lemoine Luccioni, *La Robe*

Preschool children are often asked by their educators to delineate forms by cutting shapes into blank pieces of paper. For them cutting means creating, making something out of nothing with a simple incision guided by the exploratory thrust of their sharp imagination. The novelty of cutting paper shapes soon wears off, however, while the power invested in the act of cutting remains untouched. Indeed, driven by a cutting frenzy, children often turn the creative scissors on their own body and begin to snip hair, nails, and eventually skin, which usually serves as an instant deterrent, alerting them to the pain associated with cutting the body. While they may never again touch their body with actual shears, the act of cutting becomes doubly invested as creative and destructive.

Much the same symbolic meaning applies to the act of "cutting" when performed by the poet, the filmmaker, and the psychoanalyst, an act that first and foremost defines their respective work: the lyric poet shapes language into verses; the filmmaker engages his creation by cutting, first, the prosaic text into a suitable scenario—a practice technically called *découpage* in French, literally a "cut-out," or shooting script—and, second, the filmstrip in the cutting room while editing his work; on a more symbolic level the psychoanalyst singles out and identifies traumas and symptoms out of the analysand's linguistic flow during the "talking cure." His ability to sort out the patient's language may be compared to an act of cutting through the analysand's abundant and undifferentiated verbal production. Besides being a conceivable common practice for poets, filmmakers, and analysts, cutting is more notably a symbolic act of creation and destruction performed by their male subjects on the female bodies they adore and abhor at the same time. Three brief examples taken from the works of nineteenth-century poet Charles Baudelaire,[1] new wave filmmaker François Truffaut,[2] and psychoanalyst Sigmund Freud,[3] pioneer of the unprecedented and enduring theories of the unconscious and human sexuality, will be helpful in establishing a first paradigm for the troubling, yet unshakable, relationship existing between the male cutter and the cut-up female body. In poems such as "The Hair," "The Dancing Serpent," "The Beautiful Ship," "To a Red-haired Beggar," "To a Passer-by," "Allegory," to name only a few, Baudelaire scans the female body with the precision of a laser beam splicing her symbolic flesh. In the majority of his films Truffaut's male characters fancy specific parts of the female body: legs, face, often breasts, all appearing cut off from the women's full body by the screen or other framing device. In Freud's infamous castration fable the little boy fears losing his penis as he interprets sexual differences in terms of mutilation of his mother's body.

Already at first glance it then appears essential to suggest that, in order to understand the full extent of Baudelaire, Truffaut, and Freud's work, in order to recognize the thrust behind all their representations of the female body, one cannot neglect to analyze the profound implications of the act of cutting. It is thus in the rich realm of possibilities and interpretations harbored by such a claim that I undertake here a study of the symbolic cutting of the body performed by Baudelaire, Truffaut, Freud, and the male subject in their work, of the relationship between written and filmic gestures and the primal experiences of the body: unerasable experiences of corporeal separation and cutting. This study examines the ways in which the act of cutting operates in the fields of castration, fetishism, decapitation, and birth, four instances of creation and destruction marking first the body and then the language embodying such cuts. Because cutting the body is an essential process by which we apprehend most representations of the human form, it becomes crucial to define the terms of its executions, about which Derrida writes that "they come under the 'red blade of the knife.' "[4] The cut Derrida performs is interpretative, while the artist's is creative; the blade of his "knife" is simultaneously "deciding" and "decided." Derrida would say that, no matter where you cut and no matter the type of cutter you are, with each cut a decision is being made, willingly or not.

Following the Derridian precept of the decisive nature of the cut, I propose my own cut—my decision to address the question of the cut on the body from a woman's point of view, even if my own "cutting" remains primarily inspired by readings of other interpretative (male) cutters such as Derrida, Barthes, and Lacan and primary cutters such as Baudelaire, Truffaut, and Freud. My decision to investigate the question of body cuts stems from a feminist and subversive ambition to reformulate questions of gender and identity traditionally associated with masculine representation of the female body. Indeed, if it is true that only men can account for the inner force of their desire, when this desire applies to representations of women, it may be true that only women—or "enlightened" men—can account for the perverse process that produces the breaking up of the female body. My present effort to problematize the pleasure-laden male desire that represents women skillfully cut, exploded, disseminated, by the touch of a pen, a camera, and a theory represents a feminine desire to destabilize the overbearing male subject in poetry, cinema, and psychoanalysis. Following Leo Bersani, who illuminates the connection between creation and "the loss of virility"[5] in Baudelaire's poetry, Anne Gillain, who clearly identifies the omnipresent maternal component in Truffaut's films,[6] and Naomi Schor, who demonstrates that Freud's "encoded femininity"[7] may be found in the "detail," as opposed to the male constructed fragment, I suggest that, if Baudelaire, Truffaut, and Freud engage in the perverse and often sadistic acts of cutting the female body, it is precisely to preserve their own repressed femininity. In fact, male desire will often emerge from my readings traversed by an active but sublimated feminine desire. If, in the first part of the book (chaps. 1 and 2) I argue that the initial male instinct to cut up the female body is a defense mechanism organized against what is perceived as the female power to fascinate and even entrap men who fall under woman's charms, this distinction loses its grip in the second part (chaps. 3 and 4), in which a tendency toward the feminine and the maternal blurs the vision of the male subject, whose desire to cut up the female body is displaced by a desire to reorganize the pieces into a new reconstructed body, recalling the vanished symbiosis with the original body, the vanished plenitude.

What the male artist and analyst do not comprehend about femininity, about woman's enigmatic self, her sublime beauty, her magic appearance, her reproductive body—what, in other words, they cannot assimilate—is cast as dangerously alluring, simultaneously appealing and repelling, engaging and enraging. As Baudelaire, Truffaut, and Freud cut into the magma of the female body, their initial objective is to break her defiant and beautiful body, to control and rechannel her energy to fit their male desire. Subsequently, however, this attempt is caught in a formidable paradox: in a final and decisive move, the poet, the filmmaker, and the analyst ostensibly act against their initial breaking of woman's body and attempt to capture the totality of her fragmented image. Traditional male desire thus appears to transcend fragmentation in order to be reunited with the entire female shape. Indeed, when Baudelaire, Truffaut, and Freud represent woman as a cut-up body, their exploration of male desire does not end with the fragmented pieces of that body but strives toward the return to her full form, to the *jouissance* of her uninterrupted body, to a paradoxical unity of fragments. The cut is *decisive* in fragmenting the female body, but it is *decided* by the artist's repressed desire to undo fragmentation and thus recover the pre-cut body. Such a desire remains true to its Lacanian definition as an impossible desire, since the pre-cut body can never be retrieved in its initial form but will at best become the full image of a repaired body, a freakish reassembled body bearing the scars of fragmentation. The female body in Baudelaire's poetry, Truffaut's cinema, and Freud's theory is thus an odd representation marked successively by the slashing, the sundering, and finally the suturing effects of male desire.

I am particularly interested in the suturing gesture that characterizes the final destination of male desire in the representation of the female body because it simultaneously contains and subverts the notion of the cut and that of the ensuing fragmentation. Indeed, the suture indicates the place where the cut was first administered, a critical point of erotic occurrence that must be investigated to understand the motivation behind the slashing impulse of masculine desire; it also indicates the trauma of separation that immediately follows the act of cutting as it eventually leaves the female body disarticulated and thus unfit for traditional male aesthetic and erotic yearning for totalizing pleasures. Beyond and between the cut and the fragment, the suture, a poststructuralist concept developed by Jacques-Alain Miller, "takes the place of" the void left by their passage.[8] The suture, as the third element destabilizing the binary oppositions believed to constitute the crucial models of signification in language and culture, has enjoyed many different forms in our postmodern discourse: it is what French psychoanalyst and cultural theoretician François Baudry calls a line, an "articulation,"[9] between two separate regions, a third signpost that the drunk hits while trying to go between the two posts that his impaired vision places in front of him; it is what Derrida calls "la brisure," a term borrowed from carpentry and meaning both the "breach" and the "joint" between two pieces of wood, "the hinge" standing in place of the break left by "the presence of the present," articulating its impossible representation and its projection into discourse;[10] it is the "skin" appearing and disappearing between the two flaps of a gaping garment for Barthes, who chooses this image to illuminate the place of erotic desire in the writing and reading of all texts.[11] Simply put, suture is the constant reminder that a decisive cut has been made, that a wound has been inflicted on the body; it is also symptomatic and therapeutic for the subject's trauma of separation resulting from the cut; it refers a dramatic rupture while promising healing.

In *Dissemination* Derrida explains the kind of "explosion" produced by the advent of the cut, which he sees as "a blow which parcels the seed / semen while projecting it."[12] The cut is not an origin, an incision of which the apparent singularity determines a unique and fatal fait accompli; quite to the contrary, it impels "germination," a surge of the multiplicity launched by the decision to cut. Proposing an unorthodox analogy between the symbolic realm of language and the biological realm of fertilization, Derrida suggests that in all discursive and textual forms as well as in actual inseminations "each term is a germ, and each germ is a term. The term engenders while proliferating" (338). While the outcome of such a strong analogy illuminates the thesis that the cut begets or inseminates while disseminating, it also generates a feeling of mutual dependency between language and body. The body then appears as the imperative metaphor upon which the cut is performed in order to produce multiple meanings and signs. For Derrida the body is intimately linked to the understanding of the processes of dissemination; it engenders the phenomenon of dissemination. Psychoanalyst and literary critic Didier Anzieu confirms the crucial interaction between body and language, as he invites us to think of the body as "a surface of inscription for arousal,"[13] a skin consumed by its sensitivity to the touch and eagerly awaiting the creative and explosive cut of all artists and writers. The body may then be associated with the canvas, the music sheet, the stage, the screen, and the blank page, all vibrant superstrata inviting the artist's decision. On impact the cut becomes instantly the line separating the bodily surface, exploding its materiality into decisive parts, like a symbolic lock of hair, a fetishized leg, a castrated sex, even if these partial objects generate a kind of anguish in view of what was lost in the transaction—the cut itself and the remnant of the carved-up surface—rather than complete satisfaction for their initiators. In his (psycho)analysis of the object Baudry determines from the start the importance of the cut in the formation of the object, but, paradoxically, he also notes its self-effacing quality, its concrete disappearance (leaving no apparent trace of its passage) when it engenders the line. Baudry writes that the cut is always already past and thus can only be signified as a fantasy: "a fantasy of cutting says nothing about the implementation of the cut itself."[14] Baudry adds that beyond fantasies of cutting, sadistic or perverse desire to groove the body, the artist remains bound to the outcome of a primary cut that ultimately brings forth his oeuvre.

The investigation of "primary cuts" undertaken here also necessitates a preliminary discussion of the way in which poetry, cinema, and psychoanalysis may be established as a common ground to analyze images of fragmented bodies. This book represents an effort to understand if, how, and where poetry, cinema, and psychoanalysis meet in spite of the historical gap and the personal artistic/scientific allegiances separating Baudelaire, Truffaut, and Freud and their respective work. My position is that Baudelaire's poetry, Truffaut's cinema, and Freud's psychoanalysis intersect and that their point of convergence can be identified even though their respective fields appear to accentuate their incongruity rather than their possible similarities.

Against the odds, poetry, cinema, and psychoanalysis appear to converge, if only by their common interest in the image: poetry and cinema are image makers, while, in addition to the production of images, psychoanalysis also studies their inner configuration, the psychical structures behind their formation. I propose to study the development of images in the three fields at hand and, particularly, to see how the study of images in poetry, cinema, and psychoanalysis may in fact become inseparable under the probing eye of the psychoanalyst. A rapid look into the way poetry, cinema, and psychoanalysis share similarities will soon lead us into considering psychoanalysis itself as the most efficient way to analyze the three disciplines' overlapping concern with the concept of imagistic representation.

As a point of departure for establishing the most basic connections between poetry, cinema, and psychoanalysis, dictionary definitions[15] already suggest that the three fields are grounded in a world of images organized by poetic language, cinematic motion, and mental processes. Poetry is defined as the art of composing verses using an imaginative and rhythmical language; cinema, derived from the Greek word *Kinema,* meaning "motion," as the art of composing motion pictures; psychoanalysis, as the investigation of mental activities and, as Freud argues, an "interpretative Art"[16] operating on manifestations of the unconscious like dreams that present to the subject condensed and displaced "visual pictures" (237) to be interpreted by the analyst. It appears, then, that, from the general definition of poetry, cinema, and psychoanalysis, the idea of the image (imaginative language, motion pictures, and distorted visual pictures) emerges as the undeniable point of intersection.[17] The concept of the image relies as much on the powers of the imagination (imaginative language) as on the powers of motion (motion pictures) and on the powers and intensity of mental processes involved in the construction of distorted visual images. Understanding the image in terms of motion, imagination, and mental processes represents what Cocteau, in his film *Le Testament d'Orphée,* understands as the hypnotizing effects of cinema. In the introduction to the printed script of that film Cocteau claims that it is "the screen's role to exercise a sort of hypnotism on the spectators, and to allow a great number of people to dream the same dream."[18] The film "moves" the spectators into a world of unconscious images similar to a world of dreams. In order to apprehend the process by which the fusion between cinema, poetry, and psychoanalysis may be achieved through the work of the unconscious and dreams, I will have recourse to the mediation of psychoanalysis as "an interpretative art," one that explores repressed and latent psychical manifestations of the human mind in dreams, fantasies, reveries, and images. Cinema and poetry benefit from psychoanalytic discourse just as psychoanalysis benefits from the study of poetry and cinema. Indeed, psychoanalysis offers more than a mere procedure through which to read films and poems; in this study it also becomes the object of analysis in conjunction with film and poetry.

In order to establish a possible confluence between poetry, cinema, and psychoanalysis, I will first investigate the passage of bodily images from the real world to the dreamworld and vice versa. In Truffaut's cinema, Baudelaire's poetry, and Freud's analyses the first bodily image that comes to mind as an image traveling from reality to dreams, into a world of male fantasy, is the image of woman, at times realistic, at others idealistic, and sometimes between the two, offering a fantasmatic mélange. It is this "in-between" that I propose to investigate, and that I call a cut, separating and binding at the same time, the *suturing* referred to previously, separating the image of reality from the dreamlike image while also evoking the phantasmatic passage conjoining poetry, cinema, and psychoanalysis. As modern "creators," Baudelaire, Freud, and Truffaut participate in this crucial movement that, in a certain alchemical manner, transforms the ugly into the beautiful, the evil into the good, the reality into the fiction, the body into a fantasy, without, however, abandoning the former fragment for the latter but, rather, incorporating their respective aspects into an exploded and modern view of woman in which ugly and beautiful, good and evil, reality and fiction, body and fantasy, cohabit, share features, thus creating a third entity with borrowed characteristics: a "flower of evil," a fictitious or lyrical reality, a phantasmatic body.

In his poem "To a Passer-by" Baudelaire evokes both the devastating passage of a woman in the street and her promise of a possible union in a distant eternity. In the film *Small Change* Truffaut presents two opposite images of the mother, and his camera transports us from the horror of one to the beauty of the other, from Julien's abusive and begrimed mother living in squalid conditions to Patrick's friend's mother, the loving and sensual woman he secretly admires. Finally, in 1895 Freud is shocked as he realizes that his patient Emma Eckstein's bleeding is not "hysterical," as he had diagnosed, but the result of an advanced infection of the nasal cavity due to a negligent operation performed by Fliess, his rhinologist friend. Emma's abundant bleeding marked Freud so deeply that on the night of July 23, 1895, as he so accurately reported in a letter to Fliess, he had a memorable dream in which fragments of Emma's incident became an essential part of the specimen dream known as "Irma's injection," the central dream in his acclaimed 1900 study *The Interpretation of Dreams*. Here, again, Emma's affliction became absorbed into Freud's own unconscious as Irma's injection, and it also became part of the very structure of the "dreamwork." Moving from reality to dream, from the harshness of everyday life to the lyrical world of the mind, from the unbearable and impossible sight of the past and/or present woman to her "futuristic" reconstructed beauty, her promises of eternal life and her mysterious body, this constant fluctuation between opposite representations of women retains the decisive principle inscribed in its own flow, dragging in its passage elements of the real into the constructed world of fantasies. In my analysis of Baudelaire's poetry, Truffaut's cinema, and Freud's psychoanalysis I will explore such transformation of, passage between, and explosion of images of women.

It is thus obvious that the terms of this investigation are not dependent upon a particular time in history to "prove" a theory on the "fruitful meeting" of poetry, cinema, and psychoanalysis. Baudelaire's, Truffaut's, and Freud's work share what one is tempted to call a timeless link, an "artistic" vision of women that binds them, despite the apparently unrelated nature of their respective domains. But how conceptually distant is Baudelaire from cinema, Truffaut from poetry, and Freud from either discipline? Historically, the closest Baudelaire came to any aspect of the cinema is through his involuntary and unwelcomed exposure to photography, which he excoriated vehemently as the "the shelter for all failed painters, too untalented or too lazy to finish their preliminary studies" (2:618). A great admirer of paintings, etchings, and drawings, Baudelaire finds it impossible to rank photography—a small and insignificant part of a larger category that he calls the "Industry"—among the arts because, according to his view, it involves little valuable effort on the part of the photographer and requires no creative skills, since it seeks the exact reproduction of nature that Baudelaire forcibly detests. According to him, photography destroys the artist, who now wishes to represent what he sees, not what he dreams about. Baudelaire sees photography as the unsolicited invader of "the impalpable and the imaginary" (2:619), particularly infringing upon poetry, in which imagination dominates the scene of writing. If photography must survive the test of modern times—and, indeed, it did more than survive it; it served as a direct agent of and a witness to its accomplishments—Baudelaire suggests that it should become "the humble servant of arts and sciences" (2:618), serve rather than take place among the arts. In a sense Baudelaire would seem the worst candidate for a study on the interrelation of poetry and cinema, since he undeniably refutes photography as an art form and, furthermore, depicts it as a deterrent for all artistic talents, graphic as well as verbal.

While keeping in mind Baudelaire's resistance to photography, it is also important to point to the forces of desire invested in any act of resisting. Resist, not reject. Resist only to a degree, to a point of weakness ready to collapse and bring the resisting individual on the verge of self-abandonment, toward a form of compromised recognition and acceptance of the object of distrust. Indeed, as much as he dislikes photography, Baudelaire does not discard it completely. On the contrary, to him photography constitutes yet another aspect of the "modern," for which he is one of the first true advocates. Indeed, Baudelaire's thoughts on photography appeared in his *Salon of 1859* under the title "The Modern Audience and Photography." And if the title were not explicit enough on the association between modernity and photography, the text also points to the ambivalence between the classic and the modern, between the eternal and the contingent, oppositions defining the paradox of modernity for Baudelaire, as he writes in his often-cited article on "Modernity" in *The Painter of Modern Life*.[19] Maintaining a balance between the two elements of these oppositions, creating a possible discourse between apparently contradictory notions, these are the foundations of modernity that Baudelaire articulates so vigorously. What sets the author of *The Flowers of Evil* against photography, however, is that it defaces the vital notion of the "fugitive" aspect of modern art. According to Baudelaire, the fugitive is by nature not meant to be fixed on a timeless metal plate. Yet photography captures rather than beholds that brief moment of intensity when all elements converge into what German aesthetic philosopher Gotthold Lessing calls the "pregnant moment,"[20] or what post-structuralist psychoanalyst Jacques Lacan describes as the moment of *jouissance*.[21] This intense moment cannot be preserved in a single photographic shot, only the converging elements—characters, decor, lights, colors—may be represented to recall the point of convergence that in itself remains as evanescent as the unknown woman passerby who touched the soul of the poet before disappearing forever in the urban crowd in Baudelaire's poem "To a Passer-by" (1:92–93). Then, by reproducing the environment that brought and keeps bringing such fugacious intensity so close to the artist, photography may be said to create the image of a search for *jouissance* but not reproduce its actual moment of occurrence, the impossible capture of its moment of impact.

In that sense photography shares many of its objectives with a traditional view of cinema that pursues the same search for *jouissance* through a series of carefully composed images moving toward the accomplishment of an action, a narrative moment, a visual episode aiming at bringing closure to a segment of the film before advancing in the story and thus partially satisfy-ing the viewer's pleasure. Cinema, in fact, reproduces the approach to a pos-sible coincidence of all the components of *jouissance* by setting in motion objects and subjects pursuing distant instances of narrative and visual fulfillment according to the structure established by the mise-en-scène. How well the approach is conducted by the director often determines the success of the film. In his definition of *modernity* Baudelaire takes such an approach toward the concept of modernity, whose center he may contemplate but not attain. In that sense Baudelaire's approach to understanding the modern is close to the process of creating a film. Like the filmmaker who proceeds through mise-en-scène, Baudelaire puts on the "set" of modernity "mod-ern" elements such as photography, carriages, women, garments, and makeup, thus creating a propitious environment for the elaboration of the idea of the modern, a "feeling" for modernity, without firmly establishing its concept. He thus creates a different yet fascinating image of modernity conceived like a film, or, rather, prefiguring what Stanley Cavell calls "cine-matic obsessions,"[22] strong visual motifs that can never fully satiate man's scopophilic desire to see women's bodies, cosmetic paraphernalia, gar-ments, and photographs, to name only those elements deemed modern by Baudelaire and that I will further examine in this study.

Having glimpsed the possible connections between Baudelaire's art criti-cism and the art of cinema in general, my task remains to see if the same can be claimed for his poetry. Can his poems be approached from a cinematic vantage point, from the study of some cinematic motifs such as women and their garments, and from the study of some cinematic components such as photography? Can we enrich and eventually enlarge the study of poetry by approaching it like a film? And, finally, why choose Truffaut's films when other films and filmmakers seem more appropriate for such an endeavor? For example, surrealist films such as Man Ray's 1927 *The Starfish* or Buñuel's 1929 *An Andalusian Dog* are closely related to the Baudelairean motifs just mentioned and to poetry in general. Another possibility is the highly metaphorical cinema of Jean-Luc Godard, which would provide an analogical counterpart to Baudelaire's symbolist poetry. In addition, Godard's innovative uses of techniques such as the jump-cut would also work well with Baudelaire's experimentation with poetic forms. The possible rapprochement between Baudelaire and Godard strikes us as a rich and promising one, one that would lead our analysis into an interesting observation of parallel effects used by both artists sharing a similar passion for music, painting, and literature. However fitting those filmmakers appear for the study at hand, I have selected a less *natural* association between Baudelaire and Truffaut and thus based my study on what I would like to qualify, paraphrasing Stephen Spielberg a "close encounter of *a different kind*."[23] This encounter introduces François Truffaut, a paradoxical choice, considering that he has no apparent association with poetry other than what some see as a recurrent trait of sentimentality and nostalgia, characteristics often affiliated with lyric poetry.[24]

It cannot be denied that Truffaut has consistently displayed a degree of sentimentality in his films, a tender approach to human relationships that he exploits dramatically as a fragile component of many of his characters always on the brink of emotional turmoil. This sentimental edge to his films cannot be totally ignored especially when considering the poetic quality of his work; it seems insufficient, however, to justify his possible affiliation with a type of poetry conceived as the sole expression of the poet's despair. Lyric poetry is more than the sonorous echo of a tormented soul; it is also the verbal representation of the poet's imagination, of his fantasies, and of his ideas. As a mode of representation, poetry is a process that must be analyzed in conjunction with the images it processes. In the study of poetry its mechanics are as significant as the images it produces. Truffaut may be said to produce poetic films at two levels: in their visual impact as well as in their technical designs. A film like *Day for Night* (1973), which tells the story of how a film is made, argues strongly in favor of Truffaut's desire to reveal the inner workings of the filmic process in the same nostalgic and personal tone that characterizes his cinema. In the film poetry is present visually in the representation of the incurably romantic, passionate, and moody Alphonse; it is also present formally in the representation of all the technical processes involved in the making of a film, what might be called a poetics of film.

In addition, literature is an integral part of Truffaut's films;[25] references to nineteenth-century writers such as Balzac and Zola are numerous, and, broadly speaking, references to books, reading, and writing consistently occupy a privileged place in all his films. Still, clear references to poets and poetry are scant, and mentions of Baudelaire are limited to aphorisms extracted from his personal journals and spoken by the two main male char-

acters in the 1961 *Jules and Jim,* in which the two quote Baudelaire's journal on the subject of woman: "Woman is natural and, therefore, abominable" (1:677); and "I have always wondered why women were allowed in
churches. What conversation can they possibly have with God?" (1:693).
Except for these direct references to Baudelaire reflecting Jules's and Jim's
frustrations with woman and femininity, Baudelaire, like all other poets, is
absent from the film's narrative.

Yet, despite the absence of poetry as a direct representation in his films,
Truffaut takes many his idiosyncrasies from his reading of poetry. For
example, he openly confirms his identification with poetry when he praises
the writing of French love poet Jacques Audiberti and, more specifically,
with Audiberti's poetic celebration of women: "For Audiberti, woman is
magical, supreme. I think about him when filming a man, about his work
when filming a woman."[26] It is important to notice Truffaut's intention to
put Audiberti's lyricism on screen and specifically the way his lyricism
inspired Truffaut's fetishism on the screen: "I also think of him when I see a
beautiful pair of legs passing in the street, of what he would have said about
them" (130). Truffaut's lyric cinema is, in his own words, inspired by the
poet's perception and distortion of woman's body.

On the particular subject of woman Truffaut is never far from Baudelaire's poetics. In fact, his perception of women as source of great pleasure
and pain is reminiscent of Baudelaire's own ambivalent views, sometimes
beautiful like statues and lovable like cats, often mysterious like Sphinxes
and diabolical like vampires, but always evanescent like passersby. Their
fugitive nature leads the distressed poet to attempt to capture them in writing. Truffaut's male characters seem to offer a similar tormented image of
themselves when in the presence of mysterious and beautiful women like
Catherine in *Jules and Jim,* diabolical like Julie Kholer in *The Bride Wore
Black* (1967), and "magic" like Julie Baker in *Day for Night* (1973). By analyzing representations of women in Truffaut's films and Baudelaire's poems,
I will demonstrate that female representations are more than mere poetic
and filmic characters. Instead, they force the poet and the filmmaker into the
comm(-)on(e)[27] investigation of fantasies such as castration, fetishism,
decapitation, and birth, for which the medium of poetry and cinema is particularly well suited and for which psychoanalysis is the primary method of
inquiry.

In considering questions and representations of castration, fetishism,
decapitation, and birth, I also open this study to the direct connection that
psychoanalysis shares with the other two art forms and must come to Freud
and his association with poetry and cinema. To begin with, there is Freud's

often-repeated recourse to "poetry" to illustrate a point. For example, in the introduction of his 1932 essay "Femininity,"[28] he chooses to open the question of the historical opacity and complexity of femininity by quoting a few lines from "Nordsee" by the German poet Heinrich Heine: "Heads in hieroglyphic bonnets, / Heads in turbans and black birettas, heads in wigs and thousand other / Wretched, sweating heads of humans." These heads, representing men from different times, cultures, and social classes, appear in rapid succession, as if randomly decapitated by the poet's gaze. Their morbid appearances demonstrate the fatal end of men who have searched in vain for an answer to the riddle of femininity; their decapitation echoes the myth of the decapitated Medusa, which Freud reinterpreted in his 1922 note on "Medusa's head" as a displaced act of cutting, which Freud claims satisfies male fear of castration. It is this same fear of castration that Freud reiterates as a warning against the dangerous appeal of woman to all men facing the mystery of her sexuality (including himself, whose scientific research on femininity remains "fragmentary and incomplete," as he himself admits, or even "laments," in the conclusion to his essay on "Femininity"). As he closes the subject of femininity and admits that woman remains an unfamiliar subject in his work, even after a lifetime devoted to understanding the inner structure of the human psyche, male or/and female, he also confesses that only women and poets may be able to deal with the complex subject of femininity.

If Freud's instinct regarding the poet's closeness to the female psyche is right, if, like him, we believe that the poet possesses the key to the world of femininity because of his ability to retrieve the female inside him, the hidden secret to his creativity, then we must conclude that Freud's relinquishing the mystery of femininity to poets is also a way of admitting that, unlike them, he has no access to the realm of woman, either because of his fear of admitting his own affinity with the feminine or of his dissociation from the poet's artistic ability. In short, there seems to be no poetry in Freud. A rapid overview of his 1908 essay "The Relation of the Poet to Day-Dreaming" will confirm, in spite of its title, the absence of poetic matter in his work. Indeed, if this piece appears at first to suggest the possible rapport between poetry and mental processes like fantasies, Freud is quick to dismiss our expectations as he remains unable to define the terms of the equation he sets out to solve, namely, how the poet—by way of emotional transformation and artistic talent—produces a written act of his own fantasy, of which Freud cannot even speculate the origins and the formulation. Freud is only able to consider a parallel between writer's work and child's play, as he compares the serious imaginative investment of the child in his playing with the secret fantasies shaping the poet's writing. Besides that rapprochement, Freud has little to say about the imaginative processes involved in any act of writing. Further in the essay it also becomes clear that the poets announced in his title are in fact writers of fiction—Zola, for example. To Freud the distinction between prose and poetry is completely blurred and condensed to a generic "art of fiction." Here again, contrary to what could be expected from the heralding title, there are no poets to be found, only a pretext to develop a theory on fantasies in which we will find, beyond Freud himself, strong resonances in the realm of cinema.

Freud's indirect association with cinema is indeed addressed through questions of fantasies as demonstrated by French psychoanalysts Laplanche and Pontalis. Of the substantial number of psychoanalytical studies made on the subject of fantasies, their expanded definition of original fantasies and fantasies of origins in their 1985 *Fantasme originaire, fantasmes des origines, origines du fantasme*[29] remains one of the most important and useful theoretical steps toward the understanding of the different psychic processes at work in the elaboration of fantasies. Laplanche and Pontalis restore the prominence of Freud's theory on fantasies as they occur in the earliest phase of sexual development, during the period of autoerotism, and as they continue to operate, in later sexual life, following similar configurations. The two psychoanalysts reveal the way in which the fantasy is carried out in what they call a "multiple entry scenario" (55–63), in which the subject may choose to play any role in the provided script, whether the main role or any secondary roles, and even become the main participant in the actual mise-en-scène within the given setting predicated by the scene. Laplanche and Pontalis's theoretical vision on the formation of the fantasy and the place of the subject in its configuration is heavily dependent upon an understanding of cinema, if only because of the vocabulary they borrow from the lexicon of filmmaking. They displace active elements of cinema from their ordinary and expected environment to the world of the human psyche in which they become associated with the construction of fantasies. Indeed, Laplanche and Pontalis conclude their study by confirming that fantasies are not the object of desire but *"mise-en-scènes of desire"* (75). To be able to produce desire, the fantasizing subject appears dependent upon the techniques of cinema to bring images of pleasure into a recognizable form he can access through dreams and reveries.

By analyzing fantasies of castration, fetishism, decapitation, and birth in poetry, cinema, and psychoanalysis, I will investigate images of pleasure and pain brought together in a scenario in which the subject moves freely from his role in the action to his role in the mise-en-scène, from playing an active role in the act of cutting prescribed by castration, fetishism, decapitation, and birth to becoming an active agent in the construction of the scenario underlying the scene of cutting. The contribution of Freud's theory on fantasies to examining representations of body cuts found in poetry, cinema, and psychoanalysis is optimal in redefining the subject's primal and multiple role in the production and performance of all poetic, cinematic, and analytical "scenarios" in which cutting means (re)creating.

The first chapter delineates the theoretical parameters within which the cut operates. How do the act of cutting and lyricism become associated? Can the notion of lyricism be extended to encompass the field of cinema? Who is the woman whose body bears the symbolic cuts performed by the poet, the filmmaker, and the psychoanalyst? What is her place in the lyric text? Do female body cuts contribute to the formation of a lyric cinema and a cinematic lyricism? In the second chapter I examine the way in which the image of woman from the Petrarchan lyric tradition emerges as a fragmented body and the extent to which Baudelaire and Truffaut have inherited her fragmented image while constructing their own poetic and filmic representations of her body. In the third chapter I argue that, under the precepts of fetishism, castration, and decapitation, Baudelaire, Truffaut, and Freud (and Lacan after him) perform a figurative dissection of women's bodies. In these works the fragmented female body contributes to the construction of male identity. Finally, in the fourth chapter birth is examined as an instance of body cutting negated by Freud, heavily theorized by Lacan, buried in metaphoric language by Baudelaire, visually repressed and verbally discarded in Truffaut's films. Distraught by the moment and the consequences of birth, forestalled by a culturally inbred fear of separation and pain associated with parturition, the poet, the filmmaker, and the psychoanalyst become unwilling yet engaged actors in a birth scenario that transports them into a repressed maternal fantasy in which they privately thrive and create as "mothers."

Chapter 1

Cutting the Body and Lyricism

She walks, swaying gently from such a slender waist set on generous hips! Her pale pink dress of clinging silk makes a lovely contrast with the darkness of her skin, and molds accurately her long
bust, the curve of her back and her pointed breasts.
—Charles Baudelaire, "The Beautiful Dorothea"

Women's legs are compasses which measure the globe in all directions, giving it its balance and its harmony.
—François Truffaut, *The Man Who Loved Women*

Positing the lyric as a means of exploring the presence and articulation of
woman, body, and language in both poetic and cinematic texts appears to
be a singularly appropriate approach to Charles Baudelaire's poetry and
François Truffaut's cinema, two *bodies* of work in which women are often
represented by means of their poeticized and fragmented bodies. The images
of women produced by Baudelaire and Truffaut are strikingly similar and
both are informed by the poet and the filmmaker's desire to explore the
realm of femininity for which they have developed a lyric form primarily
derived from the fragmented form of the female body. According to
Bertrand Morane, the main male character in *The Man Who Loved
Women*, the world owes its balance and harmony to the rhythmical movement of women's legs, and to the poet of *Paris Spleen*, Dorothea's walk is a
complex and graceful balance between all of her body parts. In both examples the detailed female body plays a major role in bringing the world to
tempo, in capturing its natural measure, while simultaneously devising the
sweet composition of male fantasy. The metrically and metronomically
orchestrated cadence of this fantasy shares a similar concern for movement
and poetry with the notion of the modern lyric, a new form of lyricism,
bound to the "supple and rugged" musical flow of the soul, "the undula-
tions of reveries, the jibes of conscience," as Baudelaire claims in his introduction to *Paris Spleen*.[1] As a way of exploring male fantasies of cutting in

poetry and cinema, this chapter proposes to analyze the inner movement of the lyrical text/image, thus suggesting that the concept of the lyric is closely associated with both textual/visual divisions and the detailing of the female body.

The quantitative presence of women's bodies in lyric poetry cannot be denied. One does not have to look very far into its history in order to find several famous names for these women's bodies in constant display—Petrarch's Laura, D'Aubigné's Diane, Scève's Délie, Ronsard's Hélène, Shakespeare's Dark Lady of the sonnets, Nerval's Sylvie, Adrienne, and Aurélia, as well as Baudelaire's mostly nameless eternal beauties and passing strangers. Woman is the omnipresent figure in lyric poetry, and her body is often represented in pieces, as if the predominant figure at the foundation of lyric poetry were not only feminine but feminine and fragmented, dissected even. It is as a dismembered figure or through figurative dismemberment that woman partakes in all aspects of the lyric from its prosodic forms to its metaphorical imagery.

In reference to prosodic forms, let us consider for an instant poetic terminology. In the French poetic tradition rimes may be either feminine or masculine; the *césure,* a mandatory rhythmical cut in the poetic line, may sometimes, although rarely, be qualified as a feminine cut for which there is no "masculine" cut—there are simply caesuras and feminine caesuras—to counteract its poetic action and meaning. In fact, it seems that these required poetic cuts are not defined according to gender unless they happen to be feminine. A feminine caesura, also called a lyrical cut, is considered an exceptional pause in French poetry because it occurs after a sonorous or accentuated *e* inside the line, throwing the rhythm of poetic language off balance while preserving prosodic uniformity. The feminine caesura has a disquieting effect on the natural musical quality of the language in the line, literally cutting its rhythmical essence for metrics' sake.

If the feminine manifests itself in lyric poetry through numerous representations of female body parts, the male body itself seldom appears in bits and pieces, enjoying, instead, its special status as the body of the poet, a demiurgeous laureate whose ability to manipulate language and knowledge commands respect. In the introductory poem of Baudelaire's *Flowers of Evil,* "To the Reader," the poet establishes his difference from common men and women. He becomes an exemplary figure fighting mediocrity and hypocrisy. In "Benediction" the poet welcomes and accepts the sufferings of his body as a divine trial that he must undergo in order to sit by God's side. In "The Albatross" the poet becomes the magnificent sea bird, the "monarch of the clouds" misunderstood by mortals but defiant of pain and death. This thematic line runs through *The Flowers of Evil*: the poet acquires worth, dignity, and stoicism in comparison with ordinary men and women, less worthy of esteem. Women who appear as wives, mothers, and prostitutes are portrayed as being particularly deceitful and dishonorable. In "To the Reader" and "Benediction," for example, women are repulsive characters often depicted by way of their body parts. In "To the Reader" woman is the prostitute whose breast is as dry as "an old orange"; in "Benediction" she is the abjuring mother damning her womb, which produced the monstrous poet; she is also the poet's wife whose witchlike nails lacerate his divine skin. If the women in these particular poems appear abhorrent, however, Baudelaire does not believe that woman can only be loathsome. On the contrary, many of his other poems depict female subjects who are also beautiful and fascinating to him. Nevertheless, as with the detestable women in "To the Reader" or "Benediction," their bodies are also depicted in fragments: for Baudelaire, whether detestable or adorable, the lyric woman can only be represented by way of her dismaying and fascinating body parts.

Woman's body in lyric poetry endlessly displays its beauty, infusing the poetry with feminine aesthetic qualities; as Naomi Schor claims: "The detail is gendered, and doubly gendered as feminine."[2] In fact, *feminine detail* seems a more appropriate term to use than the term *fragment* when referring to the bits and pieces of women's bodies because it signifies more than the partial trait of an unbound object; it also names the actual gesture of cutting, not just fragmenting or separating but cutting the body into minute pieces with a sharp object, as the verb *détailler* signifies in French: to cut in pieces. *Detail* also signifies the cut on the woman's body, and, as such, it precedes the fragment, which is the result of this cut. Thus, *detail* and *fragment* are related but not equivalent signifiers. The detail displays a sharper edge to the female body than the ensuing fragment.

In Baudelaire's poetry the detailed charms of woman and her body parts are multiplied and magnified to the extent that the beautiful woman outgrows human properties and proportions for the frustrated poet, who can no longer control this multiple body in a unique poetic form. The backlash of the poet's effort at multiplying her body is that her proliferation goes beyond his ability to contain each one of the resulting parts within the sphere of his writing. Indeed, the paradox facing the poet is that woman must be apprehended in pieces if her beauty is to be thoroughly relished, but the process of her fragmentation overwhelms the poet while her diffused body becomes difficult to contain in the unity provided by the poetic form. In that sense Baudelaire's lyric is indeed "a lyric of frustration," to use Northrop Frye's expression,[3] that is, a lyric born from the tension between the unattainable and disseminated woman and the poet's obsessive attempt to gather her beautiful and scattered body and assemble it in various poetic forms. Under the lyrical regime Woman appears fully subsumed into textual representations of her body. Faced with the challenging dissemination of the increasingly unmanageable female figure dispersed and scattered throughout the lyrical ages, the modern nineteenth-century poet must now organize and collect her body parts into renewed poetic forms such as prose poems like "The Beautiful Dorothea" that still retain the fragmented quality of the body from the lyrical age in prosaic forms. He thus acknowledges the insufficient matrix provided by traditional lyric forms. Already in *Flowers of Evil* Baudelaire finds it increasingly difficult to work with the classic lyric format when the modern female body appears to have outgrown this pattern. It could then be argued that the incessant and overwhelming proliferation of the female body willed from centuries of lyrical poetry and still seething in Baudelaire's poetry may have moved him to adapt, not abandon, his lyrical inclination to a more unfamiliar conceptualization of her fragmented body, which then appears reassembled in lyrical prose poems as the poet captures it in movement in the midst of the city bustle, lyrical apparition in modern attire, disarticulated beauty parading her collected body parts, walking in the streets of Paris, gracefully disjointed by the modern lyricist.

For the poet whose artistic accomplishments include the ability to produce superb and eloquent images in poetic language, the body of woman seems to represent more than just an inspiring cornucopia of fascinating thrills; it is also a literary figure transforming ordinary language into poetic language. In fact, in his unremitting pursuit of female imagery, the lyricist favors working primarily with the female form, thus mirroring both his desire and his writing. Indeed, in poetry, the woman's body often mirrors the medium representing it; it sends back images of form. On her body, a malleable form taking shape with each stroke of the artist's desire, the poet finds the ideal place to experiment with his art. In Baudelaire's poetry woman's body often appears dissected by the poetic subject, and its distorted appearance is more than simply displayed in the poems; it is actually reflected in the poetic form itself. For example, in "The Dancing Serpent" (1:29–30) the undulating body of the dancing woman affects the composition of the poem, which alternates octosyllabic lines with pentasyllabic ones. In "The Beautiful Ship" (1:51–52) and "The Jewels" (1:158) the poet represents woman's body piece by piece, as it were, and to each bodily detail corresponds a new rhythmical group, a new line, or a new stanza.

The lyric woman takes the form of a poem. Her body becomes the poem shaped by rhetorical laws, lyrical rhythms, rhyme schemes, as her fantasized body falls under the poet's surgical hand. Baudelaire himself feels the influence of this surgical metaphor of love when in *Fusées,* a section of his *Journaux intimes,* he claims several times that "the act of love is quite similar to a moment of torture or a surgical operation" (1:651, 659). Nor is this the only time Baudelaire uses the metaphor of the executioner; in "The Self-Destroyer" (1:78) the sadistic poet who hits his victim as a sinister means of ending their relationship and liberating his soul also falls victim to his own violence and becomes simultaneously "victim and executioner." As for the metaphorical surgery, it appears in Baudelaire's *Paris Spleen* published in 1869. In this collection of what I have called "lyrical prose poems," Baudelaire introduces a Parisian prostitute in the poem "Miss Scalpel," in which we witness the humorous meeting between Miss Scalpel and the poet. Miss Scalpel is described by the poetic subject as an "unexpected enigma" who mistakes him for a surgeon of love "so nice and so good to women." The poet is attracted to her enigmatic figure—enigmatic because of her incongruous fantasy of being loved by a surgeon, or a man disguised as a surgeon who would come to see her "with his bag and his apron even stained with a bit of blood" (1:355). Miss Scalpel thus offers the poet a new identity, that of a surgeon, "a man who loves to cut, and hack and carve" (353) the bodies placed in his professional hands. The image of the poet-surgeon created by "Miss Scalpel" and confirmed by the poet in *Fusées* confers on his poetic writing the metaphoric power to dissect women's bodies. In "Miss Scalpel" the poet creates and puts on stage the relationship he believes to represent uniquely the strange coming together of the poet with his female subject. He creates a fantasy in which he appears simultaneously as a lover and a slasher, a poet-surgeon simultaneously loving and dissecting the female body. "Miss Scalpel" transfigures the poet into a surgeon whose love for cutting bodies is transmuted into poetic operations of dissection.[4]

The poetic *operations* of dismemberment used by Baudelaire to control the enigmatic body of the woman may be transferred to the cinematic world of Truffaut, in which women's bodies appear as enigmatic as they did in Baudelaire's poetry. Truffaut's women are often qualified as "magic" by male characters puzzled by the mystery of femininity and examined in detail by Truffaut's inquisitive and incisive camera work. Truffaut's cinematic representations of women, mystifying and fragmented, as they compare to Baudelaire's, may then be characterized as symbolic signs of a visual "lyrical text." The lyric, although historically born as a love song in the form of poetry, is also operating outside of the traditional space of poetry, in art forms such as cinema. There is a lyric cinema that, like lyric poetry, depends a great deal on the female body to define its particular genre, and woman in cinema also lends her body to define cinematic form.

In his classic study of the cinema, *The Imaginary Signifier,* Christian Metz reads cinematic structures according to semiological codes derived from linguistics and psychoanalysis.[5] In fact, Metz claims that the semiologist's relationship to film symbolism is shaped by his desire to grasp its materiality, "its kind of body" (32). The cinema as body—and specifically as a body under the direction of psychoanalysis—finds its implicit feminine gender when Metz-the-semiologist declares, "The cinema is a body (a corpus for the semiologist), a fetish that can be loved" (80). At this point of his analysis Metz openly admits the close relationship existing between film and body, a relationship marked by an ostensibly uniquely male perversion: fetishism. Indeed, the fetish in classic Freudian psychoanalysis is solely depicted as a male perversion. According to Freud, fetishism stems from the fear of castration, which only affects the little boy, whose penis is always in danger of being cut off. In my third chapter I will address the intricacies of this controversial Freudian invention. For the time being it suffices to indicate that the fetishist locates his fetish on the female body. Metz's love for the cinema-body is analogous to the sexual attachment of the fetishist for (a) piece(s) of the female body. The cinema as body, however, is completely under the control of the critic/semiologist; it takes the form of his fantasies and his perversions. It follows an order; it borrows the shape of woman's body, but it is not her body; it does not belong to her because it is deprived of its femininity or its sense of self; it is indeed a male construction born of a private fantasy to love the compliant feminine body, dispersed into manageable and pleasurable parts. As with the prostitute, the fetishized body of the cinema referred to by Metz is only a form to be played with, and experimented with—a fragmented body that is controlled by the numerous cutting techniques used to control its visual pleasures.

In Truffaut's films, cinematographic and framing devices connote the male desire to represent parts of the female body. Close-up shots of women's legs are present in virtually all of his films and epitomized in his 1977 work *The Man Who Loved Women.*[6] In films such as *Small Change* and *Love on the Run* framing itself reflects Truffaut's desire to represent woman's body in pieces. Frames, like doors and windows, often provide the spectator with glimpses of female body parts; in *Small Change,* for instance, two little boys, using a pair of binoculars in the schoolyard during recess, observe the window of a nearby apartment in which a young woman is washing her torso, revealing her bare breasts. In other instances the natural frame of photographs, or of the filmstrip itself reveal Truffaut's incessant obsession with women's faces. The action in *Love on the Run,* the last film on the adventures of Antoine Doinel, is centered around Antoine's final pursuit of love, which begins as he finds the pieces of a torn photograph in a phone booth. Out of curiosity he tapes all the pieces together and finally reconstitutes the photograph, which reveals the face of a beautiful young woman. He immediately falls in love with the woman in the picture, decides to look for her, eventually finds her, and becomes involved with her. As Antoine Doinel feels the pull of his desire while collecting the torn pieces of the picture, his reaction of total infatuation with the woman in the picture confirms his obsession with her initial fragmentary appearance, first as pieces of the photograph and then as a face without a body, a symbolic piece of herself.

In lyric poetry love implies a total abandonment of the (male) body to the sweet torture generated by the very presence of the beloved woman. When a man sees the ravishing woman and/or hears her enchanting voice for the first time, he is immediately touched by an incurable form of love that overwhelms him body and soul. He becomes a lyric artist and sacrifices his life and body to dedicate his art to the woman who has struck his heart. In *Love on the Run* Antoine Doinel reassembles the woman's face on the found torn photograph and, similarly to the lyric artist, he relentlessly pursues the enigmatic woman in the picture and dedicates his life to her. Antoine is just like the poet in "The Beautiful Ship" who collects and reassembles in the poem the body pieces of the female passerby he pursues: he captures each piece of the torn female face within the frame of the reconstituted photograph, while the poet captures each piece of the woman's body within the frame of his poem.

In Baudelaire's poetry and in Truffaut's cinema the overwhelming presence of women partly creates the lyrical mood pervading their respective textual spaces. Woman only becomes totally lyrical, however, when she breaks into details. We have seen how the cutting of her body is as much part of lyric composition as it is part of lyric narrative in Baudelaire's and Truffaut's work. It is in order to control her enigmatic identity in fantasies that her body is not only derealized by the artist but also deformed and cut into parts, overexposed, seen in minute details, relentlessly examined, and finally collected in poems, photographs, and frames. If there cannot be a lyric without a woman, it might be also true that there cannot be lyric composition without the (de/re)composition of her body.

One might wonder why there are more women represented in lyric texts than any other natural or fabricated object. Is their constant presence in lyric texts not a clear indicator of the particular fascination they hold over the artist? In fact, this fascination is clearly expressed by Baudelaire in one of his most lyrical poems—if only in its form—"Beauty" (1:21), in which a statue speaks about her power to "fascinate these docile lovers." Although the docile poet appears here as a victim of perfect form—condemned to worship her—he also regards his poetic enslavement to form as a means to poetic productivity. Here the poet's fascination with the female object of beauty represented by the statue produces a poetry filled with feminine fragments.

Truffaut also expresses his almost mystical fascination for women, who are the main focus of most of his films. The texts of his films portray women as representations of mystery, beauty, and magic that are perhaps best expressed by Alphonse's obsessive question in *Day for Night:* "Are Women magic?"[7] It is perhaps no accident that the same actor who played Antoine Doinel in the *pentalogy* also plays Alphonse. Also, in his critical writings, partly collected in *Le Plaisir des yeux,*[8] Truffaut constantly refers to woman as a form of mystery and fascination; for instance, puzzled by the young actress Isabelle Adjani's personality and beauty, he can only repeat the phrase: "I do not know Isabelle Adjani" (165).[9] He also seems bewildered by Julie Christie's "imperfect" beauty, the effect of many fetishistic details put together: "Julie is a mix of fascinating imperfections" (171).

In his essay "The Painter of Modern Life" Baudelaire defines woman as a "beautiful," "terrible," and "unfigurable" being.[10] Throughout his films Truffaut captures men's fear of woman's mysterious femininity. The terrifying beauty of woman becomes the essence of their work, the thrust of their imagination, the endless source of lyricism permeating their poems and films.

The nature of the feminine threat posed by the myth of woman's body to the male subject in poetry and cinema is tied to philosophical and psychoanalytical considerations of the feelings of threat and anxiety associated with woman's body, and of the way in which they relate to the idea of the lyric.

The idea of the lyric surfaces whenever woman's body is suddenly engaged in the production and reproduction of a text. For Francesco Petrarch, the fourteenth-century father of lyric poetry, it is the unforeseen meeting of the poet with the beautiful Laura that hurls the young man into a deep poetic despair transposed into lyric language and form. In the nineteenth century Baudelaire, the architect of modernity, becomes inadvertently trapped in the same ephemeral moment at the precise time when the male subject of his "Tableaux parisiens" (Parisian Paintings) briefly catches sight of an unknown woman passing in the street in "To a Passer-by." Years later, and in a different genre, Truffaut creates filmic drama, each time his camera depicts the initial astounding visual contact between his male character(s) and the beautiful woman. His film *Jules and Jim* (1961) presents a particularly bewildering first meeting between the two male characters, named in the title, and Catherine, whom they initially encounter as a lifeless representation, a statue projected on screen during a slide show at a friend's house. The sculptured beauty becomes the object of an obsessive search by the two men, whose lives, from that striking first instant, will be altered forever by her sudden and breathtaking apparition.

For Petrarch, Baudelaire, and Truffaut the unexpected apparition of the woman in the artist's field of vision presents itself as the ideal situation for the potential emergence of the lyrical moment, a sublime moment filled with awe. A definition of the word *awe* reveals a paradox of emotions: on the one hand, wonder, exaltation, respect, adoration, and, on the other, fear, terror, shock, horror. The sensations provoked in the artist's mind by the accidental appearance of a woman stage the double and simultaneous effect of the wonderful and the fearful, two apparently distinct notions but nevertheless brought together in the realm of the Sublime.

The beautiful woman in herself is not the only force that plunges the artist into total awe, yet she greatly contributes to the circumstances that initially bring out the sublime effect upon the artist. "The sublime," writes Nicolas Boileau in 1694, "is not strictly speaking something that one proves or demonstrates; but it is a marvel that grips, that strikes, that one feels."[11] Boileau indicates here the violence contributing to the idea of the Sublime when he describes it as "a marvel that strikes." He also attests to the sudden feeling that grabs hold of the subject, a "gripping" feeling, and, finally, he suggests the impossibility of explaining the Sublime rationally. In his own words, the theory of the Sublime cannot be proved or demonstrated, only felt. Of course, nothing is said here of the nature and components of the vision that trigger the Sublime for the onlooker. And it is problematic to assume that any object or person would in fact be the particular catalyst for the Sublime moment. Indeed, such a fixed view of what the objects of the Sublime might be would invariably produce an almost indiscriminate range of subliminal objects, given the right circumstances. The Sublime is not the representation of any particular object or person; rather, it is a violent, sudden, and irrational feeling whose outbreak is dependent on a particular set of circumstances, not on its participants, if they exist in any fantasized shape or form. Although in *The Critique of Judgment*[12] Kant makes it clear that the only place where the Sublime may appear is in nature, he also de-objectivizes it, making it an unseizable feeling attached to the chaos and beauty of nature:

> But in what we are wont to call sublime in nature there is such an absence of anything leading to particular objective principles and corresponding forms of nature, that it is rather in its chaos, or in its wildest and most irregular disorder and desolation, provided it gives signs of magnitude and power, that nature chiefly excites the ideas of the sublime. (301)

Thus, according to Kant, chaotic and wild nature incites the Sublime because it also promises a grandeur beyond its unruliness. Let us see how this idea translates into Baudelairean terms.

We remember how in his personal writings Baudelaire makes unequivocal statements regarding his disgust for women. His notorious aphorism "Woman is natural, therefore she is abominable" (1:677) reinforces his double disgust for women and for nature, which appear mutually compatible. If we read Baudelaire's dislike of the natural woman as a subliminal disgust for her chaotic femininity, that is, for her wild yet exciting body, we begin to perceive the poetic subject as a victim of the Sublime, a sublimated subject who may only reach the spiritual and exhilarating height of poetic paradise—Boileau's "marvel"—only once he has confronted the horror of femininity. For Baudelaire the spiritual reward of the Sublime materializes once the poet has faced the natural and chaotic woman's body, a simultaneously delightful and frightful face-off that he must overcome in order to engage in the poetic representation of woman. His poetic endeavor is not faithfully to reproduce the alluring woman who ignited his imagination but to gain access to her sublime image and thus reach spiritual and poetical bliss. The poet filled with the spirit of the Sublime cannot in fact represent exactly the awesome body of woman because, to paraphrase Boileau, it strikes his unprepared poetic senses so violently and so suddenly. To satisfy his desire to reproduce her unexpected apparition poetically the poet must then collect the remains of her sublime image from his shattered imagination. She will appear in his poems as a scattered figure whose stupefying femininity generates her fragmented appearance.

For the artist, the poet as well as the filmmaker, touched by the sublime effect as he encounters a delightfully beautiful woman, there is no direct figuration of the Sublime—only a figuration of the sublime woman. In placing woman at the center of his subliminal experience, the artist attempts to *figure* what he perceives as the un*figur*able part of woman, her terrifying femininity, her subliminal body so unfamiliar to his eyes, his soul, and his body. He thus attempts to equate the unrepresentability of the Sublime with the materiality of her body, a conflation that can only be achieved in symbolic terms. Thus, he associates each part of the woman's body with a subliminal effect: her beautiful eyes with their terrifying look, her sensual legs with their awe-inspiring movement. The beauty and fear looming from her body lead Baudelaire's poetic subject into a form of poetic despair that he names "Spleen," while Truffaut's male characters are led to tragic situations, from deep amorous torment to death itself.

The various representations of woman's body, then, display a double paradox. On the one hand, each representation of her body attempts to merge the terrifying and the beautiful, and, on the other hand, as representation, it carries the inherent contradiction of representing the unfigurable. Baudelaire knows that there is a profound learning experience in any contradiction: "To learn is to contradict oneself" (1:710). What the poet hopes to learn from the challenge posed by his incongruous project to figure the unfigurable is to get closer to the mystery of femininity. This endeavor requires the artist to take a closer look at the body of woman because, as he takes a more detailed look into her femininity, he hopes to overcome the subliminal effect she has on him, to go beyond the horror. Woman's body is not a sublime representation but, rather, a condition of representability for the sublime effect. It offers a stage on which the Terrifying and the Beautiful confront each other, while the artist relates the effects of the face-off on the body upon which it occurs by way of his poetic imagination, which translates what may be qualified as the monstrous body into words and images. The body can be translated or represented; the Sublime in itself cannot—only its effects on the body may be recorded by the artist whose soul it has touched. The Sublime can emerge within any representation, within any genre, endowing it with a mystery perceived as simultaneously fearful and beautiful by the onlooker. As it fulfills the role of a condition rather than that of a tangible object, the Sublime has more than one locus of emergence. As mentioned before, it traverses genres, and for our purpose it may be said to unite the fields of poetry and cinema. The poet and the filmmaker preserve the sublime moment of their similar encounter with the beautiful woman in a lyric form adaptable to both poetry and cinema. As Louis Marin has put it, "the sublime can occur in any genre, being proper to none."[13]

If the Sublime, in the Kantian definition, resides nowhere in particular but manifests itself when all the circumstantial elements meet in a brief moment, it must then depend on an unnoticeable principle of movement. Kant accounts for the movement of the sublime as well as for the petrifying effect it has on those that are affected by it. In his 1764 essay *The Sense of the Beautiful and of the Sublime* he writes: "The Sublime *moves;* the expression of a person experiencing the full sense of the sublime is serious, at times rigid and amazed."[14] The paradox of the petrifying movement from the

Sublime to its subject is also at work in the lyric. While he is deeply moved by the vision of Laura, Petrarch is also petrified in his writing, his fixed poetic form. He is even petrified in his own name—*Petrarch,* meaning made of stone, a name that will soon become signifier for a self-constraining poetry of true and devoted love for woman: petrarchism. Baudelaire's poetic subject in "To a Passer-by" is also petrified by her brief passage; he becomes "tense like a madman," as he experiences the passing movement of the woman, her swaying body and her floating dress. In Truffaut's *Man Who Loved Women* Bertrand Morane's obsession with women's legs becomes so overpowering that he is willing to risk his life for a mere glimpse of them. When he eventually dies after being run over by a car as he was following a woman with beautiful legs, his death becomes the symbolic crystallization of his vital body. His soul outlives him, however, and beyond the grave he becomes the narrator of his own tragic encounter with the sublime woman's body.

The Sublime has a role and emerges in any dramatic spectacle of nature; for example, it mediates the feeling associated with the spectacle of the sea. In Truffaut's film *The 400 Blows* Antoine Doinel escapes from the juvenile home, and the camera follows his long run toward the sea in an interminable tracking shot. When Antoine finally reaches the sea, he is forced to end his running. At that point the long tracking shot of Antoine's running is replaced by a freeze-frame, which offers a still moment, fixing the face of the young boy on the screen for a brief but noticeable instant. In this final scene of *The 400 Blows* petrification occurs twice—first on Antoine's face, which shows a numb expression of loss as if he had reached the end of the world, the end of his world, and were condemned to eternal entrapment between two imponderable domains, the world of man and the world of nature; second, the camera freezes him in its final frame, thus leaving the spectator with a moment of photographic magnitude, a moment when the film suspends its own movement, hoping to project into the spectators' mind the emotional power invested in this final shot, its sublime effect. In *The 400 Blows* the final freeze-frame presents the boy's troubled reaction as he experiences the overwhelming sublimity emanating from the natural beauty of the mysterious sea. Nature is troublesome for the onlooker, who feels paralyzed by the mystery of its beauty, appealing and appalling at the same time.

Baudelaire is quite eloquent on the danger he senses emanating from nature and more particularly from the natural woman, from her wild animal side, which simultaneously attracts and defeats him: "Woman is hungry and she wants to eat, thirsty and she wants to drink. She is in heat and she wants to be screwed" (1:677). For Baudelaire woman is closer to animals;

she primarily wants to satisfy her bodily needs. In fact, he claims that she is a body without a soul: "Woman does not know how to separate her soul from her body. She is as simple-minded as animals. A satirist would say that it is because she has only a body" (1:694). As a body, wild with instincts and desires, and infinitely sublime, she becomes the greatest challenge for the artist, who tries to organize her chaotic and scattered image into a harmonious arrangement of fragments.

While the Kantian notion of the Sublime fails to supply a particular object of representation, the Lacanian notion of the Real is quite clear in its designation of a privileged object in which one may experience the paradoxical feeling emanating from what appears to be the terrifying unfigurability of sexuality. This object is the body of the woman—to be more precise, its unsettling interiority. For the male subject intrigued by female sexuality there is something abysmal about her body, something sublime exuding from its hidden flesh.

Of the ternary system—"Real, Imaginary, Symbolic"—that Lacan proposes as a means of grasping "human reality," the concept of the Real while essential has been the most unattended of the system, by Lacan himself as well as by schools of literary criticism naturally attracted to the Imaginary for the study of fantasies and images and to the Symbolic for the study of language and culture. The Real offers nothing that the Imaginary and the Symbolic do not already cover. Chronologically speaking, it is placed in a relation of anteriority to the Imaginary and of posteriority to the Symbolic, the Imaginary being everything that exceeds the Symbolic. In other words, the Real is outside the realm of representation by images or by words; it is behind the screen of representation. Any part of the Real that touches the human mind appears to our subjectivity in its represented form; there is never a reality of the Real that is not already caught in the nets of desire and therefore imagined or symbolized. When Lacan tries to inscribe the Real, the Imaginary and the Symbolic in a mathematical formula, the Real is represented by the unknown sign, thus demonstrating its unfathomable nature.

As mentioned earlier, for Petrarch, Baudelaire, and Truffaut artistic production begins with the traumatic apparition of woman. When they meet with woman either in dreams or in fantasies, they never meet with her reality, and that is what causes the lyrical trauma in their texts. It is at this point that Lacan's Real offers a line of theoretical understanding for the devastating lyrical moment of meeting with the unknown woman. Lacan defines the Real in terms of a "missed encounter," as "un rendez-vous auquel nous sommes toujours appelés avec un réel qui se dérobe."[15] This missed encounter with a fleeting reality he chooses to call "la Tuché," a term that he borrows from Aristotle, simply meaning an encounter. In psychoanalysis the *Tuché* becomes synonymous with a profound trauma associated with the subject's realization that life and beauty are always passing him by: "Isn't it remarkable that the analytical situation begins with reality in its utmost unthinkable form, as a trauma determining its direction and imposing on its development an accidental point of departure" (55). This sentence could very well be describing the lyric situation if we were to substitute the word *lyric* with the word *analytical* in the phrase "the analytical situation begins." Let us put such a substitution into context: isn't it remarkable that the lyrical situation begins with reality in its utmost unthinkable form, as a trauma determining its direction and imposing on its development an accidental point of departure? Indeed, the accidental trauma at the origin of the lyric experience is a brief encounter with woman, her devastatingly beautiful body, for the artist who reconstructs its image fragmentarily in the poem and on the screen.

In fact, when in the *Séminaire 11* Lacan asks, "Where does one meet with this Real?" on/in the body of the woman is the answer he has already put forth in his *Séminaire 2*. There, as he reexamines Freud's specimen dream, during which the analyst looks down his female patient's throat, Lacan describes the feminine sexual organs displaced symbolically in Irma's mouth in the following terms:

> There is there a horrible discovery, never yet seen flesh, the very depth of things, the back of the cover, the other side of the face, secretions, flesh engendering everything from its deepest mystery, flesh in pain and deformed, flesh provoking anxiety. (186)

The site where the terrifying moment of encounter with the Real occurs is the inside of woman's body. What inside the body of woman is so traumatic for the analyst searching for a "formal" science of dreams, for a relatively set system that can then be used with some accuracy to interpret most dreams? Inside her body the analyst finds precisely the opposite of what he is looking for. In place of the anticipated form he finds the "informe," that which has no form. He finds feminine flesh and secretions that constitute the other side of the face—"la figure" in French. For the lyric artists who encounter such a feminine *figure* of the unfigurable, there seems to be no simple artistic means by which to represent her as much as there is no analytical means of representing the Real in psychoanalysis, only a fantasy turned ugly, a nightmare filled with grotesque images of the woman's corporeal privacy. Behind the *figure*—behind Irma's face, according to Lacan—

lies the monster of femininity that makes the Real the most unreal encounter with the feminine.

It is as they encounter for a few fleeting seconds the terrifying implication of femininity in Laura, the passerby and Catherine, that Petrarch, Baudelaire, and Truffaut embark on the lyric adventure during which they will attempt to give a face, a *figure,* to the Real and Sublime woman whose terrifying Reality and Sublimity they can only imagine with an adventurous sense of fear. They will then represent her beautiful body as they remember it best from their striking first encounter, dispersed and fetishized; they will reproduce the circumstances surrounding that encounter, and for each attempt at representing the woman of their fantasies they will let their imagination be guided by that ambiguous subliminal feeling associated with the vision of the female body.

As we combine Kant's Sublime with Lacan's Real, it may be put forth that for Baudelaire and Truffaut the mystery of femininity motivates the feeling of the *Sublime* emanating from Woman's *Real* body, from her dark and frightening side. The desire to relate the astounding moment of their first meeting will then always be tinted with the fear instigated by the *subliminally Real* woman, the frightening female living inside the beautiful female, the fearful *gynumculus.* Thus, in their aesthetic pursuit of the ravishing woman who so swiftly stole their heart and soul at first sight, the poet and the filmmaker always run into moments of creative insecurity as they approach the terrifying female lying in wait behind the beautiful woman. No representation of the female body in their work will ever be free of the inherent threat this figure poses to the artist who comes too close to the privacy of her body. In response to such threat the artist will apply lyrical patterns of representation to what he perceives as her wild and chaotic femininity. The woman then appears in the lyric text (in the poem and on the screen) as a derealized, dehumanized (turned goddess), defeminized (ridden of her sexuality), and detailed body, one that is so disfigured in order to appease man's fear of Real femininity but one that also appears reassembled and reorganized to quench the artist's desire to represent Woman's Sublime beauty. In this context lyricism appears as a displaced poetic enactment of what might be ironically called the "taming of the lyrical shrew," a textual and visual act of cutting used to overcome the culturally predicated lawlessness of Woman's body.

Chapter 2

The Woman in Pieces in Petrarch, Baudelaire, and Truffaut

Petrarch and the Fragmented Body of Laura: The Lyric and the Fragment

If, as I have argued in the first chapter, the concept of lyric expression is intimately and permanently linked to the representation of woman's body, we can turn to Petrarch to find one of the most eminent examples and decisive historical sources of that connection. The 366 poems of Petrarch's 1374 *Rerum Vulgarium Fragmenta,* also known as the *Canzoniere* (songbook) or the *Rime Sparse* (scattered rhymes),[1] have as sole obsession the figure of Laura, a source of limitless, painful poetic inspiration. This languishing devotion to a single female figure inspired much of the tradition of French lyric poetry up to the twentieth century by providing the model of the encounter between the poet and the woman who frustrates his desires, giving rise to an impossible love that in turn generates the possibility of lyric poetry.

Acknowledging the importance of Petrarch at the origin of the lyric tradition does not mean that the history of the genre begins with him. In fact, with Petrarch that tradition may be considered to be already on the wane, insofar as it has diverged from the earliest forms of sung poetry developed in Provence by the troubadours in the eleventh and twelfth centuries. By the time of Petrarch lyric poetry has lost its literal lyre, its strict connection to instrumental and vocal music, giving way to a more metaphorical "musicality." The incorporation of harmonies into verbal forms gives rise, for example, to Petrarch's *Canzoniere,* whose poems have no need for actual music in order to exploit the resources of voiced song. After all, the *Canzoniere* is a songbook composed of written poems intended to be brought out of the materiality of the book into the world of sound.

In his *Petit traité de poésie française* (1871) French Parnassian poet Théodore de Banville reiterates the fundamental Petrarchan idea that identifies lyric expression not with actual musical performance but with some inner music, a more interior song whose effects are equivalent to those created by the musician/singer. For Banville, as for Petrarch, poetic language becomes musical without music. Banville defines the role of lyric poetry in the following terms: "What are verses for? For singing. To sing a music whose expression has been lost, but that we hear inside us, for it is the true song."[2] For Banville authentic song is song that has lost its expression, sung by no mouth, heard by no ear. The truest music of lyric expression is unheard music, songs muted by being internally sung, deafened by being interiorized, heard only by our inner ear. It is this internalized music designated by Banville that Petrarch transcribes skillfully from his inner ear to the blank page upon which the lyric poem will be born. Petrarch's contribution to the development of the lyric does not only dwell in the altered musicality it proposes; its originality lies as well in a new conception of lyric form.

With Petrarch the lyric also reaches a decisive moment in its history when the poem detaches itself from the unity and singularity of sung ballads in order to approximate the scattered, disparate, strangely formless form of the fragment. The lyric poem incorporates fragmentation into its form and does not distinguish itself from the scatteredness of its nature, as Petrarch himself announces in the first line of his introductory sonnet: "You who hear in scattered rhymes the sound / of those sighs with which I nourished my heart."

In his introduction to the translation of Petrarch's lyric poems Robert Durling points to the novelty of the association of the fragment with the lyric. Commenting on the Latin title of Petrarch's collection, *Rerum Vulgarium Fragmenta* (*Fragments of Vernacular Poetry*), he writes, "This may well be the first use of the term fragment to describe a kind of work of art."[3] The work of art in question here is lyric poetry, poetry that cannot be conceived outside fragmentation, whether of its poetic form, the poetic subjectivity it expresses, or the object of Petrarch's poetic representations, the body of Laura.

The entire object of Petrarch's lyric experience is constituted by the person of Laura; her sudden, unexpected appearance to the man about to become poet simultaneously awakens his love and his lyric talent. Out of the initial brief encounter with Laura, Petrarch constructs an immense poetic space entirely devoted to the symbolic representation of her body. Petrarch's poetry lives paradoxically between the microcosmic brief instant and the macrocosmic textual space that the brief encounter generates when the poet immediately engages in the monumental enterprise of recovering and repeating in verse that instant of fulguration. In the prodigious poetic space created by Petrarch out of this short-lived moment, the body of Laura is celebrated, both embalmed and fragmented, in the private crypt that the poet has built and where he jealously keeps her.

Indeed, throughout the *Canzoniere,* which aims to recollect her fragments for the purpose of celebrating and monumentalizing her, Laura is always implicitly represented as lost or dead. The entire lyric tradition makes extensive use of the figure of the dead, fragmented woman, lifeless and objectified, as a means of protecting her image from time and change. Her immortalized form is able to cross centuries of poetry safely, and the crypt in which she has been placed is the legacy that is passed on to other lyric poets.

The predilection of the lyric poet for representations of the "dead" woman, of her fragmented body, enhances the pathos of his duplicitous project of memorializing, of marmorealizing, woman. He writes as if his aim is to give her life, to preserve her life against the loss occasioned by his brief first encounter and her subsequent death. In fact, she of course only "lives" in his verse, entombed within the poetic language that dismembers her body and embalms her memory. In the *Rime Sparse* the poetry itself that preserves Laura's body in bits and pieces assumes a fragmented form, as if to become her body, the better to preserve her from the double loss suffered by the poet. In the fifth sonnet the association of woman's body with poetic form is textually established through the use it makes of the familiar form of Laura's name, Laureta, in which we recognize the play of the double syntagms Laura and Lauro (laurel).

> When I move my sighs to call you and the name that love wrote in my heart, the sound of its first sweet accents is heard without in LAU-ds.
>
> You are RE-gal state, which I meet next, redoubles my strength
>   for the
> high enterprise; but "TA-lk no more!" cries the ending, "for to do her honor is a burden for other shoulders than yours."
>
> Thus the word itself teaches LAU-d and RE-verence, whenever anyone calls you, O lady worthy of all reverence and honor;
>
> Except that perhaps Apollo is incensed that any mor-TA-l tongue should come presumptuous to speak of his eternally green boughs.
>   (40)

The name Laura simultaneously refers to the beloved woman and alludes to Apollonian laurels with which the poet is crowned. Whenever the poetic voice mentions the one, we are compelled to hear a reference to the other.

The language that thus expresses regret for the loss of Laura's body may be taken as well to reflect Petrarch's poetics. Devoid of any totalizing form, poetry for him can only be a fragmented language that expresses nostalgia for the woman's body once seen as a total object and now reduced to elliptical and scattered forms. Lyric poetry speaks in the form of fragments about fragmentation, the dismemberment of woman's body. There is in the lyric form an attempt to figure ellipses in the blank spaces that cut the poetic line, that shape the length of verses and stanzas. That is, lyric poetry speaks in fragments about fragmentation, displaying not only the pieces of an inaccessible whole but also itself cut up into pieces.

Petrarch acknowledges the elliptical form of his poetic writing when in his twenty-third sonnet he states: "My pen cannot follow closely my will; wherefore I pass over many things written in my mind [. . .] Words spoken aloud were forbidden me; so I cried out with paper and ink." The last verse establishes an equivalence between the physical and the textual as the poet cries out with paper and ink. The corporeal voice is *incorporated* into the mute letters on the page. As a result, the lost body of the woman is incorporated into the fragmented forms of the poem; Petrarch's poetry itself may be said to be feminized. Femininity here assumes the figure of a voice signified in the line "Words spoken aloud were forbidden me." We must recall Banville's definition of poetry as "music of which the expression has been lost, but that we hear inside us," in order to understand the equivalence between the lost body of the woman and the lost physical sonority of music. This equivalence represents the double loss of woman and music that initiated the passage from oral to written poetry. What is graphically materialized in the written form of the poem is the incorporation of the musical and feminine loss that still resounds within us, "that we hear inside us" (Banville) as we read/write lyric poetry.

If the feminine transgresses the written language of the poet, "she" does so by way of "her" voice. As such, as a speaking/vocal signifier, the feminine disturbs the writing mode of the poetic "I." The first-person singular characterizing lyric poetry thus shares its subjectivity with a vocal feminine other. And it is her "cry" that transgresses Petrarch's writing when he writes, "I cried out with paper and ink."

To build his fragmented poetic space the poetic subject looks back into his memory, which brings to his inspired self the nostalgic image of Laura's fragmented body. Her absent body triggers his poetic impulse. Laura is indeed a specter in the *Canzoniere,* and Petrarch represents her ghostly body as he best re-members it: in fragments. He exerts his memory and his poetic art to restore her absent body. As a consequence of her absence, Laura remains an imprecise figure of his past, and she never offers a complete and accurate image of her body to the poet, who, in spite of his effort to recapture her unified and uniform body, can only remember her in pieces. Petrarch is not left empty-handed, however, by his sporadic recollection of the woman he loves. In fact, he endows the fragment with a high poetic status by turning it into a means of preserving Laura's image as scrupulously as possible. What the fragmented representation of the woman's body comes to signify is less the failing memory of the poet than his desire to signify a perfect poetic object by descriptively exhausting each fragment of her body. The poetic fragment itself becomes in turn a rich whole, a microcosm of multiple nuances. These nuances composing the lyric poem are themselves overwritten synecdochic details of the largest fragments of the woman's body.

Petrarch's poetry embodies a conception of the poetic detail that we find again in Hegel's *Aesthetics* (1835),[4] in which he defines poetry's focus on detail in terms of the absolute value of the particular:

> But, in a poetic treatment and formulation, every part, every feature must be interesting and living on its own account, and therefore poetry takes pleasure in lingering over what is individual, describes it with love, and treats it as a whole in itself. Consequently, however great the interest and the subject may be which poetry makes the center of a work of art, poetry nevertheless articulates it in detail. (981)

In its relentless poetic pursuit of the disseminated body of Laura, in its search for the totality of her scattered body, Petrarch's *Canzoniere* epitomizes in its very form this focus on detail. Because he can only recollect her body in details, Petrarch gives each one of the fragments of his text a more condensed poetic richness than epic poetry could allow. In order to better serve her body in pieces, he breaks the formal poetic pattern of graphic and narrative continuity defining epic poetry. In place of the lengthy uninterrupted composition of the epic poem, Petrarch creates autonomous poetic fragments, short poems of fourteen lines, built around a particular set of prosodic rules. The sonnet, as a fragmented yet autonomous poem, mimics the fragmented body of Laura. In order to reinforce his argument on the wholeness of the detail in poetry, Hegel himself writes, "In the human organism each limb, each finger is most delicately rounded off into a whole, and in real life, in short, every particular existent is enclosed into a world of its own" (981). Hegel anthropomorphizes poetry in general by comparing it to a living organism and the poetic fragment in particular by giving it the status of a limb, a finger. In other words, poetry may be said to possess a corporeal thickness, and its inherent fragmentation recalls the terms of dismemberment. Thus, Petrarch's poetic gesture consists of dissecting Laura's body, of dismembering it while re-membering it. But, even if the poet intends to remember Laura's body by re-membering it, he composes a poetic text that, in fact, does the opposite. Petrarch's effort to rebuild from memory a complete but fragmented image of Laura emerges in his writing the *Canzoniere,* as Giuseppe Mazzotta suggests: "*The Canzoniere* is, to be sure, the attempt to restore the pieces, to give an illusory unity to the fragments. [. . .] The point is that the unity of the work is the unity of fragments and in fragments."[5]

This remark points to the impossibility of the *Canzoniere's* recapturing of the original unity of Laura's body, if this unity ever existed, or, rather, if it ever existed under the name of Laura. For there is a generic virtual human body behind the fragmented construction of Petrarch's poetry, a potential human form whose unity it is impossible to retrieve. Petrarch gives himself the impossible task of recapturing the woman of his dreams in a poetic construct. His continuous efforts to write poetry where he hopes to find her again is similar to the task that the inhabitants of Italo Calvino's *Invisible Cities* have set out to accomplish as they build and rebuild the city of Zobeide in which they hope to capture the Ideal woman who haunted their dream. Teresa de Lauretis explains that for the men of Zobeide "desire provides the impulse to represent, and dream, the modes of representing."[6]

Similarly for Petrarch, desire to capture Laura in full by writing a succession of sonnets about her is complemented by her dreamlike apparition that provides the poet with means of representation. Further in her analysis of *Invisible Cities* de Lauretis assimilates the body of the dream woman to the body of the city that men built to entrap her: "The city is a text which tells the story of male desire by performing the absence of woman and by producing woman as text, as pure representation" (13). In a sense the same is true of Petrarch to whom we could apply the same comment in relation to his lyric poetry: Petrarch's lyric is a text conveying male desire by performing the absence of Laura, the ideal woman, and by producing woman as text, as pure representation. As pure representation, Laura proffers to the text her fragmented body, which becomes the founding mode of lyric poetry: simultaneously fragmented and corporeal. It is the nature of lyric poetry to be fragmentary and organic while its endemic substance remains feminine. As a book of poems, the *Canzoniere* acts as the unifying agent of the ever disseminated woman's body; as such it never offers a uniform image of that body. In fact, Laura's body may be compared to a puzzle the poet tries to put together piece by piece by writing his poetic fragments. The *vision* of the finished puzzle is the best that the poet can do to satisfy his desire for unity, but the reconstituted image of the woman's body still displays unerasable cracks formed by the edges of the puzzle pieces. Her reconstructed image indicates that her passage in poetry has left her body scarred by the imperative of verse writing. Thus, the completion of the poetic puzzle of the woman's body preserves in each one of its pieces, each one of its sonnets, an indelible mark of separation at the same time as it presents a full fragmented image of her body.

It is also important to notice that the poetic tradition of fragmentation is faithful not only to the cutting up of the woman herself, but also to the specific selection of certain of her body parts. In her study of the mythical inspiration of the fragmented body in Petrarch's *Canzoniere,* Nancy Vickers makes the following remark on the selection and nature of the body pieces articulating the poet's poetics of fragmentation: "Laura is always presented as a part or parts of a woman. [. . .] Her textures are those of metals and stones: her image is that of a collection of exquisitely beautiful dissociated objects. Singled out among them are hair, hand, foot and eyes."[7]

This remark brings together Petrarch's *Canzoniere* and Baudelaire's *Flowers of Evil* within the poetic tradition of the fragmented body of woman initiated by Petrarch. Not only does this tradition survive in the selection of bodily parts chosen by Baudelaire the lyric poet, but it also respects to some extent the texture of these bodily parts. As I will demonstrate, the Petrarchan model of the fragmented woman remains virtually untouched in its form and texture throughout Baudelaire's poetry.

Baudelaire's Fragmented Women: Ideal Statues and Modern Bodies

In Baudelaire's *Flowers of Evil* the poet chooses to represent woman in scattered fashion, often referring to her presence by the mention of isolated bodily parts, such as her eyes, hair, legs, feet, arms, hands. He displays female body parts in metaphoric fashion imparting to those body parts the texture of metal and stone. Eyes, as they appear in various poems, are represented as cosmic: "eyes, as large and deep and brown as your skies, spacious Night" (1:161); cutting: "cleave and rend like lances" (1:35); shining like lights in the dark: "like feast-lanterns glare" (1:56), "where intermittent glimmers dwell" (1:165); and sparkling like gems, they are metaphoric jewels: "where everything is gold, light, steel, and diamonds" (1:29). The description of the woman's hair in "The Hair" (1:26–27) evokes simultaneously the qualities of stone: "hoard of rubies, pearls, and sapphires in your mane"; and feather: "among your fringe's tight-curled filaments." This incongruous account of her appearance blurs his vision: "you hide a dazzling dream, O ebony sea," while also intoxicating him: "In this dark sea, I'll plunge my head, in love with drunkenness." In "To a Passer-by" (1:92), "the rich hand" evokes a highly ornate hand covered with jewels, and "the statuesque leg" evokes the beauty of sculptured marble.

Most of these metaphors insist on the metal and stone textures of the fragments of the woman's body. It is as if, in *Flowers of Evil*, women were preserved in their ideal and beautiful form in the shape of precious stones and marble statues. It is this aspect of the precious and beautiful fragmented body that Baudelaire's lyric woman retains from Petrarch's Laura. Baudelaire goes further than Petrarch, however, in establishing woman's body as his fragmented object of poetic predilection. In his poetry not only is her fragmented body precious and beautiful; it is also the place where beauty and ugliness meet, where qualities of metal, feathers, stone, and flesh are simultaneously exhibited. The contiguity of these opposite elements and contrasting textures is an essential characteristic of the descriptions of women in *Flowers of Evil*. In order to accommodate such a mélange of textures, Baudelaire describes many different types of women. The plurality of his feminine world opposes itself to Petrarch's singular poetic world inhabited by a single feminine figure: Laura.

Baudelaire's poetry presents a body of women, which gives an undeniable sense of feminine plurality to the poetic world of *Flowers of Evil*. The expression "a body of women," however, suggests more than the omnipresence of women in the book. It juxtaposes the "singularity" of a body within a plurality of women. This expression also suggests the incorporation of different bodies of women into one poetic body, namely *Flowers of Evil*. In order to signify this incorporation, I will use the word *body* in a purposely ambiguous manner to refer simultaneously to the corpus of poetry represented by *Flowers of Evil* and to the bodies of women inhabiting and shaping this corpus of poetry.

Irreducible to any particular social or mythical model, the women in *Flowers of Evil* resist immobility and undergo changes in consistency (stone, flesh), form (statues, passersby), and color (white, brown) of their bodies throughout the collection of poems. In an effort to accommodate the fleeting nature of women and the various metamorphoses of their bodies, the poetic forms of *Flowers of Evil* also undergo change. This constant transmutation at work between the women and the poetry uses the body as its medium. This "body" convenes on the poetic scene the two realms of the physical and the formal. As stated by Yves Bonnefoy,[8] *Flowers of Evil* is "a theater of the human body" in which the body plays its physical part and poetic language gives (bodily) shape to the scene/seen.

The poetic body of *Flowers of Evil* includes feminine figures such as divinities, muses, angels, nymphs, vampires, old women, prostitutes, beggars, and passersby, not to mention a host of others. The very eclecticism of such an extensive list hints at a division between ideal women and modern women. In some respects this separation follows Baudelaire's division of "Spleen and Ideal," in which the women belonging to the world of Spleen are often depicted as modern women—women always on the move, often living or passing in the streets and offering sensual pleasures, real or fantasized—whereas women belonging to the world of the Ideal poems appear more often as divine creatures, as pure and inaccessible as goddesses. The distinction between the two types of women, however, is not so clear-cut. Ideal women and modern women meet on common ground, which allows their bodies to share each other's distinctive characteristics without relinquishing their original particularities. Women do thematically what the title of the section "Spleen and Ideal" does syntactically: the two categories "Spleen" and "Ideal" appear in an undivided title form, while the conjunction *and* keeping them together also marks their division and differences, like a cut. By bringing together two seemingly opposite ideas, Spleen and Ideal, for the purpose of separating them, Baudelaire ends up dealing with them together in the context of a single section of his work, as if they were separable and inseparable at the same time and only tenable in the untenable form of a poetic body in which they unceasingly move from one pole to the other. If the women, in Baudelaire's text, appear to move within distinct groups (ideal women, modern women), their bodies are subjected to the same movements. Built upon these fundamental figures of women, *Flowers of Evil* in turn delineates two bodily forms: the Ideal body and the Modern body.

This paradox heals the breach between two distinct notions, Ideal and Modern, and also becomes the crucial element of what Baudelaire calls "modernity," of what Michel Foucault calls the "heroization of the present"[9] and of what I will call here the idealization of Spleen. Modernity is more that just a disruption in time, in Foucault's view "a rupture of tradition, feeling of novelty, dizziness for what passes by" (67); it is the result of an "attitude" that the critical artist adopts in recognizing the Modern in Ideal terms, in valorizing the representation of modern woman using an evaluation system based on the representation of classical woman, immortalized in precise aesthetic codes from a distant and respected past. Baudelaire seems to substantiate such an affirmation when in *The Painter of Modern Life* he argues: "For any modernity to be worthy of one day taking its place as antiquity, it is necessary for the mysterious beauty which human life accidently puts into it to be distilled from it" (2:695).

When Baudelaire begins his critical investigation into the possible emergence of modern art in nineteenth-century painting, he seems primarily concerned with the passage from what he calls "modernity" to "antiquity." The anachronism of the proposed shift from modernity to antiquity does not remain unexplained. According to Baudelaire, this is a movement by which modernity would enter the pantheon of art history as a "worthy" art form. Baudelaire argues, however, that before it can be recognized as a valuable piece of work, the modern composition must be amended to conform to classical aesthetic values. But, to be celebrated as a worthy classical work of art, which are the elements in the modern work of art that should be retained or deleted? Baudelaire proposes that the mysterious beauty of human life must be distilled from the modern work of art and that, once singled out, modern beauty may find its place in an artistic eternity also referred to as antiquity, a symbolic realm in which Baudelaire places celebrated art forms withstanding time and trends.

Yet, beyond Baudelaire's perplexing suggestion that the value of modern art may only be assessed in relation to ancient and established art forms, he also offers an insight into what may constitute the modern work of art in the first place. He suggests that the idea of the modern crystallized when the aesthetic abstraction known as "the beautiful" encountered human life, in other words when the aesthetic principles defining a certain idea of classical beauty were reoriented to accommodate a growing visual interest for the ordinary surroundings of the observer, the poet-*flâneur* caught in the beauty of everyday life. It appears that Baudelaire is indirectly indebted to contemporary human life for releasing a "mysterious beauty" into the symbolic arena of modern representations. To paraphrase his own words, the ephemeral, fugitive beauty emanating from the human body is the essential basis for the aesthetic conception of the modern work. Once captured on a canvas or a poem, beauty is given eternal life. Baudelaire's apparent dismissal of the body as the accidental bearer of modern beauty must then be understood as a desire to combine both the passing trends of everyday life and the established classical figures of the past into the same pattern of representation that he calls modernity: "By 'modernity' I mean the ephemeral, the fugitive, the contingent, the half of art whose other half is the eternal and the immutable" (2:695). The body is then an integral part of the modern project in which it actively participates, even if only partially.

In his critical assessment of modern art Baudelaire does not wish to retreat behind a definition of art that favors tradition at all times; rather, he is willing to challenge the aesthetic notion of antiquity with contemporary representations of life. Consequently, the double presence, the coexistence of transitory beauty and eternal beauty, constitutes the true nature of modernity, and it is the movement from one to the other that interests us in the present analysis, in particular as it affects the female figures in the poetry of Baudelaire. We shall see that Baudelaire experiments with the double edge of modernity by infusing the poetic representation of classical beauty embodied by the Greek statue with the distinctive charms of the modern woman and modern woman with the immutable features of the classical statue. It is the crucial poetic shifting from the body of stone to the body of flesh, and vice versa, that I propose to analyze here as a way to stress the decisive implication of the woman's body in the poetic construct of modernity.

The "ideality" of woman's body emerges principally in three poems of the section "Spleen and Ideal": "Beauty," "The Mask," and "Hymn to Beauty." Frozen in the purity of its lines and cast in stone, woman's body assumes the dimensions of a statue that immobilizes the poet with its stability. Her inviolability lends the poet the reassurance of her permanence, fixed and immutable; the poet's search for ideal forms culminates in the vision of finality she embodies. Accomplishing his poetic desire, however, she kills poetry, petrifying its very movement, as when the statue in "Beauty" affirms, "I hate the movement that disturbs lines." The fluidity of poetic verse is threatened by the frozen form of her ideal perfection. Like the solidly fixed forms of the lyric tradition, her petrified body, by analogy, threatens the mobility of line with which the modern poet seeks to embrace the fugitive passage of time. The threat is clearly suggested in the following verses of "Beauty":

> Poets will spend their lifetime in austere
> study of grand poses I assume
>
> I charm these docile lovers with pure mirrors:
> my great eyes whose light, eternal, clear,
> reflects to them a world of things made fairer.

The specular glitter of her Medusan eyes fascinates the gaze of this poet-lover, freezing his discourse, which the speaking statue identifies as "austere study." The words spoken by the statue displace the austere impenetrability of her body onto the poet's language and its forms. Fixated by his fascination with her ideal perfection, he is compelled to become the guardian of traditional verse forms like those in which "Beauty" is cast: twelve-syllable alexandrines, regular rhymes and unvarying rhythms, the fixed form of the sonnet. The eyes of the statue, these "pure mirrors," repress the poet's desire to free himself from traditional forms. Agents of repression, her eyes are isolated from the rest of her body in the poem; capturing his gaze, they confine his poetic impulses to the specular realm of ideality that sight, the most abstract of all the senses, uniquely conveys. Isolated from her body, the eyes are also a synecdoche for the totality of its consoling immutability, resisting time and seducing the poet with its promise of immortality, as suggested in the poem's last line: "My eyes, my great eyes filled with light, eternal and clear." To gain access to the eternity her austerity proffers, the poet must in turn isolate his poetry from other sources of inspiration, exile himself from the chaos of the modern world in order to devote himself to the cruel beauty of this poetic goddess, this goddess of poetry.

In other poems, "Allegory" (1:116) among them, Baudelaire finds some release from the ideal woman's power to petrify body and forms by informing her appearance with some aspects of modernity, not enough to desecrate her almost divine apparition but enough to weaken her petrifying power of fascination. Now her body appears fragmented, diversely composed of ideal and modern features. The beautiful woman in "Allegory" is indeed a woman displaying statuesque and eternal features, "her granite skin," as well as human and mortal ones, "who lets her hair trail in her cup of wine." In a single line she appears like an immortal goddess and sprawls like a luscious exotic queen: "She walks like a goddess, and rests like a sultana." The allegorical woman represented here retains the nostalgic texture, the granite, of the sculptured goddess while exposing the lasciviousness of her beautiful mortal body. She is a hybrid, presenting a double image of eternity and mortality. She is eternal in stone and mortal in flesh.

She also becomes a beautiful monster, or a monstrous beauty, as in the two poems "The Mask" and "Hymn to Beauty." In "The Mask" heterogeneous details of her body come to constitute the monstrosity hidden behind the image of the perfect woman, the ideal body of stone:

> O Blasphemy of art! O dread surprise!
> From that fair body's promise of content
> Two monstrous heads on shapely shoulders rise!

In "The Mask" the perfection of the divinely beautiful woman dissolves as the poet's gaze circumvents her body in order to admire her more completely from front to back. In this circling movement to the back of the statue, we recognize the impulse of the modern poet, who varies the perspective of his gaze and avidly seeks to view her beauty *obliquely,* to envision her forms from unexpectedly different angles. In changing his visual perspective of the subject, the poet resembles the filmmaker's camera panning around the statue to discover her hidden face. Just as the visually inquisitive camera aims to establish aesthetic continuity in prolonging a panoramic shot on a subject, the eye of the poet examines the statue patiently and continuously hoping to maintain the uninterrupted scopophilic pleasure emanating from her total beauty. As he circles the statue, however, the poet discovers a terrifying face beneath the beautiful one that appears in the classical vis-à-vis. The treachery of the petrified model of beauty betrays itself in the poem in altered rhetorical modes that violate, or break up, the serenity of classical forms. With trepidation, stumbling on new sets of forms, the poet invents monstrous figures whose metaphor is the statue's horrifying other side, a face that conveys, in Lacanian terms, the face of the Real hidden behind the idealized mask of feminine beauty.

Like the tercet just quoted, separated from the body of the poem, the woman's head carries the sign of her double nature, reflecting a conflict of opposite elements. This separation provides a formal correlative of her menacing fragmentation. A similar scenario occurs in "Hymn to Beauty":

> What matter whether you come from heaven or hell,
> O Beauty, monstrous, dread, ingenuous one!
> if you open the door with your foot, your eye, your smile,
> to an Infinite which I love and have never known?

In these lines the eye, the smiling mouth, and the foot are cut from the body of the monstrous statue. The gesture of severing these body parts says more about the fragility of the poet's model of feminine beauty than about the psychology of the sadistic impulse that mutilates it.

The fragmentation that produces the isolation of three corporeal parts (the foot, the eye, the smile) enables the poet to escape the petrifying fascination produced by the synecdochal eyes of the statue in "Beauty," now "open[ing] the door" in the poem's last line, to "infinite" possibilities that contrast with the unbroken unity, the immobile uniqueness of stonily fixed poetic forms. The infinite possibilities offered by the lovely but not flawless beauty of the woman's body, with its implications for the evolution of poetic forms, invite us to examine the representations and the reality of modern woman as she is figured elsewhere in *Flowers of Evil.*

Having located the danger lurking in the immobile form of the ideal woman, I propose now to uncover the threat posed by the modern woman to the integrity of the poet who appears as both the writing subject and the written object of the poem's figuration. In the familiar presence of modern woman poetic consciousness is no longer menaced as before by the stony ideality of a unified appearance; instead, it discovers a further danger in the fragmented multiplicity of her fleshy body parts. Like shards of glass, the bodily parts, cut out from the totality of her person, turn their sharp edges against the poetic consciousness that has invested them with its desire.

Who is this modern woman endangering the poet with the dispersed fragments of her body? She is, in fact, not one but multiple. She is the figure of many different women Baudelaire/the poet encounters on the street, in cafés, at the theater. She is often a total stranger as in "To a Red-haired Beggar Maid" or "To a Passer-by," but she is frequently his mistress, real or imagined, as in "The Cat" or "The Beautiful Ship"—and, as such, familiar and reassuring. Unknown or all too familiar, she nevertheless retains a mysterious, uncanny, and dangerous quality, more dangerous in fact than the ideal body of stone, necessitating, in response to her threat, that the poet render her more docile in his hands and accessible to his pen by cutting her up into bits that are ever more minutely and scrupulously observed. In "The Cat" the danger of her gaze, displaced from the cat to the woman, is felt like a cold blade cutting and splitting his body:

> Come to me, pretty puss, my lullabies
> To hear. Come, draw those sharp claws in,
> And let me dive into those mottled eyes,
> Metallical and agatine,
>
> When I have stroked, with leisurely caress,
> Your head and supple back, and felt
> A thrilling tingle as my fingers press
> Electric sparkles from your pelt,
>
> A woman comes into my mind, whose glances,
> Like yours, my cat, my pet, my sweet,
> Are deep and cold, and cleave and rend like lances,
>
> And from head to foot,
> A nimble air, suffused with feral smells,
> Around her brown body swells.

In this sonnet the cat is the source of tactile experiences and visual pleasure. The series of verbs in the imperative mood, "Come to me, draw, let me dive," reiterates the imploring poet's desire for pleasures that are taken as signs of love. His position is vulnerable and avowedly dependent on another for satisfaction. In a sense the poet appears here as helpless as the young child primarily sensitive to his mother's love and body. And, in light of Lacan's reading of such an ancillary bond, the poet's demands of the cat's body may be interpreted as the outcry of desire expressed by the child craving his mother's body, which he believes to be the sole provider for all his needs and pleasures. Indeed, an analogy can be drawn between this relation and the Lacanian analysis of the infant's desire for the mother. This desire arises, according to Lacan, out of the tension between the infant's physical needs, satisfied by the mother's breast, and its limitless demand for love that no material satisfaction can fulfill. The poet, like the infant, craves love from the other (here the cat/woman), but his desire cannot be satisfied by any object and certainly not by isolated body parts—"your sharp claws," "your mottled eyes," "your head and supple back," "from head to foot"—that he perversely enumerates. His imperative demand, expressed in the first stanza ("And let me dive into those mottled eyes, metallical and agatine"), seeks his total immersion in the oceanic eyes of the cat in order to merge their bodies in an undifferentiated union of perfect pleasure. Eyes become the partial object emblematizing the totality of the beloved body into which the poet wishes to lose himself in an experience of timeless gratification, ecstatic intoxication, and energizing sexual contact: "with leisurely caress; a thrilling tingle; electric sparkles from your pelt."

When, however, the body of the woman is substituted for that of the cat, "a woman comes into my mind," there is also a sea-change in the nature of the eyes the poet at first wishes to plunge into. In the third stanza they give way to "glances deep and cold"—a pointed weapon attacking, perhaps castrating the poet: "cleave and rend like lances." Here the gaze cuts and splits up the body of the poet, who, in the first stanza, had dreamed of merging into undifferentiated union with the other. Eyes have shifted from being sources of pleasure to objects of pain; they project a threatening gaze pointed in the poet's direction. Against this threat he reacts by turning away from the fragmented body of the other, ostensibly to return to the totality of the woman's body he now embraces "from head to foot." But the unified totality of her body denies the promise contained in the cat's "electric body" in the second stanza. Ultimately, the body of the woman proves to be just as dangerous to the poet as her eyes, as can be seen in the poem's last lines: "A nimble air, suffused with feral smells, / Around her brown body swells."

Here the "feral smells," the dangerous perfume, could be interpreted as a physical corporeal detail cut off from any corporeal locus, a scent detached both from the woman's body and the poet's but nonetheless charged with the penetrating sensuality Baudelaire unvaryingly attributes to perfume. The ambiguous origin of this dangerous scent enhances the danger it conveys. As an emanation from the woman's body, it persists even in the absence of contact as a more powerful, self-sustaining fragment of the woman, more pervasive and correspondingly more dangerous to the poet's integrity. At the same time, its uncertain origin could make it a material correlative of the poet's floating consciousness enveloping the brown body of the woman with its dangerous scent or sense.

. The perfume emanates from and envelops the "brown body" of the modern woman, which here is in contrast to the white body of the statue. Through this designation of body color Baudelaire wishes to associate modern woman with the nineteenth-century image of oriental sensuality, as it is the case in "Allegory," in which the sultana displays her vulnerable, sensual body. Here the modern woman becomes a sensual icon of otherness, intelligible only through her body. Her sensual body is central to the construction of the modern poem, and it unleashes a powerful poetic and/or feminine perfume—a sensual detail whose ambiguity of origins forces both the poetic body and the feminine body to share the agency of and the submission to fragmentation. In the end, as we have seen in "The Cat," what constitutes the true image of the Baudelairean woman is less her modernity—or her ideality in "Beauty"—than her fragmentation. Her fragmented body reflects its dissemination onto the other body of the poem, onto its form.

The modern and ideal woman, understood as distinct categories, represent for the poet two mystifying absolutes that provide him with two precisely delineated models of femininity expressed through their bodies. Since Baudelaire's objective is to capture the absolutely feminine in the totality of the woman's body, his poetry involves the art of observing, gathering and pasting together various fragments of her modern body and ideal body disseminated from the lyric tradition and preserved in fragments by modern poetry. Baudelaire is partly lyric in his desire to celebrate woman's body in detail; however, he is also partly modern in his desire to piece together her disseminated image, even if in the end the modern women appears as a collage of anachronistic body parts.

Baudelaire has very little taste for absolutes. His female figures are neither totally ideal nor totally modern (nor, as in "All of Her," totally complete). In his poems women are figurations of a constant confrontation of ideal and modern, stone and flesh, whole and fragmented. If, in order to situate the Baudelairean woman in relation to these binary oppositions, we drew a line spanning the space between the oppositions, we could never locate her at any one fixed point. Instead, we would see her multiple, ambivalent figure move in either direction but never reach either end of the line. Women in Baudelaire's poems evolve in a vast and flexible medium, a Pascalian "vast expanse" "where we drift, always uncertain and floating, pulled from one end to the other."[10] The Baudelairean woman is always moving between two infinites, the infinitely ideal, mineral, whole, and the infinitely modern, fleshy, fragmented. It is from this *in-between* space that an immense number of women appear on the poetic scene of *Flowers of Evil.*

According to poet and critic Michel Deguy, the woman's body in *Flowers of Evil* is "[in] the middle."[11] As such, she presents a feminine body joining and exchanging body parts and textures as she moves on the infinite lines of binary oppositions. Deguy refers to her body as a monstrous body, "an expanding monster which gathers and distributes its microcosmical hemispheres" (338). Woman in Baudelaire's poetry may have a monstrous body, but she strikes the poet as a perfect monster to whom he dedicates his love: "Indeed, in my quest for the very cream of Evil and wishing to love nothing but a perfect monster, truly, my old monster, I love you still" ("The Monster" 1:166). Baudelaire's modern creation of a feminine monster consisting of different shapes and textures brings female representation closer to an equally monstrous figure of antiquity: the Sphinx—the creature who is half-animal, half-woman—one of the many beautiful and horrifying creatures of Greek mythology that fascinate Baudelaire ("Spleen LXXVI," "When She Puts On That Dress That Glints and Waves," "Cats"). It is perhaps in "When She Puts On That Dress" that Baudelaire gives the most explicit description of the monstrous woman whose nature is "strange and symbolic," composed of "gold, steel, and lights, and diamonds," caught between two opposite representations, "the inviolate angel" and "the ancient sphinx," between the purity of the angel and the monstrosity of the sphinx.

If, according to Deguy, the Baudelairean woman is best represented as a "woman of the middle," she should not, however, be confused with the representation of a middling woman of banal or average appearance. Indeed, she is not ordinary; on the contrary, the magnitude and complexity of her character greatly preoccupy the poet, who dedicates his art to exploring the vastness and greatness of her body. Baudelaire confirms the "vast expanse/middle" she occupies in the poetical imagination in *The Painter of Modern Life,* in which he situates her undecidable nature neither on the side of the animal nor on the side of the "pure beauty," which would be insufficient "to explain her mysterious and complex spell"; instead, he locates it on both sides at once. She is "that being, terrible and incommunicable," "terrible" because of her monstrous appearance and, as such, impossible to convey; yet she also paradoxically remains the most exhibited artistic figure "for whom, but above all through whom, artists and poets create their most exquisite jewels" (2:713).

My reading of Baudelaire's poetry has followed the transformation of the beautiful statue into a sublime and dangerous female apparition, the conversion of aesthetic pleasure into poetic pain. Regardless of the sense of visual security provided by the fixed form of the statue, women of stone in *Flowers of Evil* display a power to move the poetic subject from a blissful admiration of their marble surfaces to a horrified state of poetic paralysis. To fight the crippling effect generated by these representations of past beauty, Baudelaire "de-idealizes" women of stone by infusing their classical representations with another model of feminine figuration: modern urban women. In turn, modern women relate to their sisters in antiquity by retaining some of their ideal features. As bearers of classical attributes of beauty, modern women become as artistically valuable and viable as classical statues. We have thus seen the way in which the modern woman who emerges from both Baudelaire's imagination and his everyday world becomes a true subject of poetry. Baudelaire's curious proposition that in order to become a valuable work of art modern representation must rid itself of the human element left by the passage of the cosmopolitan woman has not eliminated the crucial role of the woman's body in the construct of modernity. However disjointed and monstrous her body appears in Baudelaire's poetry, it remains poetically modern.

Truffaut's Magical Women

In Truffaut's *Day for Night,* Ferrand (played by Truffaut himself) is portrayed directing his film *Meet Pamela.* We see him dealing with all aspects of his work not only as a director but also as a man who cares about the personal lives of his crew. One of the members of this crew, Alphonse, is a moody, emotional character whose personal life hinders his performance as an actor. He awkwardly manages his relationships with women; in fact, women in Alphonse's life are as tormenting and haunting as the question he randomly and obsessively asks: "Are women magical?"[12] This question produces resonances in Truffaut's entire film production. Indeed, each one of his films deals with mostly unsuccessful relationships between men/boys and women, as if women brought something more tragic than magical to his films. For Truffaut's male characters the tragedy of their lives is always connected to the degree of fascination they experience with the women they encounter. Magical women become responsible for men's personal dramas and psychological traumas, the two major emotional components valued above all by Truffaut in his films.

In her excellent study[13] focused on Truffaut's ability to make films "instinctively" rather than "intellectually," on the emotional sensitivity on which he depends to "short-circuit" logic and reason, on his art for cultivating secrets meant to remain opaque, Anne Gillain demonstrates that part of the secret linking all of his films is due to a particular type of rapport between man/boy-woman, an early intimacy and connection between two bodies endearing boys forever to their mothers. Whether or not the heroes of Truffaut's films are actual boys or boys trapped in men's bodies, they always seem to be searching for imaginary and ideal mothers to replace or supplement the dysfunctional one who has left their desire for maternal love unfulfilled. According to Gillain, cultural entities such as the city, the postal system, the amusement parks,[14] the interior of a house or a room, the chapel, and other symbolic structures become metaphoric mothers by way of natural and functional analogies. She argues that the only woman the men/boys in Truffaut's films enshrine in their most private fantasies is their mother. Gillain reads men's fascination for women, for their "magic," as a fascination for the mother's body, a feminine maze inside which they like to lose themselves.

As he reflects on filmmaking in *Day for Night,* Truffaut is also commenting on the important part played by the various aspects of "the feminine" in his films. The magical characteristics associated with the women on the screen form and inform another kind of magic, the one created by filmmaking. For example, by using numerous close-up shots and framing techniques, Truffaut isolates and magnifies woman's face in order to insist on particular elements of her beauty. Through the "magic of filmmaking" he thus brings the spectator visually and psychologically closer to the mystery and the magic that her beautifully expressive face may contain.

The close-up shot that Truffaut often uses to frame women's faces may be understood as a technique reflecting his desire to understand the mystery of/behind a face by enlarging it in order to expose all of its details. While maintaining the integrity of the image, Truffaut's close-up shots satisfy his desire for proximity to the details of the female subject, but they also activate his desire for truth. Indeed, it seems that Truffaut's insistence on representing women in close-up shots indicates his eagerness to pay close attention to her detailed features in prolonged fashion. By often closing up on the female face, he offers the viewers the opportunity to exercise their own interpretation on woman's detailed representation. Better yet, Truffaut establishes the possibility for the viewers not only to read feminine details but also to receive information from the enhanced images of her body. Thus, Truffaut generates the possibility of a discourse between the spectators and the magical woman on screen. His close-ups translate woman's face into a rich surface of information that the spectator in turn reads according to personal assumptions and values. Truffaut's cinematic fantasy to expose the magical realm of woman may be anchored in his visual questioning of her face: can her face speak? Can it reveal the secret of femininity to the men it confounds? The truth about women sought by Alphonse (and Truffaut) in *Day for Night* is correlative to the discovery of woman's being, presumably hidden behind the magic of her face.

In *Day for Night* Ferrand/Truffaut focuses his camera on the face of Julie/Pamela as a way to provide Alphonse—as well as the spectator—with the specular circumstances that aroused his curiosity about women and lead him to formulate the question about their magical appearance; it is also a way to allow Truffaut himself the opportunity to provide a visual answer to Alphonse's verbal question. The first time that Alphonse directs the question to Jean-François, the assistant director, he is told that women are not magical, because they have numerous affairs with different men: "When a woman tells you: 'I met exceptional human beings' it really means: 'I screwed many guys.'" Jean-François's answer indicates the moral implication of the word *magic,* which is here associated with the "proper" sexual conduct of women. According to Jean-François, only nonpromiscuous, and thus virtuous, women ought to be considered magical; however, looking at some of Truffaut's other films, we know that he finds promiscuity just as magical as virtue. Among his less virtuous female characters we find Antoine Doinel's mother in *The 400 Blows;* Theresa Saroyan in *Shoot the Piano Player;* Thérèse and Catherine in *Jules and Jim;* Anne in *Two English Girls;* Camille Bliss in *A Gorgeous Kid like Me;* Liliane in *Day for Night;* Hélène in *The Man Who Loved Women.* And the list is not exhaustive.

The second answer to Alphonse's question is given by Bernard, the prop man. To him the magic of women lies in (between?) their legs. Bernard's answer indicates Truffaut's predilection for women's legs, that is, for his representation of women in pieces. Women's legs are a major motif in Truffaut's films, from Antoine's mother sensuously rolling up her stockings in *The 400 Blows* to the anonymous legs passing above Julien's basement office windows in Truffaut's last film, *Confidentially Yours.*

The third answer to Alphonse's question is given by Julie, the main actress of the film(s) and herself the incarnation of feminine charm. To her, either everybody is magical, men and women, or nobody is. She purges Alphonse's question of its gender specification by creating a possibility for films and individuals to be understood outside of any sexual differentiation. In other words, she tells Antoine that the mystical charm of an individual is unrelated to sexual determination. The word *magic* operates independently of sexual categories. She tries to undermine the masculine belief about the mystical nature of women by desexualizing the word *magic*. Her way of eliminating sexual discrimination by erasing sexual differences appears, however, as an ineffectual effort at feminist cinema. In fact, she is totally dominated by Truffaut's intention of making an ancillary character out of her. She is instrumental in Alphonse's search for the truth concerning feminine nature; she provides him with a feminine point of view, an insider's opinion on the question of femininity, but her opinion is inconsequential for a female audience wishing to hear some degree of "feminist" wisdom from the only feminine voice allowed to speak about the misunderstanding affecting the male conception of the nature of femininity.

Julie is not herself; she has no independent thoughts outside Truffaut/Ferrand's directorial orders. In fact, Truffaut illustrates the way in which he dominates Julie's language and her acting in the scene that follows Julie's nervous breakdown after Alphonse has called her husband to inform him that he has slept with Julie. Julie has locked herself up in her changing room and refuses to see anyone. She finally accepts to see Ferrand, who eventually manages to calm her down. She pours her heart out to him and explains that life is unfair. The next day she feels better, and, while getting ready for her next shoot, she reads aloud the freshly written script for her next scene. While doing so, she soon realizes that Ferrand, making full use of real-life situations, real personal dramas, has recycled the monologue on the unfairness of life that she had shared with him the day before in total confidence. Truffaut, via Ferrand, reappropriates the most private expression of Julie's feminine despair by placing her own words in the text of his script without her consent. As an actress in his film, her life on and off of the set cannot be differentiated, and it is as her total person—woman and actress, private and public—that she falls under his directorship. In her critical study of Truffaut's cinema Annette Insdorf confirms that his women characters have no identity except that which male desire imparts to them: "Truffaut's females are often portrayed as existing less in, of, and for themselves than as realizations of male visions" (115). Like other women, Julie is a man-made character with no voice of her own. She is a creation of his fantasy, even when his fantasy includes her own language transposed into his cinematic language.

Behind Julie's answer to Alphonse's question on the magic nature of woman, we can hear Truffaut's voice saying that a woman cannot answer questions about the true nature of femininity because she denies the possibility of sexual difference and therefore the possibility of a self-standing feminine identity. With Julie, Truffaut sets up a controversial background for Alphonse's question; he provides a mild female opposition that self-destructs and conveniently consolidates his masculinist cinema. As far as he is concerned, of the three individuals presented with Alphonse's question, Julie offers the least convincing answer. Indeed, for Truffaut women are magical because they are sexually different from men, because they are a strange mix of promiscuity and virtue, and because they are only representable through particular pieces of their bodies.

For the purpose of identifying the lyric woman in Truffaut's cinema, the promiscuous, virtuous, and fragmented woman, I will concentrate on two of his films, *Jules and Jim* and *The Bride Wore Black*. In *Jules and Jim* Catherine is the promiscuous woman whose magnetic powers are intrinsic to the many different details of her face delineated by the camera, and in *The Bride Wore Black* Julie is the virtuous woman whose body is also represented in a fetishistic manner by Truffaut, who confirms his obsession with feminine details by repeatedly framing her unemotional face either in close shots or within the visible frame of the painter's easel. In both films the lyric woman is represented as she was in Petrarch's and in Baudelaire's poetry: in pieces.

In *Jules and Jim* we are invited to continue our investigation of detail, since the face of Catherine is persistently framed. In choosing her face as the predominant feminine representation in his film, Truffaut stands in a long lyrical tradition of faces in French poetry: the medieval adoration for the angelic face of the Lady, the Renaissance blason, the Nervalian and Baudelairean scrutiny of female facial details. For French lyrical poets the face in and of itself functions as a detail in relation to the rest of the body, and it also contains an abundance of details (eyes, mouth, eyebrows, etc.), each of which is so full of secret passions and emotions that they become as important as the woman's face from which they are detached. The configuration of the sexual body usually includes breasts, belly, and genitals as its centerpieces, all of which are available for a display of passionate and amorous vicissitudes. The decentered displacement of poetic interest from the sexually connoted body to its idealized extremities is less an exclusion of sexuality than a form of moral and aesthetic control over the conceivable risk of its breaking out into culturally prohibited performances. This libidinal and poetical energy displaced onto the extremities of the woman's body is a form of sublimation as well as a rhetorical exercise that results in the spiritual elevation of what Naomi Schor calls the "humble and prosaic detail"[15] of woman's body. Her face is brought into the field of poetic representation once its details have been purged of their realistic and libidinal contents. Each detail is highly idealized and stylized, creating a beautiful and untouchable dismembered woman as in the case of Petrarch's Laura and Baudelaire's unnamed beauties.

When woman is visually represented on Truffaut's lyrical screen, her body and her face are also broken into details as a result of the director's fascination with the enigmatic beauty of the particular woman he wishes to examine more closely. To view woman in detail is also to escape the fatal attraction that accompanies her essential and absolute beauty—the same dangerous beauty that Barthes evokes when he analyzes Garbo's face, describing it as "a kind of absolute state of the flesh, which could be neither reached nor renounced."[16] The threat of death ("mystical feelings of perdition" [72]) hanging over the aesthetic effect one experiences being in contact with Garbo's deified face is subverted by her heavy white makeup, which Barthes identifies as a white mask enhancing the details of her face such as her eyes ("two faintly tremulous wounds" [70]), her nostrils, and her eyebrows. It is these "human" details of her face that disrupt her fatal goddess look. Barthes explains that the mask of facticity, the white makeup applied to Garbo's face, allows for the emergence of her "human" facial details. Garbo's mask, as it reveals rather than conceals physical details of her face, creates what Barthes calls "a lyricism of woman" (71) opposed to her essential beauty. In *Jules and Jim* Truffaut's camera technique exhibits details on the face of Catherine that make her the incarnation of Barthes's lyrical woman. In fact, it is not Catherine's face alone but her detailed face that makes her a lyrical figure.

For Annette Insdorf, Truffaut's lyricism lies mainly in what she calls, along with Truffaut, "a cinema in the first person singular" (173–218). Viewed this way, Truffaut's autobiographical cinema qualifies as lyrical in the same way that Wordsworth's "Prelude" stands as a lyrical recounting of the life of the poet. Besides the autobiographical content of Truffaut's cinema, Insdorf is inclined to compare Truffaut's imagery with the images found in poems by Keats, Tennyson, Donne, and Robert Frost. And, in order to identify the degree of lyricism at work in Truffaut's representations of statues, she also evokes the poet and filmmaker Jean Cocteau, whom Truffaut[17] deeply admired: "Death in Cocteau's *Blood of a Poet* (1930) is a statue that becomes a woman—as would be figuratively true of Catherine in *Jules and Jim*" (195). Death and Catherine experience the same lyrical metamorphosis as they turn from stone to flesh, both poetic subjects displaying their lyrical transformations on the screen. By comparing Cocteau's female representations to Truffaut's, Insdorf reinforces the poetic qualities that constitute Truffaut's female characters. As she compares Julie's dressing in black and white in *The Bride Wore Black* with Death's similar dress code in *Blood of a Poet,* she makes the following remark concerning the odd characterization of women on screen: "Both women [Julie and Death] are alternately human and frozen, and fundamentally revenge figures" (195). Women in Truffaut's films are Baudelairean figures of the same kind that we identified as modern women and ideal women, human in flesh and frozen in stone.

In his book *The New Wave: Truffaut, Godard, Chabrol, Rhomer, Rivette*[18] James Monaco evokes the lyricism of female figures in Truffaut's films in terms of their relationship to art in general: "More often than not, since the men are artists—musicians, writers, painters—the women appear as art works, mysterious and confusing, variable and a little frightening" (70). In the opinion of Truffaut's critics who have considered the implication of the lyric in cinema, it is the mystery and the danger emanating from the women on Truffaut's screen that best characterize their lyrical content. The cliché that consists in making lyrical all images of women based on their mysterious and dangerous nature might explain the paucity of interest that film criticism has shown for Truffaut's cinema. His sentimentalist and masculinist cinema have appeared on the critical charts as a cinema of classical dimensions inasmuch as most of its themes revolve around male-female relationships.

Even if in *Le Secret perdu* Anne Gillain dramatized such relationships by analyzing their connection with the figure of the mother, the fact remains that what Barthes calls "the lyricism of woman," the detailed construction of her image, has been of secondary interest for critics naturally attracted to the "narrative harmony" running deep in Truffaut's construction of a cinematic world in which women carry their magic images like poetic icons while holding the role of destructive fictional heroines in the male characters' lives. While the implications of storytelling as a genre cannot be denied in the search for a common analogy to all the women in Truffaut's films, it is as poetic icons that they offer the crumbling image of their body.

In *Jules and Jim* the first feminine detail represented on the screen is less a body part than a body function: Catherine's voice. How can voice be effectively represented by an apparatus historically designed to capture and frame images?[19] When the voice belongs to a woman, what is the role played by gender in this problematic of visual representation? These are some of the questions raised by the voice in the dark that opens *Jules and Jim*.

While the screen is still black, a woman's voice is heard. No musical background, no other artificial sounds, accompany this voice so crisp and clear that it sounds like an earnest statement purposely isolated to underscore the intensity of a vocal feminine presence from the start: "You said to me: I love you. I said to you: wait. I was going to say: take me. You said to me: go away." The voice is deep and sensual; two qualities defining the voice of Jeanne Moreau, the woman behind the voice and the actress in *Jules and Jim*. It mixes childish and mature tones in the same breath; it speaks of love, frustration, and separation. In this section I will first attempt an uncovering of the filmic status of this voice "singing" in the dark and then a questioning of the effects of this voice on the spectator expecting visual, not aural, pleasure. Whose unexpected voice do we hear coming from the darkness of the screen?

Plot provides us with an immediate answer to this question. This voice is the disembodied voice of Catherine, the main female character in Truffaut's 1962 movie *Jules and Jim,* in which two young men, Jules and Jim, fall victim to their dream of *ideality* represented by the sublime statue of a woman, a work they come across by accident during a slide show. The beautiful statue on the slide triggers their desire to search for the actual woman represented by the statue. This woman is Catherine. When they meet Catherine, they know that she is their sculpted desire come true. Catherine's complex nature leaves her out of psychological reach, however, and, despite her coming into Jules and Jim's human world, she remains an unattainable object of desire throughout. As an impossible representation of desire, she raises the question of feminine figuration in *Jules and Jim,* a question prompted by the mysterious female voice opening the film.

The voice in the dark prefacing the visual experience that is about to begin dramatizes the distinction between the vocal and the specular, a distinction thoroughly investigated by Kaja Silverman in her 1988 book *The Acoustic Mirror: The Female Voice in Psychoanalysis and Cinema.* I will first refer to Silverman's argument on the female voice and particularly on the maternal voice[20] in order to understand the dichotomous nature of *Jules and Jim,* in which the division between the vocal and the visual is made clear from the start. In the process I will unmask the performing presence of the maternal figure invested in the voice prefacing Truffaut's film *Jules and Jim*.

For the purpose of defining as accurately as possible the female subject represented in cinema, Silverman uses Guy Rosolato's phrase "the acoustic mirror,"[21] which indicates the double function of the voice for any subject that simultaneously receives and produces sounds, internalizing the voice of identification while also externalizing it as an object of projection. Seen/heard through the acoustic mirror, the voice "violates the bodily limits upon which classic subjectivity depends" (Silverman 80). The bodily limits evoked by Silverman are determined by modes of identification built on the specular order alone. In psychoanalysis the primacy of the specular over any other modes of perception coincides with the critical oedipal moment when the infant identifies its own body, for the first time separated from the mother's body. According to Jacques Lacan, this first coming into subjectivity occurs in the life of the infant between the sixth and the eighteenth month.[22]

For the infant's first meeting with its subject, Lacan proffers a symbolic object, a mirror in which the infant first catches sight of its full body image. Lacan's mirror is less an actual mirror than a metaphor for the mother's body, where mental separation of bodies first takes place. Past the mirror stage, the child continues to enhance the contours of her or his own subject while growing into a social and cultural being. The child acquires her or his individual image in relation to the bodies the child sees evolving around him or her. These "other" bodies act as mirrors that send back images of differences and similarities to the subject, who, subsequently, assumes its identity and the limitations of its own body. Rosolato's concept of the acoustic mirror adapts the optical relation that the subject has with the mirror in psychoanalytical theory as if the mirror were reflecting sounds rather than images. The subject constitutes itself as it first differentiates sounds through the acoustic mirror. Rosolato claims that the process of identification starts from birth and that the child, born with reduced visual powers, first distinguishes sounds[23]—especially the mother's voice—and incorporates them as if they were its own sounds. Rosolato associates the mechanism of emission and reception of the voice with "the images of entry and departure relative to the body" (Silverman 80). In Rosolato's theory the voice of the mother creates the vocal subject in similar ways that the imago in Lacan's theory of the mirror stage creates the specular subject. Rosolato gives the speaking mother the status of a vocal mirror in which the child recognizes the mother's voice as its own voice. Thus, according to Rosolato, subjectivity is not solely dependent on the image of the mother, but, rather, her voice has already set into place the structures of individuation. In the acoustic mirror the mother is first perceived as a speaking subject before being perceived as a subject of speech. She is a speaking voice before being an image/body spoken about; as the acoustic mirror, she becomes the subject's voice providing a vocal model of identification.

Silverman examines the two paradoxical functions of the acoustic mirror that she reads as a sonorous envelope that initially provides pleasure and later must be rejected. In the early life of the infant the voice of the mother is perceived as a swaddling envelope of sounds protecting him. Once the infant becomes an individual subject caught in the cultural structures in place, the mother's voice represents maternal "abjection," in which the subject "hears all the repudiated elements of its infantile babble" (81) that he must reject. The central problematic raised by Silverman questions the constant shifting of the subject's position vis-à-vis the acoustic mirror. Is the infant inside or outside the sonorous envelope created by the maternal voice? Is the mother inside or outside her own vocal envelope? Is the mother's voice a voice of pleasure or a voice of fear?

In answering these questions, Silverman first invokes Michel Chion's theory of the "uterine night," a sort of nightmare within which the child is trapped by the maternal voice.[24] In the uterine night the mother is outside producing the sounds that form the confining walls of a dark prison. Chion's view of the traumatic implications of the maternal voice on the formation of the cinematic subject lie in sharp contrast to Guy Rosolato's theory on the cinematic voice perceived as a "protective blanket," an aural environment of pleasure. Rosolato indicates that child and mother live in an undifferentiated state of vocal plenitude. According to him, they are both situated inside the circle of sounds created by the mother's voice.

In light of these different approaches to voice in cinema we come closer to understanding a little more clearly the odd beginning of *Jules and Jim,* a beginning in which there are no images to be seen, only a female voice to be heard. This voice seems to cradle the spectator in the dark as it naively narrates/sings a simple, repetitive riddle: "You said to me: I love you. I said to you: wait. I was going to say: take me. You said to me: go away." In duplicating the simplicity of a nursery rhyme, this riddle bestows maternal qualities upon the voice. Silverman's question about the position of the mother and the child in relation to the sonorous envelope created by the voice is fully dramatized in this "preface" to *Jules and Jim.* In a single instant Silverman's distinctive critical positions on the role of voice as maternal pleasure or maternal fear conflate. I will now attempt to restore both positions and to see how they determine the double presence of pleasure and fear within the same vocalic representation of the mother.

The voice in the dark at the beginning of *Jules and Jim* dramatizes

Chion's "uterine night" and, as such, speaks from outside the vocal darkness it creates. Catherine's riddle lures its listeners into the darkness of her femininity, and the dark frames accompanying the voice serve as a metaphor for her unappealing dark womb. The spectators, sitting in the dark movie theater, their eyes riveted to the screen, expecting it to produce images, are thrown into total confusion by the dark frames that pull them into the uterine night, in which they become the infant-subject trapped by the maternal voice. In the first few seconds of *Jules and Jim* the spectator experiences a moment of anxiety as he or she is forced to become a listener against his or her own will and desire to see. In place of the expected visual pleasure—an anticipated pleasure for which he or she has paid his dues by buying a ticket—the spectator finds himself or herself trapped in the undesirable interiority of the vocal uterine night.

Rosolato's theory of first auditive bliss suggests a different scenario for the spectator thrown into total darkness; the spectator loses all visual sense of subjectivity and returns to the undivided world of presymbolic plenitude and bliss where the only "other" object is the maternal voice enveloping the subject in its blanket of pleasure. In Rosolato's terms the spectator listening to the maternal voice at the beginning of *Jules and Jim* introjects the voice and makes it his or her own. As through an acoustic mirror, phonic utterances detach themselves from their original maternal voice to fill the subject with a sonorous and rhythmical identity.

This moment of vocal identification with Catherine's voice precedes the visual bonding between the spectator and the images of the film. Whether nightmare (in Chion's thesis) or bliss (in Rosolato's thesis), the maternal voice prefacing Truffaut's *Jules and Jim* reenacts a primal scene of subjectivity, a vocal fantasy for blinded spectators.

What happens to Catherine's voice once the film's visual mechanism is under way? Her maternal voice that once protected and cradled the child/spectator with the simplicity of its rhythms and sounds becomes the voice of a woman expressing sexual desire. Even as the voice in the dark sings its mysterious riddle, Catherine's sexuality can already be differentiated in terms of what she says as opposed to how she says it. In other words, her sexuality depends on the meaning of the words rather than on the musicality supporting the words. Indeed, the female voice that asserts, "I love you; wait; take me; go away," utters words of a sexual significance depicting in simplistic terms a scene of frustrated love. In this scene an unidentified lover declares his love ("I love you") to a woman who does not feel ready to respond immediately to such passion. She asks her lover to wait ("wait"). When she feels that the moment has come for them to consummate their passion, she offers her body to her lover ("take me"), but the latter, tired of waiting, casts her off ("go away"). The sexual connotation of these four verbal injunctions leaves behind the maternal resonances of Catherine's rhythmical voice. Understood for what it says, the voice in the dark becomes the voice of sexual desire, a seductive voice speaking a lover's discourse.

The first auditive instant provided by the chanting voice at the beginning of *Jules and Jim* mixes the cradling sounds of motherhood with the riddling language of sexuality. The mother behind the voice in the dark is also a sexual being seducing the blinded audience into its feminine darkness.

We begin to wonder whether the feminine voice singing in the dark belongs to a loving mother or to a seductive temptress. Much of the ambiguous nature of the feminine figure is based on the conflict I have just traced between voice and language, sounds and words, rhythms and meanings, and these conflictual terms in turn delineate a conflictual feminine figure, maternal in essence but divided in nature between platonic love and sexual love. Similar questions on the nature of maternal voice are raised in *La Jeune née*, in which Cixous views voice with a capital *V* as the legacy of motherhood resisting symbolic codification. The voice of the mother is a powerful stream of sounds that cannot be cut off by the symbolic order, the paternal order of language. In *La Jeune née,* a poetical analysis of the feminine unconscious in relation to the female body, Cixous offers an alternative to the psychoanalytical views of Freud and Lacan based on the infant's visual apprehension of the world. Instead, she proposes a feminine reading of the child's psychological and cultural development based on the specificity of the maternal drive, on the importance of its role, which Freud and Lacan's male-oriented theories have downplayed. She develops a comprehensive view of woman, and she evaluates woman's power to participate in all intellectual discourses while involving her own body into the force of her argument. According to Cixous, the maternal substance always informs the feminine subject in its making. Voice is a maternal element sustaining the specific nature of woman. The voice of the mother is pleasurable and unthreatening; it is

> a song prior to Law, prior to breathing cut off by the Symbolic, reclaimed by the separating authority of language. The deepest, oldest, and sweetest apparition. In each woman sings a nameless first love. Within the woman's psyche there always is something of "the mother," repairing, nurturing, and resisting separation, a force which does not let itself be cut off but rather tires out all the codes. (172)[25]

According to Cixous, the maternal voice stands outside the "law" just as Catherine's voice prefacing *Jules and Jim* stands outside the actual limits of the film, before the credits and before the film's first images. Cixous's view on how the "Symbolic" interrupts the respiratory function of the voice lends itself to the odd beginning of *Jules and Jim* when the female voice in the dark is interrupted by the written credits and the first images, two symbolic occurrences marking the official beginning of the film. In *Jules and Jim* the voice in the dark permeates the film's visual order throughout.

Beyond its vocal introduction the film itself provides some answer to the ambiguous nature of the feminine figure. The nature of the female voice prefacing *Jules and Jim* owes much of its ambiguity to the fact that it does not accompany a body or an image. The disembodied maternal voice Silverman evokes in *The Acoustic Mirror* is always a voice-over, a voice separated from its original body but initiating a relation of signification with the images appearing on the screen as it speaks. The voice in the dark in *Jules and Jim* is a voice(-)over nothing, a voice for voice's sake. As the film progresses, the voice becomes associated with the visual image of Catherine. Yet, even when the voice has claimed Catherine's body as its originator, the dichotomy between music and language, between maternal rhythms and sexual signifiers, does not dissolve into the film's visual order.

Catherine's singing voice resounds again during the film when she performs a song entitled "The Swirl of Life" in front of her three lovers. Catherine's song is written by Albert, one of her three lovers; the voice is hers, the lyrics are his. We may view the singing as an emanation of her maternal self and the language of the song as an emanation from the masculine/paternal other embodied in the three male figures who participate in Catherine's love life. Indeed, either directly or indirectly, the three men listening to her have established a relationship of paternity with her. Jules is the real father of their little girl, Sabine; Jim is the short-lived would-be father of Catherine's miscarried child; and, finally, Albert is the "adoptive" father ready to marry Catherine and, in his own words, become Sabine's stepfather. Thus, with this audience for her performance the division between maternal voice and paternal language manifests itself more clearly as Catherine sings "Le Tourbillon de la vie." The song has a simple and repetitious melody; it has "a catchy tune" eliciting a desire to hum along. The pleasure of singing along is somehow reminiscent of the aural pleasure in early infancy during which the infant incorporates the mother's voice as if it were his or her own. The melody of the song creates the acoustic mirror in which sounds are reflected upon the subject able to receive and produce the song at the same time. The lyrics, however, retell a familiar love scenario in which a man meets a woman, a singer whose voice coaxed him to love her: "she sang with a voice that immediately beguiled me." He loses her to the swirl of time, but later in his life he finds her again in a café, where she sings with her "fatal voice." He gets drunk while listening to her wheedling voice—"I got drunk while listening to her"—and finally he wakes in her passionate embrace. The fantasy leading the powerless male into the arms of the femme fatale is initiated by the bewitching voice of the woman-singer. She is a siren enchanting him with her voice of pleasure. In the myth of the sirens pleasure rapidly recedes, and the sailors are eventually destroyed by the nymphs's ensnaring song, a song that represents the destruction of male subjectivity. "The Swirl of Life" has the intoxicating quality of the siren's song, for it describes a chaotic love story for which the woman is responsible. Such chaos also marks the song's composition; indeed, the long ending repeats ad nauseam the two lovers' separating and meeting over and over again, thus creating a vertiginous and dizzying effect justifying the title of the song.

The narrator in the song, the "I" speaking the dizzying words of the love affair, is male. There is complete identification between Albert, the writer of the song, and the male narrator in his song. In his composition Albert projects the powerful and seductive effect of Catherine's voice on all men listening to her. In fact, Catherine's voice enacts the vocal seduction already signified by the lyrics. She is the female voice singing a male song for a male audience. She represents the voice, and Albert (as well as Jules and Jim) represents the language dismantled by the power of her voice.

The separation of voice and language retroactively bestows meaning upon the first "vocal scene" of the movie. The female voice singing in the dark becomes separated from the content of the opening riddle. As melodic voice, it falls under the maternal category, and, as spoken language, it delineates the sexual content imposed on its maternal musicality by the fathers of Catherine's born and unborn children. The analysis of Catherine's performance of "The Swirl of Life" dissipates the ambiguity behind the voice opening the film because, in the final analysis, it casts each component of the act of singing to its particular role: to the mother the voice and to the father the language.

Thus, the maternal voice emerges from our analysis of *Jules and Jim* as a feminine detail separated from the corpus of female images and language generally constituting the elements of representation most accounted for in film criticism. Situated outside images and language, the maternal voice belongs to a psychoanalytical category outside the Imaginary and the Symbolic, Lacan's Real. As I have already indicated in the previous chapter, Lacan defines the Real as the missed encounter between subject and language that translates into a terrifying unknown territory standing beyond all representations.[26] The fear generated by Lacan's Real may account for Chion's negative view of the uterine night. The inside of the womb belongs to the biological reality of maternal interiority, and therefore it is not accessible to the subject of language. Outside its metaphoric representation the maternal womb cannot successfully be conceived of by the subject. It is the maternal body that the subject must reject in order to function linguistically and culturally. A voice capable of recreating the uterine conditions of the prelinguistic environment surrounding the infant would also recreate the horror standing beyond all possible representations of the mother's body. The voice that brings the subject closer to the maternal womb also destroys the subject of language. Lacan's Real stands outside representation just as, in the unsettling darkness preceding the film, Truffaut's maternal voice stands outside the film's actual limits. In *Jules and Jim* the initial voice catches the spectator unawares, unprepared as he is to receive its poetic of blindness and pure sound.

The spectator may well confront the initial voice with fear as he is reminded of Chion's uterine night, the paradigm for the threatening female interiority that the male subject must reject in order to function in his cultural environment. He may also allow himself, however, to be wrapped up inside the pleasurable sonorous envelope of the female voice suggested by Rosolato, thus giving full power to his fantasy of being led back to a lost state of union with the mother. Jules and Jim are Truffaut's creation of male subjectivity fighting the maternal force deployed by Catherine's voice and finding refuge in the visual pleasure provided by filmic representations of her body. As a way to negate the power of the voice singing in the dark, Jules and Jim set up a search for the body belonging to the feminine voice heard at the film's outset. As their search progresses, the unidentified woman's voice becomes a figure of reality embodied by Catherine. Throughout the film, however, Catherine will always remain the feminine and maternal force that can never be captured; she will escape the logic of Jules and Jim's world, and, at very best, she will only give Jules and Jim the frustrated love life foreshadowed by the lyrics of her opening riddle.

At the end of the film, at Jim's funeral and Catherine's, Jules feels almost relieved by her tragic disappearance. He is not afraid to lose her anymore because, as the voice-over declares, "it was done." Her body had been cremated, her image had finally disappeared, she had returned to her initial condition of a presence without a representation, of a voice in the dark. Catherine's maternal presence continues to live beyond the death of her body, and the voice-over accompanying the final images of the film reveals the undying force of motherhood manifesting itself as it mentions the great relief that Sabine, Catherine's daughter, will provide for her father now that Catherine is dead.

The voice-over tells us that Jules feels released from the nauseating vertigo that Catherine created in his life; it also tells us about his faith in a better future thanks to Sabine: "They [Catherine and Jim] left nothing of themselves. Jules had his daughter. Did Catherine like struggling for struggling's sake? No, but Jules felt dizzy ad nauseam from her struggle." Jules believes that the nausea that ripped through his tormented self while Catherine was alive is finally over when Catherine dies; however, he is literally reminded verbally (by voice-over) that Sabine is here to replace the void, the "nothing" left behind by the tragic disappearance of Catherine and Jim. Although Sabine is also Jules's daughter, we are led to question this paternity in an early scene of the film. During a conversation at the German chalet between Catherine and Jim, the latter expresses doubts about Jules's claim to fatherhood by declaring how different Jules and Sabine look. As if to maintain a certain level of doubt in the spectator's mind, Catherine denies Jim's insinuations in a dispassionate, almost indifferent, manner: "Believe what you will, she is his."

Whatever the case, Sabine, the undeniable daughter of Catherine, continues to represent the presence of her maternal power. In the melancholy darkness that fills Jules's mind after Catherine's death, the incorporated voice of motherhood invested in the final voice-over offers to Jules the undying figure of female oral/aural presence represented by Sabine ensuring Catherine's lineage, the natural legacy of the maternal voice. Although Sabine does not appear on screen after the scenes at the German chalet, the final voice-over designates her as the unquestionable continuation of Catherine's presence in Jules's life. She offers a filmic version to Cixous's unbreakable chain of maternal sounds.

Beyond representation and beyond life itself voice(over) confirms the undying force of feminine presence in the film. The initial voice in the dark has mothered a final voice-over confirming her presence by way of her child. Even though the female voice is cut off from the female body it belongs to when Catherine dies, it still survives the terminal cut represented by her death and lives on as a representation of the feminine detail inexorably present in and through the techniques and narrative of the film. As he introduces *Jules and Jim* with the overwhelming effect of Catherine's chant, it may be argued that Truffaut consciously staged the vocal in opposition to the visual as part of his primary concern for the film. It cannot be denied that the lingering voice motif running throughout, even beyond death itself, appeals to such theory. The female voice, however, remains a voice in the dark, a feminine detail that may be said to belong to his own "dark continent," his repressed desire to "represent voice" with a medium primarily designed to offer visual thrills. Truffaut's recurrent use of the voice-over technique in all of his films reunites him, consciously or unconsciously, with the pleasure of working closely with the vocal component so intrinsically attached to woman while also, as we have argued, remaining cut off from her visual representation.

Brought together in their search for their dream of the perfect female by the enchanting and mysterious voice in the dark, the vocal fantasy for Jules and Jim slowly becomes a figure of reality embodied in Catherine. Yet the feminine voice ultimately lends its initial feelings of fear and pleasure to another type of feminine detail, this time belonging directly to Catherine's body, to her feminine image as it changes from stone to flesh.

Although the spectators watching *Jules and Jim* have already been introduced to Catherine vocally, it takes some time before the two free-spirited bachelors in the film themselves fall sway to her compelling presence. In the beginning of the film we are able to follow them in their active social lives: they enjoy the company of women, late nights, café life, art and literature, and a good game of dominos. There is, however, a shadow over their solid friendship, a slight imbalance in feminine conquests. Jim has numerous affairs, while Jules needs to be initiated to the love game by extroverted women like Thérèse. Jules is a sentimental and nostalgic character with a strong desire to find the ideal woman. In fact, the day he loses Thérèse to a stranger she meets in a café, he draws with chalk the Matisse-like contour of a woman's face on the table, as if he were transposing visually and in his own artistic terms the face of feminine perfection that he has not yet met but will encounter one day. Indeed, the drawing on the table acts as a visual forerunner to another framed female face that stirs the greatest passion for both Jules and Jim. The immediate editing response to the scene in which Jules draws the woman of his dreams is a cut to the scene in which Jules and Jim finally meet on screen the woman's face, which will determine the course of their lives. The transition between the two scenes is quite abrupt, as if Truffaut did not want to delay any longer the crucial moment of encounter between the two men and Catherine's face. In the scene immediately following Jules's impromptu drawing on the café table, Jules and Jim pay a visit to their friend Albert, of whom we know nothing except that he is "the friend of painters and sculptors," and without further explanations the lights are turned off, and Albert shows his two friends a series of slides representing statues of women. Suddenly, a beautiful sculpture appears on the screen, and, in an instant, the destiny of Jules and Jim is changed, as they embark on a passionate journey that will take them from the slide to the statue itself and finally to the body of the actual Catherine.

In the film we are visually introduced to Catherine through the representation of her face on a slide. This time, however, unlike the very beginning of the film when her soothing voice is heard, there is a feeling of both inaccessibility and imminent danger in the way Catherine's face first appears on the screen. Catherine's face is frozen, first onto the stone and second onto the slide. Her twice-immobilized face acts as an extra protection for the two men, whose attraction and eagerness may bring them too close, too fast, to her Medusan face. Catherine's face appears to Jules and Jim like a Medusa's head, that is to say, a face with powers to turn to stone the men who look at it. We know that for Freud the myth of the Medusa's head serves as an illustration of the threat of castration. It is indeed the specter of castration that Jules and Jim face in the presence of the statue, although at the time they see the slide they are still protected by the rigidity imposed by the slide and the stone on the dangerous Medusa. Immobilized in its form, the statue remains primarily the exciting object of a male fantasy that Jules and Jim can make appear or disappear at will.

Catherine's first frozen appearance on the screen suspends her Medusan powers; at that point they are powerless to reach the active world outside the slide, allowing Jules and Jim to contemplate Catherine's ideal beauty at greater length and with greater pleasure. Aesthetic considerations also seem to have motivated Truffaut's first representation of Catherine's face. Her quiet beauty endows her with a divine quality, making her an inaccessible goddess to Jules and Jim. Catherine's Medusan figure—that is, her representation of mythical danger—and her ideal beauty widen the gap separating her from Jules and Jim. She appears on the slide as the impossible goddess on a pedestal, the essence of a masculine dream of perfect beauty and contained danger.

Jules and Jim's tenacious desire to bring the statue from the realm of dreams to that of reality slowly materializes. Before she comes to life, Catherine's masks of immobility must fall away one by one. From the face on the slide Truffaut takes Jules and Jim to the statue on the island, thus bringing them closer to both the danger and the goddess. On the island the two men spend a great deal of time with the statue, which they examine meticulously—an activity reminiscent of the poetic subject circling the statue in Baudelaire's poem "The Mask." Their detailed observation of the statue is conveyed by Truffaut's editing technique of quickly cutting from one particular feature of the statue's face to another.

At last the two men move from the statue to the apparition of the real

Catherine. When Catherine initially appears on the screen, a series of close-ups of her eyes and lips recalls the same editing movements, the same meticulous cutting, at work on the face of the statue. These camera movements not only indicate the similarities between the statue and Catherine; they also place her face under the sign of fragmentary detail. In fact, now that Catherine has become a living woman, Jules and Jim confront the inherent danger and beauty of this feminine apparition of pure lyrical love. By coming to life, Catherine does not abandon her goddesslike powers, but, as she steps out of the slide's rigid frame, the danger of her liberated beauty is activated and allows Jules and Jim to believe that they can finally capture her through their undivided love for her. In fact, Catherine sets the film narrative in motion as she fills the lives of Jules and Jim with the unexpected dangers that were only latent in her first appearance on the slide.

For Jules and Jim to think they could meet and live with a goddess without risks is a foolish dream. She is the incarnation of the otherwise unseizable fantasy of two romantic men, and, even though she appears in human attire, she still displays details of her divine powers that the camera singles out (the camera follows and focuses on her eyes and lips in close-up shots). With her framed image occupying most of the screen, she is always the object of the camera's gaze, even when Jules and Jim do not look at her—in fact, the camera often appears as the third male subject that cannot take its fascinated eye off of her—and she often occupies the first and last shot in sequences in which the three characters are together. In fact, Truffaut's camera work, more than Jules and Jim themselves, contributes to Catherine's identification as a demigoddess, metamorphosed from stone to flesh.

Like most goddesses, she is beautiful, unpredictable, and her immortality is underlined by her indifference to death. Twice, Catherine confronts death. The first time, at a point when Jules and Jim no longer seem to be paying attention to her, she jumps into the Seine, determined to disappear even if momentarily, from the lives of both men, thus punishing them for ignoring her. Here we must mention that Catherine's leap into the Seine is motivated by a misogynous conversation between Jules and Jim, who refer to Baudelaire's worst statements on women in order to feed their own antifeminine dialogue. In substantiating his position that woman is solely a sexual object and an inferior being, Jules cites numerous misogynistic passages from Baudelaire's *Journaux intimes:* "Woman is natural and, therefore, abominable" (1:677); "Scarecrow, monster, art killer, you idiot, you slut . . . utmost ignorance combined with utmost depravation" (1:698); "I have always wondered why women were allowed in churches. What conversation can they possibly have with god?" (1:693). These misogynist quotations from Baudelaire have a provocative effect (on the spectator and) on Catherine, who prefers to simulate her own death by drowning rather than suffer the reappropriated language of Baudelaire's worst "poetics."

Because she did not really intend to die but, rather, to scare her two companions, she emerges from the water after taking her unexpected leap, and she has a smile on her face—a smile of satisfaction at Jules and Jim's sudden terror at the prospect of losing her. Her intention as a woman to disappear momentarily from the lives of Jules and Jim by drowning herself is counterbalanced by her nature as a demigoddess taking revenge on their unbearably misogynist language. Her smile can be read as a sign of revenge while also recalling the statue's smile, a smile of stone that remains unaltered by the human concerns expressed by Jules and Jim, who have just realized that losing Catherine would represent an incomparably traumatic experience for them. Her smile indicates her belief in the nonfinality of death.

This same peaceful smile freezes on her lips when, in the company of Jim, she drives her car over a bridge and finally kills them both. In fact, the scene of Catherine's leap into the Seine foreshadows the scene in which she drives off the bridge. In both scenes death is not perceived as a tragic end to two lives but, on the contrary, as the sealing of two fates, Catherine's and Jim's, while Jules is left with the pain of this double loss. The day after Catherine's jump into the Seine, Jim is suddenly touched by a striking vision of tranquillity, an ethereal moment of peaceful union between Catherine and him only possible beyond life itself. Compelled by an unknown force to draw Catherine as she disappears into the water, he imagines them both swimming away together, while Jules worries about Jim's simulated death by asphyxiation. In fact, Jim's "flash of admiration" for Catherine's leap offers the premonitory terms of their future death aboard the car she drives off the edge. In the scene of the fatal car accident the smiling Catherine and the tranquil Jim are portrayed as serenely going to their death. We can only imagine that, as the car disappears under the water, Jim finally realizes his earlier dream of swimming away with Catherine, who has now completed the full representation of the siren, whose voice and beauty have led her male victim into the depths of the water. As for Jules, left behind at Catherine's request specifically to watch death in action, he is overtaken by fear, as Jim had pictured him in his vision, while the car goes over the bridge.

First Jules then Jim are victims of Catherine's smile, for they both cut themselves off from their active sexual lives (before Catherine, Jules and Jim—Jim more than Jules—have numerous affairs). Their frivolous and carefree lives cease almost immediately when they meet Catherine, from whom they become inseparable, as shown, for example, throughout the long sequence in Provence. Finally, at the outbreak of the war Jules marries her, and Jim, while vaguely keeping in touch with an old flame, becomes a solitary writer slowly consumed by his attraction to her. They have both fallen under the magnetizing effect of her smile, a smile that becomes a facial detail of her indifference to their "human" love, a detail for which Jim, finally, has to die. Truffaut's fixation on Catherine's smile, a mark of her divinity, is duplicitous. First, the repeated shots of the smile indicate his desire to recall forever this seductive and dangerous feature of the woman's face. Second, he knows the danger of such a seduction, and, in order to protect himself against these lips, he immobilizes them in an everlasting smile. This petrification of Catherine's smile by the camera is a rhetorical form of fragmentation. Catherine's smile is a synecdoche for her unattainable body, and it is cut off from the rest of her body by a director all too well-aware of her power over the men at whom she smiles.

Catherine's smile, her nose, lips, and her voice (all of her partial representations) contribute to the fragmented construct of the lyric image that sustains the feminine figure on Truffaut's screen. Her fragmentation, however, has a double effect on Jules and Jim—and perhaps on Truffaut as well as on the spectators. Indeed, her feminine pieces act as agents of separation as well as agents of reparation for those whose gaze enacts a detailed examination of her body. Her voice has suturing effects, while her smile has rupturing effects. As a voice, she evokes *jouissance;* as a smile, she evokes pain. As such, she takes lyricism a step backwards in its history to the time when the lyric was primarily a song, a voice before becoming a face, a figure, a fragment, a symbolic set of broken pieces.

In *The Bride Wore Black* Julie Kohler is five women in one as she assumes the task of killing the five men who accidentally shot her husband to death on the steps of the church where they had been married a few minutes before. Driven by her ordeal, she becomes the ideal woman for each of the five men she plans to murder. She matches to perfection the ideal woman of their dreams, a dream come true but a dangerous one for which they must die. Bliss, whose name ironically signifies absolute pleasure, is the first victim: he falls over a balcony on his engagement day as he politely tries to retrieve the scarf of the mysterious woman—Julie—who has seduced him in an instant; the same woman poisons Coral, an introvert and a dreamer who is enthralled by her magical appearance; then she shuts the arrogant politician Morane in a cupboard, where he suffocates to death. It is at this point of Julie's unexplained series of killings that Truffaut chooses to reveal her motives; while listening to Morane suffocating, she begins to tell the story of two happy children, David and her.

A flashback scene accompanies her narration, and we see the two children simulating a wedding ceremony and promising each other eternal fidelity. This scene finally brings to light Julie's determination to avenge the death of David, the boy she grew up with and unequivocally loved throughout the years and to whom she had just been married when Bliss, Coral, Morane, Fergus, and Delvaux accidently shot him. The spectators are now able to identify better with Julie and to observe her crimes with more compassion and empathy.

After postponing the killing of Delvaux, who is arrested by the police before she can activate her fatal plan, she enters Fergus's life as a model for his painting of Diana the Huntress, an opportune character to help her accomplish her deed. As she regularly pauses for him, her arrow often pointed in Fergus's direction, she has ample opportunities to kill him; it is only after some hesitation, however, that she finally releases her bow and kills him. (I will examine her unexpected hesitation further along in this chapter.) Finally, she purposely shows up at his funeral in order to be arrested and brought to prison, where Delvaux, the last victim, is serving time. In prison she manages to get closer to him by volunteering to serve food to the prisoners. A large kitchen knife and a shrill scream indicate in a very Hitchcockian moment when she has accomplished her deadly mission. The film ends with the paradoxical sound of the wedding march, which represents the dramatic event that triggered Julie's killings in the first place and the time of her own symbolic death. Throughout the film she often appears with an expressionless face placing her outside the usually responsive world of humans. She unflinchingly performs her deadly mission like a mysterious corpse back from its demise, one that, for her, occurred on her wedding day, as her soul dies the minute David is fatefully shot. Her symbolic death is confirmed by a failed suicide attempt: she then realizes that she does not need to kill herself, being already dead inside.

Julie plays the role of the perfect object of desire five times, each time with true efficiency and complete success, as we see her five male victims blindly fall into her feminine snare. Although Truffaut was at that time completely under the influence of Hitchcock, to whom he had just dedicated an entire volume,[27] he also seems to offer his own visual opinion on the vulnerable nature of male desire; the strong lyricism that characterizes his own work remains intact. Julie is the ideal object of desire for the five men she plans to kill. She successively represents feminine conquest for Bliss, a dream of pure love and magic for Coral, the perfect female housekeeper and governess for Morane, long-awaited aesthetic perfection for Fergus, the pleasures of eating for Delvaux. As the prototypical object of desire, Julie becomes increasingly more dangerous as the five men reduce the distance between her ideal image and her actual body. Distance is the only way to preserve desire's unfulfillable nature, its true ideal form, which implies its movement from one fantasy to the next.

As Bersani observes in *Baudelaire and Freud,* ideal desire may only survive if satisfaction is imperfect, thus leading the subject to build excitement for another fantasy.[28] The inherent inadequacy of desire represents its only chance of survival, its only chance to stay away from a single locus of satisfaction. But, if and when desire meets its true match, its fully realized center, its real body, the desiring subject goes to his tragic end, he cannot outlive the absolute pleasure of perfection. In that sense Julie embodies the devastating effects of a totally fulfilled desire, and she knowingly becomes the fatal object of desire for the five men she kills. As a real incarnation of desire, or desire made flesh, she fulfills the destruction of desire and of its bearers. The image of unparalleled desire provided by Julie's five personalities implies the death of the subjects—Bliss, Coral, Morane, Fergus, and Delvaux—and the devaluation of the power of desire. Truffaut's most powerful and symbolic dramatization of the objectification of desire in *The Bride Wore Black* is contained in the few scenes in which Julie meets Fergus, the painter, the artist.

Julie insinuates herself into Fergus's life as the perfect model for his painting of Diana the Huntress. It is in this episode of Julie's metamorphosis into a femme fatale that the lyrical symbolism of her appearance, linked to the figure of the goddess Diana, acquires its full development on Truffaut's screen. Her transformation into Diana triggers yet another metamorphosis: that of "Fergus the woman chaser" into "Fergus the lover" consumed by his adoration of Julie/Diana. Julie becomes Diana for the purpose of using the goddess's powers to kill her adoring admirer, and Fergus wishes to be pierced symbolically by the goddess's arrow, to die out of love for the mythical figure he has fixed on his canvas, to give his life in exchange for his fulfilled desire. He confirms his willingness to die when, caught in the passion of his painting, he asks Julie/Diana to direct the aim of her extended bow in his direction. This impassioned artist is the only man in the movie to declare his love for Julie. We can wonder, however, whether he loved the woman or the myth and, more important, whether, in the final analysis, the nature of his love was not in fact primarily narcissistic, turned toward his own artistic ability to represent Julie/Diana.

Fergus's metamorphosis from a frivolous man into a true lover and an impassioned artist is analogous to Acteon's metamorphosis from ruthless hunter into subjugated man struck by the arrows of Diana's beauty in

Ovid's *Metamorphoses*. For Acteon, as well as for the lyric artist—poet or painter—the brief instant of ecstasy provided by the vision of Diana's beautiful body has tragic consequences for his own body. As she scatters water over Acteon's face, Diana punishes the audacity of his gaze, not only creating an obstacle to his ability to recount but also changing his human body into a stag hunted and dismembered by his own dogs. In contact with the beautiful woman, he cannot preserve the integrity of his own body. Similarly, Fergus's lyrical vision of Julie/Diana has tragic consequences for his body as he becomes the target and the victim of her fatal arrow.

Nancy Vickers[29] discusses how this Ovidian myth acquires all its lyrical value when it becomes part of Petrarch's poetic imagery and when it makes the subject of lyric poetry contingent on the metamorphosis taking place from one text to the other. In Petrarch's "Poem 23" the question of subjectivity is raised in the text when the poetic "I" asks itself the question: "Who am I? Who was I?" In this poem, known as the poem of metamorphoses, the poetic subject successively assumes the identities of six mythical creatures. This accumulation of different identities is analogous to Julie's incarnation of different personalities when she plans to murder the five men responsible for her husband's death. In Petrarch's "Poem 23" none of the mythical creatures is expressly named, but each is easily recognizable as Daphne, the laurel; Cygnus, the swan; Battus, the stone; Byblis, the fountain; Echo, the voice; and finally Acteon, the stag.

Much critical attention has been given to this particular poem because, on the one hand, it characterizes the lyric as poetry of the fragmented self and, on the other, it appropriates the classical text of Ovid's *Metamorphoses*. From Ovid's text to Petrarch's, omissions, transformations, and adaptations are textual reflections casting images that embody the different representations of women in the lyric, some of which, the silent woman or the woman of stone, for example, we have already encountered.

Vickers has no doubt that the woman in Petrarch's lyric is a silent woman. In her essay she studies the transformations that occur between Ovid's text and Petrarch's. Her analysis is centered around the final metamorphosis undergone by the poetic "I" identified with Acteon, who becomes a stag hunted by his own hound. She focuses on the differences between Ovid's original story of the careless hunter Acteon, who could not resist looking at the beautiful goddess Diana bathing nude in a stream and Petrarch's retelling of the same story. In Ovid's text Diana throws water in Acteon's eyes to punish him with a symbolic gesture intended to blind him. Acteon had violated her sacred and divine body with his eyes when he allowed himself to be enthralled by its beauty and purity. But in Ovid's story

Diana's punishment is both performative and verbal. As she splashes Acteon's face, she says: "Now you can tell that you have seen me unveiled, that is if you can tell." Vickers rightly remarks on the absence in Petrarch's "Canzone 23" of Diana's verbal rebuke, which "negates the possibility of telling" for Acteon or for the poet. Her vocal presence in the Ovidian text is eliminated from Petrarch's "Canzone 23." Yet the force of Diana's statement is present in Petrarch's *Canzone*, since Vickers believes that Petrarch eliminated Diana's words from his version of the Ovidian story in order to eschew the danger that the woman's language represents for poetic expression. In the omission of Diana's words from Petrarch's poem, Vickers sees an act of silencing the female voice in poetic production. Petrarch's Diana is said to be silent in order to allow the poet—and his imitators, that is, the lyric poets who inherited his poetic form and content—to tell his story:

> Silencing Diana is an emblematic gesture; it suppresses a voice, and it casts generations of would-be Lauras in a role predicated upon the muteness of its player. A modern Acteon affirming himself as poet cannot permit Ovid's angry goddess to speak her displeasure and deny his voice; his speech requires her silence. (Vickers 278–79)

By placing the silencing of Diana at the conclusion of her study on the fragmented body of the woman in lyric poetry and by invoking a further silencing of female figures in poetry producing a "generation of would-be Lauras," Vickers suggests that the poetic voice in the lyric can only be heard when the "threatening" female voice is reduced to silence. Vickers appears to extend what she rightly understands as a poetic eviction of a threatening woman's language in Petrarch's work beyond the boundaries of his lyric to "generations" of women subsequently represented in poetry. She thus concludes her analysis of the determinative involvement of the female subject in Petrarch's poetry by accentuating both her silent presence and the creation of a silent female prototype upon which the lyric tradition has built its poetic force.

Yet we have seen that the following generations of women in the lyric are not as silent and harmless as Vickers seems to imply. The statue in Baudelaire's "Beauty" speaks about the danger that her beautiful body imposes on the fascinated and enslaved poets. In *The Bride Wore Black* Truffaut's Julie, as she poses for Fergus, shows signs of her dangerous self when she becomes Diana. Like Petrarch's Laura and Baudelaire's women, Julie is the embodiment of a true lyric persona. As such, she is always ready to endanger the men defying her mythical order. It is true that, if Julie is dead inside, her body carries outside marks of this death, and throughout the film she remains expressionless as she faces each one of her crimes. She never loses sight of her criminal intentions and allows herself no mistakes, no emotions. Her irrefutable insensitivity is almost challenged, however, by Fergus's charisma. Her determination to kill all five offenders appears to slacken when Fergus becomes truly passionate about and devoted to the character she represents: Diana, the ruthless and impervious goddess. With the help of Diana's callous identity, Julie's task of killing Fergus should be even simpler than it is for any other one of the four victims, since, as Diana, she represents the least appealing female persona in the entire film, but, paradoxically, it is as she incarnates Diana that she also shows slight signs of vulnerability. Indeed, she does not kill Fergus in the first attempt. He is saved first by her own hesitation—visually accounted for by a slight trembling of the arrow—and the sound of the doorbell, for which he must momentarily leave the potential scene of the crime. Why is Julie so hesitant in fulfilling her irreversible mission? Is she touched by the depth of Fergus's adoration for her? Does she realize that to his loving eyes she may only represent Diana and not Julie? If the answer to this last question is indeed that Fergus is a modern Acteon in love with the impossible female goddess and ready to die for loving her, then Julie's crime is less her crime than the dramatization of Fergus's own desire to die. Julie does not kill Fergus, Diana does, and her releasing the fatal arrow on her bow is the result of the unspoken request of the impassioned artist. When Julie finally allows Diana to kill Fergus, her fatal gesture may be interpreted as an act of self-punishment motivated by her sense of betrayal for allowing herself to feel forbidden emotions for Fergus.

Historically, Ovid's story of Diana and Acteon as it becomes a component of the lyric in Petrarch, Baudelaire, and Truffaut is the story of a "sublime" female body that cannot be seen or represented, a virtual body that can only exist in a phantasmatic form resisting all artistic representations. It is the same fundamental scheme that articulates the relation between Fergus and his representation of Diana. Fergus's death seems unavoidable as his lyricism reaches extremes. In addition to painting Julie/Diana on canvas, he also paints her on his bedroom wall, next to his bed, thus making her symbolically closer to and available for erotic as well as artistic pleasures and therefore suggesting that she could be both goddess and human, desire and reality, representation and body. Fergus's death can be read as Truffaut's denial of the double presence of woman—representation and body—in the lyric text of his film. His death also represents the destruction menacing the lyric artist who wants too much from his lyrical fantasy and so introduces into the "real" world the represented figure of his dreams, the impossible image of the woman in pieces.

Chapter 3

Freudian Clips: Castration, Decapitation, Fetishism

Freud has widely explored the concept of cutting with his theory of castration, based on a scenario in which the little boy fears for his virile member after convincing himself that the women around him (mother, sisters, friends) were castrated as a punishment for masturbatory pleasures. Bypassing, even denying, the umbilical cut as the primary traumatic separation for all subjects, Freud posits the moment of castration at the origin of human sexual development, and as the fundamental cut to the understanding of all subsequent psychological traumas. French psychoanalyst Jacques Lacan insists on the notion of cuts when he analyzes the construction of the subject, its coming into the signifying world from "nothing" to something "divided."[1] Yet the division cutting the subject into a signifier and a signified seems so remote from the concept of the body that the question as to the actual signification of the body in psychoanalysis must be raised.

In psychoanalysis the body is the human prototype for all separation to come, it is the place where primal divisions take place. In short, the body is the locus of the cut. In order to understand the body, in order to speak about the body we must first cut it up: "We understand the meaning of the body only when we cut and organize it with the signifier," says Serge André, a French psychoanalyst who pursues the same course of action proposed by Lacan with regards to the role played by the body in the formation of the subject of language.[2] Once brought to signification, once represented by language, once, in Barthes's words, "gathered to be expressed,"[3] the body is cut again, fetishized by language: "The total body must go back to the ashes of words, the slow dripping of details, the monotonous inventory of parts, fragmentation: language undoes the body, returns it to fetishism" (120).[4] It is the dissecting and signifying action of language on the body that defines the existence of the body in language. The body is figured in the discourses of literature, cinema, and psychoanalysis as a symbolized object cut off from the real body but inseparable from the action of cutting that determines its representation.

Psychoanalysis has in other words become a discourse centered around the question of body cuts, starting with Freud's theory of the castration complex. This theory relies heavily on an acceptance of the figurative cutting up of the body. The body most deeply implicated in this symbolic cutting is that of woman; her figurative dismemberment is the basis of the Freudian theories of castration, decapitation, and fetishism, the foundation upon which the principal building block of psychoanalysis, the Oedipus complex, rests. Because castration, decapitation, and fetishism are so central to Freudian psychoanalysis, I will investigate the way in which their dissecting mode may be traced not only in Freud's analyses but also in Truffaut's films and Baudelaire's poems. By focusing for now on the dissecting function in these three bodies of work, my objective is to show that the psychoanalyst, the filmmaker, and the poet share a number of views on the representation of the female body and that they may be understood by critics as influencing one another's creative and analytical productions as well as participating in the construction of woman's cultural image, something that each could probably not have achieved within their isolated, individual disciplines.

Castration

"Do you like music, Antoine?" asks the mysterious and beautiful Fabienne Tabard to a distracted Antoine Doinel held captive to her charms. "Yes, sir!" is his unexpected answer, which creates a sudden embarrassment for the young man who then prefers to flee the scene as he feels unable to explain to himself and to Fabienne the reason for this incongruous Freudian slip. Can we try to explain what in Antoine caused him to utter an injunction so radically inappropriate to the person it refers to? Indeed, how can anybody point to any masculine attributes in Fabienne Tabard's appearance or personality? On the contrary, she seems the most feminine, graceful, seductive, of all the female characters in *Stolen Kisses,* perhaps in all of Truffaut's films. She is the true embodiment of a certain feminine ideality: celestial appearance, soft blond hair, sublime smile, and gracile body. In place of Antoine's baffling answer one would expect him to respond "Yes, angel!" or else "Yes, sublime apparition," thus accidently voicing his unadmitted thoughts on the beauty sitting across from him. Instead, Antoine's unconscious chooses to verbalize his fascination for Fabienne by calling her "sir."

In the *Psychopathology of Everyday Life* Freud points to the active part taken by the unconscious that often manifests itself in written and/or oral slips thus allowing the representation of a secret wish, of a repressed desire at the level of consciousness. Can Antoine possibly wish for Fabienne's transformation into a man? Or do his words represent less a wish-fulfillment than a typical military automatic response to a superior—as indicated by the soldierlike dictum "Yes, sir!"—to someone who has total control over the subordinate's language and actions, someone commanding respect, and even fear? It seems that the character of Fabienne could in fact generate both possibilities: in Antoine's mind, she becomes the man whose intrinsic authority he unconsciously acknowledges. By giving a masculine identity to the woman he secretly adores, Antoine suggests an intriguing reversal of roles in a classically Freudian castration scenario in which it is the boy who traditionally fears for his phallus after speculating that his mother, his sister, or any other woman in his entourage has already been emasculated. Fabienne is overly feminine, so much so that, to Antoine, she seems to belong to a different sexual reality, a subliminally threatening one that puts him in the position of the young boy fearing for his masculinity. Fabienne's overwhelming beauty becomes her most dangerous attribute, a symbolic sign of castration directed against Antoine whose only defense is to run away. His fleeing the scene of castration may be associated with his sudden realization that the dream woman represents in fact a real danger to his own sense of masculinity.

We must understand Antoine's Freudian slip, then, as a manifestation of a Freudian "clip" and the beautiful woman he mistook for a man as a powerful apparition that instills the fear of castration in him. Later in the film Antoine does overcome this fear of castration when he finally sleeps with Fabienne; however he only retrieves his potency after she has stooped to a more human level and explained to him that she is a common mortal simply seeking a few hours of pleasure in his company. In fact, it is only after she has received a goodbye note from Antoine in which he finally admits his attraction to her, comparing his impossible dream of loving her to that of Felix de Vandenesse for Madame de Mortsauf in Balzac's famous novel *The Lily in the Valley*, that Fabienne decides to pay him an unexpected visit, and to make his impossible dream become reality. As she enters his bedroom, she explains that she is not the Madame de Mortsauf from Balzac's love story *The Lily in the Valley* whose impossible love with Félix Antoine had interpreted as a beautiful but inconceivable dream. Arguing against his idealistic viewpoint, she puts forth a different portrait of Madame de Mortsauf, that of a woman who does not wish to die before sharing her intimate feelings with her lover. Her renewed perspective on the unrealizable love affair at the center of Balzac's story, simultaneously destroys Antoine's romantic interpretation of the same tale and his celestial vision of Fabienne Tabard. As a revised and ordinary Madame de Mortsauf, she is now "cut to size," welcome in his bed, open to the pleasure of intimacy. At the end of the sequence Fabienne establishes the terms of their love agreement by taking the key off the lock and dropping it into a vase, a gesture loaded with sexual implications, but most importantly a gesture that she initiates and to which he responds with a smile. The key as it drops in the vase restores Antoine to his sexual potency, becoming the fetish associated with their love affair. With the key as symbol of sexual union, the impairing effect of castration has been replaced by the regenerating effect of the fetish, pleasure in lieu of pain.

As with the significant example of Antoine's slip, the filmmaker may be considered to give woman the role of a direct agent of castration and her beauty, like Fabienne's, thus becomes "sharp" and dangerous to male identity. Beauty instills fear of castration, and the beautiful woman takes the form of a Medusa depriving her secretly adoring devotee from his masculinity with one brief look. As we have seen in the previous chapter, the encounter with Beauty is mercurial, but its effects can be ever-lasting. The fear of castration connected to the sudden meeting with the exquisite enchantress subsides to give way to the lasting pleasure of a reconstructed scenario whereby male identity secures its masculinity by constructing a safer object of love, a fetish reminiscent of and associated with the blissful body of the enthralling Venus. In the process, however, he keeps her real body at a safe distance, like an inaccessible reference, replacing his fear of her dangerous beauty with a feeling of creative fulfillment as he makes a selection of aesthetically delightful parts from her fantasized body of pleasure. While the encounter with the beautiful woman symbolizes castration, its fetishistic upshot means pleasure at all times.

Fear of Castration: The Case of Antoine Doinel

In "Antoine and Colette," an episode from Truffaut's *Love at 20*, the director reconnects with the life of Antoine Doinel, last seen desperately looking for a way out of his young boy's life of misery and imprisonment in *The 400 Blows*. In this short piece, the second of the five-film series constituting the adventures of Antoine Doinel, Antoine has legally severed all relationship with his mother and, despite his youth, has become financially independent by taking a job in a music store. Forced into maturity and solitude by the unhappy circumstances that left him without a family, Antoine is nonetheless starving for true romance, for an ideal love that could wipe out years of maternal indifference. When he meets a young woman by the name of Colette at a concert hall, he immediately falls under her charm, and she becomes his life's sole preoccupation. Love hurts, however, especially the first time. Antoine experiences difficulties in matching his desire to love Colette passionately and romantically with her desire to be loved nonchalantly by a more modern man than him. As with other Truffaut films, it is Colette's legs that first attract Antoine. A few scenes later, when he sees her again, he is fascinated by her hair and her neck.

What puts Antoine in a state of adoring contemplation for the young woman are specific parts of Colette's body, her legs, her hair, and her neck. He seems to construct his love for her and her body bit by bit, and each piece of her becomes her as Antoine's desire to know her grows stronger. The fetishistic manner in which he visually composes her body remains the only way he is able to love her, since as a complete female—body, soul, and language—she literally escapes him. Indeed, if at the very beginning she finds his persistent sentimental inclination touching and flattering, she soon expresses her aloof attitude toward his passion when she casually indicates that his romantic nature and physique have certainly seduced her mother, not her. Antoine is an unlikely lover for Colette because he is out of context, out of time, out of fashion. Despite his repeated efforts to get romantically closer to her, Antoine fails to initiate in Colette the same feelings he has nourished for her idealized image. In a sense she resembles the lyrical woman for whom the passionate lover burns unabatingly while she remains unattainable and fragmented as when he first saw her, lovable only in dreams and reveries, captivating only in bits and pieces. Antoine's lyricism does not fit, however, with the present times of casual encounters and simplified relationships. His sentimentalism leans toward the past, toward the nineteenth century, as his literary taste for Balzac demonstrates.

His outmoded style may be the main cause of his failure to seduce Colette, and Truffaut captures the lyrical drama of their impossible liaison by isolating particular visual signs marking the inherent principle of their incompatibility. For example, Truffaut chooses hair as a symbol representing both the cultural and the sentimental gap separating the two adolescents. Different hair styles become associated with different ways of loving. The story takes place in the 1950s, a time when a clean, short look was in style for men, puffy and semi-long hair for women. Antoine's longish hair seems to indicate that he is not in tune with the times. After receiving a love letter from Antoine, Colette comments on Antoine's hair length, declaring that it certainly appealed to her mother who thought his coiffure gave him a "romantic" look. Indeed, Antoine is profusely romantic and incurably passionate in his pursuit of Colette. He goes as far as moving into a small apartment across from her parents' in order to be close to her at all times. Colette's hair, although puffy, is shorter than that of most women her age; her hair is cut like a man's; in fact, her hairdo is quite similar to Antoine's. They look alike, and their relationship feels like one of familial closeness and similarity, Antoine becoming nothing more than a brotherly figure for Colette.

The question raised about hair style is literally spelled out in the film in the following terms: can a man love a woman with short hair? A question already suggesting the query formulated in *Day for Night*—"Are women magical?"—and underlying all of Truffaut's films. In *Antoine et Colette* the magical quality of women may be associated with their long hair: can a woman still be magical without her long hair? It is René, Antoine's only friend and soul mate, who provides an answer to this question when he admits that he finds women more attractive with long hair and that his cousin, with whom he is very much in love, has decided, much to his dislike, to cut her hair. He does not know whether he will be able to love her with short hair. When she does have her hair cut, however, he is surprised to find out that his feelings for her have not changed, although she now looks like "Joan of Arc."

What René indicates in his assessment of a woman's changing hairdo is that, by cutting her hair, she liberates herself from the image culturally constructed around a feminine look inseparable from the soft bounce of her long hair. With short hair she becomes manly and rebellious, like Joan of Arc. For his part Antoine is far too romantic to accept being loved by a woman looking or even acting like a man. He tells René how much he hates Colette talking to him as if she were a male friend. Unlike René, he cannot bear her boyish attitude, his desire has set high feminine standards for the ideal object of his love. In fact, René's fear of loving a woman with short hair mirrors Antoine's fear of loving a woman acting like a man. It is Antoine's fear that woman deprives herself of a part of her femininity when she cuts her hair. She is still a woman but the act of cutting her hair may be seen as an act of castration that leaves her in an ambivalent sexual position: that of a masculine woman, whose masculinity is threatening while counterbalanced by her appealing femininity. As a "mannified" woman, she offers Antoine a reversed castration scenario in which she becomes a man, a Joan of Arc with short hair and long pants. Antoine is horrified by the type of masculine woman she embodies, even if his peers, René among them, have found the appeal behind the new look of the modern woman.

Antoine does not openly oppose his friend René on his changed attitude toward the new sex appeal generated by women in manly gear; however, he unconsciously offers his censorship of the type of "Joan of Arc," for whom René provides an unacceptable image at the end of the scene, when he shows Antoine his cousin's last love letter, which she has covered with lipstick marks as a sign of her amorous thoughts for René. Antoine, who reacts as if he admired and recognized these feminine imprints as marks of a true passion, lets out a singular cry: "Oh, terrible!" that, in French, may be read in two different manners. First as an admiring sound: "Oh, terrific," second as shocked speech-act: "Oh, terrible!" In fact, we can easily detect that behind his pretended admiration contained in the outcry, "terrific," Antoine *is* indeed shocked by what he perceives as disgraceful marks printed on the letter, and he cannot refrain from expressing his feeling of profound disgust by really saying: "How terrifying!"

A further look at the actual scenario adds an interesting detail to this scene; it reads: "The letter is covered with lipstick, or, more precisely, with the shape of lips imprinted in bright red" (84). The radiant color of the lipstick remains invisible on screen because the film is shot in black-and-white. Although it is true that most representations of women's lips are generally perceived in color and that the degree of female passion often translates into bright red tones of lipstick, the director shooting in black-and-white is clearly unable to convey the direct visual significant impact of the color red on screen to his spectators. The reading of the scenario, however, offers more than the mere confirmation to the cultural assimilation of women's lips with the *rouge* of passion, it reflects an unconscious association— between color and lip, between red and woman—that for Antoine has roots in another displaced unconscious scenario causing his adverse feelings for women looking like men.

Indeed, if for René the color red is that of a woman in love, for Antoine it is the color associated with a woman whose hair she has cut, a woman compensating the loss of femininity caused by her haircut with a heavy layer of red lipstick; her red lips become the sign of her lack of femininity. This seems to be the case for Antoine for whom the color red represents less the passion expressed by René's cousin than her horrifying loss of femininity translated onto her lips as if they were red with blood from her body (hair) cut, not with lipstick. As in a dream or, rather, a nightmare, Antoine condenses the cut of the hair, with the red of the lips into a single symbol of horrifying proportion bringing a feeling of immediately unsuspected terror behind Antoine's twofold exclamation: "*oh, terrible!*"

For Antoine, fear of castration takes on a double meaning, fear of being loved by a masculine woman who would challenge his manly ways, and fear of seeing his feminine side, his sentimental self symbolized by his longish hair compete with the women he meets. When in pursuit of Colette, whose short hair points to her masculine side, Antoine's masculinity literally freezes as he explains to René: "Whenever I try to get serious, she thinks I'm funny. I spend hours waiting in front of her door, freezing my balls off!" In his familiar manner of speaking Antoine expresses his anger at being regularly stood up by Colette, but he also literally points to his "frozen" male parts, thus indicating his inability to perform in a virile manner whenever Colette acts like a male friend with him. The castrating effect of her masculine behavior throws Antoine off the gender track, putting him in a position from which he is unable to perform as a man. Still, Antoine's temporary emasculation does not leave him crippled forever; he is still a man, but his sexual happiness depends on a delicate balance of the man/woman component of the loved other. His ideal woman cannot be either too masculine or too feminine.

As we have seen, the much too feminine Fabienne Tabard possesses a castrating beauty that paralyzes Antoine's desire to fulfill his dream to love her. Her refined charms transform her into a phallic character that he accidentally names "sir" and that he ultimately leaves, completely ashamed of himself. Twice castrated by the overly feminine Fabienne and the unduly masculine Colette, it appears that Antoine's chance at asserting his masculinity depends on his loving a conservative woman—not too beautiful, not too boyish, not too flamboyant, someone like Christine, whom he meets in *Stolen Kisses* (1968), marries in *Bed and Board* (1970), and divorces in *Love on the Run* (1979). His failed relationship with Christine, who appears to represent the best possible choice to undo Antoine's fear of castration by bringing into his life the stability generated by their uneventful love affair, leaves little alternative as to what type of woman Antoine can truly feel happy with: one who could restore both his confidence and his sexual identity.

In the last film of his adventures, *Love on the Run,* Antoine meets Sabine, a woman who does not quite fall into any of the categories of women perceived as either too feminine like Fabienne or too masculine like Colette or even too conservative like Christine. Unlike other women in Antoine's life, Sabine appears as a little girl trapped in a woman's body, and as such she escapes the denomination usually reserved for fully sexual adults. Besides her girlish looks and attitudes, Sabine revels in the childlike habit of speaking in puns and children's rhymes: at the beginning of the film, she gives Antoine a collection of books, several volumes of "Léautaud's journal," that Antoine comments on by saying: "See all the troubles he had with women this poor Léautaud." To Antoine's genuine concern with Léautaud's complicated love life, Sabine offers a pun based on the sound of his name: "Léautaud ou tard" (the last syllable of *Léautaud* sounds like the adverb *tôt*, meaning "early," which she juxtaposes with its opposite *tard*, meaning "late"). Nothing about Léautaud's dramatic love life—for instance, the fact that he really wanted to make love to his mother—seems to incite repulsion toward his incestuous tendency or even any mature response at all in Sabine whose sole observation is reduced to a silly play on words.

Later in the film a flashback offers another sample of Sabine's naive views of the adult world: before leaving on a three day trip she makes Antoine swear that he will remain completely faithful to her in action and in thoughts. They conclude their arrangement by saying: "Done deal." Sabine, however, cannot help adding one of her ingenuous aphorisms: "OK, but the liar is a pig." Antoine is quite taken aback by her unsolicited sentence, he does not understand it, and thus fails to respond adequately; he can only briefly articulate his surprise by repeating: "What? What?" two quick inquisitive injunctions that cry out for explanations. Sabine smiles and offers no solution to her unfamiliar and puzzling language, but it is precisely her genuine spontaneity that makes her an endearing character in Antoine's life. She becomes Antoine's uncomplicated playmate. In fact, "playing" the game of love with Sabine helps him relive part of the childhood that he missed in *The 400 Blows*. As a little boy, Antoine was forced out of his childhood by an unloving mother and a rigid education. By the end of *Love on the Run*, Sabine admits her refusal to grow into the seriousness of life by attesting her fear of commitment and subsequently proposing a make-believe relationship to Antoine who gladly accepts its playful terms:

> *Sabine:* We cannot be sure that we are starting something that will last a long time.
> *Antoine:* Why not?
> *Sabine:* But we can always pretend.
> *Antoine:* Yes, yes, that's right, let's pretend.

As is the case in all children's games, players can pull out even if the game has not been conclusive. The terms of the playful relationship upon which Antoine and Sabine are building their amorous association seem to be the only way they can both retain their childhood, their innocence, their pure imagination. For Antoine, in particular, the pretend relationship has momentarily eliminated the fear of castration that he had experienced so far with the women in his life: his unloving and berating mother in *The 400 Blows;* his aloof and amazon friend in *Love at 20;* his cruelly beautiful lover in *Stolen Kisses;* his cold and conservative wife in *Bed and Board.* With Sabine his masculinity is safe because it is not challenged by the demands of a woman but allowed to thrive in a playful environment created by a fun-loving inamorata.

To Antoine, Sabine is just the opposite of the classic Freudian adult woman, one who operates under the assumption that the role naturally assigned to her by her given sex is secondary to the male's and that her sexual identity only finds its place as an instrument for establishing the phallic role of man. Because Sabine does not act under the terms of castration, she does not contribute to Antoine's process of maturing into a fully developed Freudian man. For Antoine to keep his passion unscathed by the female Medusas who confronted his masculinity in earlier films, he must give in to Sabine's uncontrived world of ingenuous pleasures. The relationship she proposes to pursue with him is reminiscent of the flashback scene of two children engaged in a playful ceremony of marriage in *The Bride Wore Black.* In the film Julie and David's simulated wedding is distinctively the only happy moment of the story, purposely set up in contrast with the dark mood carried throughout by Julie who vows to destroy the five men who killed David on their actual wedding day. In fact, the film epitomizes in reverse the course of Antoine and Sabine's liaison: a relationship can only—literally—survive under the playful terms of a make-believe agreement and is doomed to failure once sealed by psychological and social obligations. Antoine and Sabine vow to make-believe, "de faire comme si," thus saving their own integrity as lovers and individuals. It appears that for Antoine to engage in a relationship in which mature commitment has been ruled out means to deny the fear of castration for himself and what Freud calls "the fact of castration" for Sabine.

The "Fact" of Castration: The Case of Freud

From a feminist standpoint, the long-standing debate on castration needs to be addressed over and over again as a means of disrupting what classical psychoanalysis has normalized and culturally absorbed as the irrefutable "fact" of the woman's castration. The more we investigate the psychoanalytical terms that prompted the question about woman's castration, the more difficult it becomes to assign a specific sexual role to either gender and the less we are able to accept the classic castration scenario and its set of culturally accepted idiosyncrasies. Let us discuss one of these idiosyncrasies—the symbolic cutting on the woman's body—in the hopes that, by questioning its triviality one more time, we might be able to better understand the woman affected by such a cut.

According to Freud, the cut involved in the castration complex would have left woman's body mutilated and therefore inferior to man's body: "She [the woman] acknowledges the fact of her castration, the consequent superiority of the male and her inferiority, but she also rebels against these unpleasant facts."[5] Thus, woman faces her castrated condition with anger, and Freud grants her room for rebellion "against the facts." What is striking here is the reliance of psychoanalytical discourse beginning with Freud—on through Lacan—on the legend of the missing penis, which constitutes the crucial element of the story on the formation of sexual identity in psychoanalysis. Although claiming the status of science, psychoanalytical discourse relies heavily on a number of fictitious accounts borrowed from classical mythology: the Oedipus story and the Medusa legend, to name only the most renowned ones.

Besides deriving their sexual models from ancient tales, it can be said that Freud and Lacan have dealt with their scientific findings on the human psyche in a creative manner. Critics such as Samuel Weber and Catherine Clément have argued that Freud and Lacan have created a psychoanalytical discourse based on literary works that eventually teach us to better understand the analysts' respective modes of writing and interpreting. Freud and Lacan, just like creative writers offering their versions of the "missing penis," have construed a plot centered around woman's deficient body standing as the crucial requirement for man's "superiority." Such a story leaves her no significant place in the symbolic order as if her femininity were valuable in the Imaginary only, that is in the oedipal phase of a boy's sexual development.

The linear order according to which the individual progresses in the scientific chart established by Lacan from the Imaginary to the Symbolic fails to include the progress of woman in the same order. For her the scientific model is replaced by a looser but nevertheless potent narrative, one by which she acknowledges her failing body, "the fact of [her] castration," in order to empower her man's body. When Freud compares woman's body to man's body, the missing penis is the element he singles out in order to take his psychoanalytical mission toward its goal: understanding the dramatic and even traumatic formation of male sexuality. It seems clear that the penis missing from the female body manifests its presence in Freudian discourse in order to legitimate his views on male sexuality. Freud must return to the missing penis in order to authoritatively establish his discourse on castration. In Freud's oedipal story the female body is the visual and symbolic deterrent to man's private bodily pleasures. As he searches for the perfect scenario, Freud mixes the inventiveness of his enterprise, his creative sense, with the analytical processes informed by the available scientific discourse. It can thus be said that his psychoanalytical discourse comprises both imaginative and scientific elements, or "imaginary facts" (like the missing penis) with which he creates the castration story.

In "What Is an Author?"[6] Michel Foucault explains how a discourse builds itself following a movement of return to a point of omission in a primary text. He gives a convincing account of the importance of the missing textual element—"the interstices of the text, its gaps and absences"—to which intellectuals must return in order to form new discursive practices. Foucault offers the examples of Freud's and Marx's writings as initiating texts that have respectively been reformulated by Lacan and Althusser. According to Foucault, it is a reading of the blank spaces in Freud's and Marx's original texts that creates a legitimate new discourse for Lacan and Althusser: "We return to those empty spaces that have been masked by omission or concealed in a false and misleading plenitude" (135). The discursive relationships that the psychoanalytic text on castration establishes in relation to the castrated body of the woman—from the Freudian text on the woman's missing penis to its Lacanian reformulation into the phallus she does not possess—is based on a principle equivalent to that enunciated by Foucault. The primary text contains a crucial moment, that of the cutting of the penis in Freud's castration theory, a moment that is reformulated and enhanced in Lacan's concept of the *phallus*.

With the inheritance of Freud's missing penis Lacan turns away from its "flesh" and replaces it with a signifier, the *phallus,* an analytical invention *standing outside* the reality of the body that it signifies; yet, according to *Petit Robert,* the phallus is "the virile member in erection." Can a signifier—even without a signified—be thus paradoxically chosen so as not to designate what its connotative function so strongly states? Despite his questionable naming of the "universal signifier," Lacan neutralizes the sexual codification of the phallus by claiming that it is neither a fantasy, nor a real object, and even less an actual sexual organ: "In Freudian doctrine the phallus is not a fantasy, if by that we mean an imaginary effect. Nor is it as such an object (part-, internal, good, bad, etc.) in the sense that this term tends to accentuate the reality pertaining in a relation. It is even less the organ, the penis or clitoris, that it symbolizes."[7] According to him, however, it is an object signifying desire in general: "a privileged signifier of that mark in which the role of the logos is joined with the advent of desire" (*Ecrits* 287). In other words, it is a signifier without a signified, a desire without satisfaction. And, as signifier and desire, it stands at the junction of the castration theory where Freud builds the oedipal drama of the missing penis.

In Lacanian terms what is inherent in the idea of castration is a moment of loss that does not affect the body so much as it affects the logic of sexual difference. This logic is spelled out by Jane Gallop, when in *Reading Lacan* she understands the moment of castration as "a moment of loss [. . .] always to come [for the boy] or gone by [for the girl]."[8] Caught in a past that never was and a future that never will be, the cutting moment of castration has no actual place in space or time within the theoretical development of psycho-analysis, but the potential loss it represents is deeply felt by both male and female subjects, to the extent that it acquires the signification of a violent moment of inscription on all bodies, so violent that it has no identifiable role in symbolic representations. The role of the cut body within the theory of castration is thus limited to a missing yet marking and marked symbolic moment insuring the proper functioning of the Oedipus complex.

From what we have seen, psychoanalysis seems nowhere more incomplete and insufficient than when it deals with women and female sexuality. On this subject Freud admits the incompleteness and unfriendliness of his discoveries in the concluding statement of his late essay on "Femininity": "That is all I had to say to you about femininity. It is certainly incomplete and fragmentary and does not always sound friendly."[9] He adds, however, that the woman in whom he is "scientifically" interested is the sexual woman and, although "the influence [of her sexuality] extends very far; we do not overlook the fact that an individual woman may be a human being in other respects as well" (135). Freud does not name any of the limited "other respects" whereby woman appears in "friendly" light, and it seems certain that feminism is not one of them as it precisely deals with the re-assessment of the sexual nature of women in all disciplines, cultural, social and political. In fact feminism may sometimes be perceived as an "unfriendly" discourse when it raises its voice against a male oriented discourse. Its unfriendliness, however, cannot be interpreted in terms of feelings of individual instances of resentment against men but, rather (and similarly to Freud's suggested unfriendliness regarding his analysis on female sexuality), a discourse addressing women's issues in a "professional" manner encompassing the full range of experiences and emotions.

The incomplete "scientific" results of Freud's research on female sexuality led him to admit that the question of femininity should be investigated by other researchers. In the very last statement of "Femininity" Freud acknowledges that he has continuously opened up the question of femininity for others to pursue—women, poets, and future scientists. "If you want to know more about femininity, enquire from your own experiences of life, or turn to the poets, or wait until science can give you deeper and more coherent information" (135). I have here taken up Freud's challenge to better understand femininity by starting to question and problematize the femininity about which Freud admits his inadequacy; the future scientists, and in particular, female French psychoanalysts like Françoise Dolto, Janine Chasseguet-Smirgel, and Julia Kristeva have certainly made great contributions to the understanding of feminine sexuality, to which we will refer in the next chapter; before we can proceed to newer scientific ground on femininity, I would like first to "turn to the poets," and particularly to Baudelaire, and, as suggested by Freud, to focus on the poet's knowledge of and association with the feminine part of his poetry, the intrinsic and intimate part of himself.

The Pain of Castration: The Case of the Poet ("A Voyage to Cythera")

Baudelaire's poetry remains primarily an expression of male desire; however, his poems reveal the presence of femininity captured by the lyric subject, who feels its stirrings with great pain, as if the woman within his text suggested to the male poet the terms and the suffering endured by what Freud calls her "mutilated" body.[10] Although Baudelaire's poetic examination of the female body contributes to its mutilated image, it is the vision of a mutilated male body in "A Voyage to Cythera"—a poem from the section of *Flowers of Evil* also entitled "Flowers of Evil"—that creates the circumstances by which the poet fantasizes about his own castration, the cause of his feminization. As he endures the masochistic fantasy in which he undergoes the double suffering of his body and his mind, the poet absorbs the pain of mutilation and emasculation of the hanged man he sees on the island of Cythera.

Baudelaire wrote "A Voyage to Cythera" in 1851, after reading Gérard de Nerval's impressions of his trip to the Mediterranean, when the latter recalls sailing by the island of Cérigo—a British possession—that plunges him into a dream about ancient Cythera, the island of all pleasures. The rhapsody of pleasure is broken by the morbid reality of the gibbet implicitly forcing Nerval into a reflection on the destruction of the island by its British occupant. As he in turn captures the tragic duality of the scene, in which the island of pleasure becomes the island of horror, Baudelaire recasts Nerval's vision of the hanged man into a different meditation on the inevitable physical and moral pain awaiting the sensualist.

The poem's moralistic tendency has been glossed as Baudelaire's endorsement of Christian mysticism by literary critic J. B. Hubert who sees the poet as a Christ figure whose body must expire in pain in order to redeem man's sinfulness incarnated in the poem by the hedonist from Cythère.[11] The poet's final imploration to the Lord: "O Lord, give me the power and the courage / To regard my heart and my body without loathing" certainly contributes to such an interpretation. As he pleads for the "mortal" vulnerability of his body and soul, however, the poet's prayer goes beyond his desire for spiritual redemption by pain, as pain is detached from its Christian model for eternal salvation while it simultaneously keeps all its didactic value. What the poet learns in considering the pain felt by the hanged man is the overwhelming power of his own "masochistic" desire to suffer, and his final beseeching represents a desperate call for protection against castration observed on the body of the hanged man. We will consider the poet's masochistic fantasy as we examine his paradoxical desire to endorse the hanged man's pain while refusing the terms of his castration.

Although relatively rare, Freud's remarks on the phenomenon of pain and its relation to the psychological processes have indirectly influenced his concern with the problematics of pleasure. Freud never developed a full theory of pain, concerned as he was with the pleasure principle to which he opposes the reality principle. According to him, pain is part of the pleasure principle, it relates to pleasure in terms of "the quantity of excitation that is present in the mind [. . .] unpleasure corresponds to an increase in the quantity of excitation and pleasure to a diminution."[12] Freud's understanding of pain remains linked to his speculation on the degree of tension received by the mental apparatus: an increase in tension translates into an augmentation of pain and a decrease into a release of pleasure. Besides this fluctuation of tension, pain in and of itself remains for Freud "an obscure and inaccessible region of the mind" (7). Later on in his 1925 essay, *Inhibitions, Symptoms and Anxiety,* Freud saw pain as a form of mourning due to the loss of an object by which he means principally the separation from the mother at birth experienced by the individual as an unretrievable loss, a kind of symbolic death for which he mourns and feels pain. Pain is a reaction to a situation of loss, such as the missing of the mother.

Does Freud mean that any loss of an overvalued object is responsible for a kind of "mourning" pain? Would, then, the loss of the penis also occasion a form of mental pain for the little boy in the pangs of castration? Because pain always follows the separation from or loss of a "loved" object, Freud speaks of castration as masculine anxiety prior to and related to the danger of losing the penis: "anxiety is a reaction to a situation of danger" (57). While characterizing castration for man as related to anxiety, fear of losing his penis, pain would then occur in the unlikely case when castration has occurred and the penis has been lost. The "morbid reality" of castration would trigger a reaction of pain on the part of the emasculated individual, who, as we follow Freud in his theory, becomes woman by virtue of the cut that transformed his body, a body feminized by castration. In other words, in the castration story pain can only be associated to woman whose castration has caused her to lose and mourn the penis. Beyond/against the fable of castration she has become associated with the "painful sex."

For the purpose of engaging the concept of male castration on a different and productive layer of the poet's imagination, I will present a reading of "A Voyage to Cythera" in which the poet endorses the castrated man's pain in order to envision his *feminized* body. Baudelaire's poem "A Voyage to Cythera" offers the unique and hallucinating tale of the indirect emasculation of the poet and his realization that, through the poetic handling of his vision, he has feminized himself by absorbing the painful processes of castration, by overcoming the fear that Freud associates with what he calls the mutilated sex of woman, by becoming women beyond castration.

The central figure of this poem is the enigmatic body of the hanged man seen from a boat by the poet during a trip to an island known for having sheltered Venus, the goddess of love. But love and Venus seem to have abandoned Cythera and the goddess's presence is characterized as a "superb ghost," a spectral figure haunting the imagination of the romantic and nostalgic "old bachelors." Images of a beautiful past are soon replaced by images of a terrifying present. The island is "sad and black" and resembles "a rocky waste where strident voices sound." The seductive and beautiful body of Venus "hot and burning to uncover" is in turn replaced by the mutilated body of the hanged man. Finally, the feeling of love and tenderness is replaced by a feeling of horror and repulsion for the sea traveler who gradually catches sight of the forlorn island, its desolate nature, its destroyed and violated bodies. Yet the unexpected emergence of the repulsive body in the visual field of the poetic subject will not cause him to turn away from the horror of mutilation; instead, it attracts him and leads him to investigate his own desire to become a different body, a horrible body torn to bits and emasculated, a body in pain.

In this poem the body upon which the metamorphosis takes place is the mutilated body of a man. His dismembered body becomes the allegory for the poet's past, the memory of his body subjected to the same "sweet torture" represented by the fantasy of castration. Although the poet exchanges his body and his identity with another man, the metaphor of the body in this poem soon reveals traces of feminization behind the figure of the mutilated man: "the torturers, the corpse had perfectly emasculated." This image of emasculation points to the poet's fascination with castration as the primary cut on the body, a cut by which he envisions the painful feminization of his own body.

In "A Voyage to Cythera" it is through imagining and acknowledging the pain of a dismembered body that the poet finds a feminized poetic body with which he exchanges his poetic body. Even though no actual representation of woman—Venus is only a "spectral goddess"—appears in the poem, the feminine is represented through pain emanating from the dismembered male body. The poetic subject represented by the "I" of the poem goes from its first encounter with the body of a hanged man, to a transitional feminized body, then to the poetic incorporation of pain and finally to the unconscious recapturing of an early moment of traumatic separation involving the poet and his hallucinated image, his materialized Other.

In the very first line of the poem, the "I" compares itself to a happy bird flying around a boat: "My heart, like a bird, was coasting happily." This feeling of serenity and freedom embodied in the figure of the bird diminishes as the highly spirited bird becomes the weary passenger of a boat approaching the sinister island of Cythera. As the boat draws nearer to the coast of the island, the "I" is totally absorbed by the vision of a man hanging from a gibbet. This vision becomes the focus of the poem at the same time as it becomes the sole preoccupation of the "I." Two stanzas of the poem offer a specific and explicit description of the hanged man's body hacked by ferocious birds and offering the unbearable spectacle of its torn flesh: the "bleeding foul decay," the "perforated stomach," the "intestines hanging down to the thighs."

The horror raised by such a description slowly and painfully escalates to a paroxysmal moment of castration, which ends the direct visual contact between the poet and the lacerated body. Although dealing with the poetic subject's visual contact with the gibbet scene, the following stanza pulls the onlooker back from the actual mutilated body; the poet detaches himself visually from the tormenting spectacle of the shredded body and his gaze goes "below," under the feet, to observe an ominous faunal scene in which ferocious animals are competing with the birds for a piece of the mangled body and referred to as "jealous beasts." It is as if the poetic gaze had to digress from the site of the body after its last and unbearable glimpse. Castration represents the most untenable vision for the poetic subject, and such vision must be broken yet mediated by another vision. Paradoxically, the prowling beasts of prey coveting the dead body provide visual and mental relief to the poet who must look away from the castrated man. As horrible as this vision of relief may seem, it represents horror to a lesser degree whereas, comparatively, castration represents the unsurpassed vision of horror.

The hyperbolic language used to characterize the traumatic sight of castration accounts for the poet's intention to make castration man's worse fear. Worse than any other type of mutilation, castration embodies the utmost violation to the male body. It demonstrates that a man can actually lose his penis, that the threat of castration may become the irremediable "fact of castration." What the poetic subject sees in the repulsive image of the castrated hanged man is the clear message that he must take the threat of castration seriously in order to establish his male identity, and that the failure to construct a symbolic male identity may result in the destruction of his body. Yet there is much excitement in the sinister path awaiting the poet: an inexplicable attraction for the mystery of darkness, even if it can lead him to destruction. Indeed, the poet's desire to acknowledge his otherness sends him exploring the possibility of emasculation, in spite of the danger he runs of undergoing his own castration.

It is the poet's imagination and his ability to fantasize about otherness that make it possible for him to bypass any detrimental effects involved in his transmutation into the mutilated body. As he adopts the emasculated condition of the hanged man, the poet never loses sight of his own masculinity. In fact, castration is not the essential factor in his desire to embrace his feminization, pain is, as indicated in the following verse: "O swinging joke, your griefs are those I know." To separate the threat of castration from the fear of losing one's masculinity is a means of de-emphasizing the exclusive dependency of masculine identity upon the sole possession of the penis. In "A Voyage to Cythera" the poetic subject does not wish to be castrated, he wishes to reach out for his feminine self. To that effect, he is able to accommodate the presence of the other body inside his own, the presence of another sex alongside his.

In order to remain untouched in his virility while becoming the other sex, the poetic subject experiments with the pain of emasculation without enduring the act of castration. And pain can be magically isolated from the act of castration; the only "magician" capable of separating them is imagination. In *The Salon of 1859* Baudelaire explains that no other human faculty has greater power for the artist than his imagination. He calls imagination "the queen of all faculties." In terms recalling Genesis, Baudelaire places the emergence of Imagination at the time when the world began, at the time when language began: "At the dawn of creation, she engendered analogy and metaphor." Imagination is the creator and the ruler of the artistic world; imagination disturbs the world's logic; it creates a new world under its own rules: "It breaks up all of creation, and with the material gathered and positioned according to rules whose origin may only be found in the deepest part of the soul, it creates a new world, it produces a new sensation" (2:621). The new sensation produced by the fragmenting imagination of the poet in "A Voyage to Cythera" allows him to remain at a distance from castration while at the same time experimenting with the suffering generated by its horrible representation. In the poem pain stands as the poetic figure by which the poet secretly hopes to become a woman without giving up being a man.

In "A Voyage to Cythera" what are the implications of the concept of pain on the poetic subject's unconscious desire to find the terms of his latent femininity? The description of the mutilated body once again raises the question of the language of pain, and its ability, or inability, to express in poetic terms the sensation felt by the passenger on the boat, the "I," spectator of this scene of dismemberment. As a spectator, the poetic "I" stands outside of the locus of pain and it can only speculate on the feeling of pain located on the body of the other. The sensation of pain is foreign to him, since it is played out on the other body. As he tries to understand the linguistic value of sensations such as pain, Wittgenstein asserts in *Philosophical Investigations* that the feeling of pain cannot be communicated in and of itself because it is private and does not denote any object.[13] Pain plays a part, however, in what Wittgenstein calls "language-games," but obliquely, through observation of the behavior displayed by the person in pain.

Logically, we are led to assume that the hanged man in "A Voyage to Cythera" feels no physical pain while the birds are tearing his body since he has been dead for a while. The painful circumstances of his death belong to the past. His pain, however, is very much present throughout the poem, perfectly represented by means of the poetic language, fabricated by the imagination of the poet who observes patterns of painful occurrences such as "his eyes were holes," "the stomach perforated," "the dark intestines hang down to his thighs." Pain in the poem is "ornamental," a poetic object that holds no truth other than the aesthetic component of the image of mutilation and castration observed by the poet. Because pain lives beyond the castration scene that initiated its emergence in the first place, the poet's association with the hanged man's pain does not include the incorporation of his castration. The poetic "I" defies the threat of castration by adopting the pain generated by the spectacle of the hanged man's mutilated body, feeling its pain, the beaks and jaws of the ravenous beasts.

The poetic "I," at first only the simple spectator of the mutilated and castrated body of the hanged man, becomes the hanged man through the adoption of his pains. He opens a poetic dialogue with the castrated man using a direct style, which reduces both the narrative distance between the two subjects and the distance between their two bodies: "O swinging joke, your griefs are those I know." Here the word *griefs* is literally placed in the middle of the line. The mediating position it holds in the line corresponds to the mediating role it plays between the body of the hanged man ("swinging joke") and the body of the poetic "I" ("those I know"). It figures the moment of painful transition whereby the poetic subject becomes the other body; pain become the metaphoric means by which the poet passes from one body to the other. It is through pain that the poet can be one with the object of his poem.

In the last four stanzas of "A Voyage to Cythera" the poetic subject, having traded his place for the place of the hanged man, is now in position to receive directly the pain of being under attack by a number of ferocious animals: "I too felt all the beaks and all the jaws / Of the black panthers and jabbing daws / Who once so loved to shred my shrinking flesh." The crows and the panthers are devouring his flesh as they were devouring the hanged man's flesh. Does this mean that, like the hanged man, the poet must now endure the pain of mutilation, including castration? After enduring such pain, the poet feels nauseated ("I felt . . . like vomit rising sour against my teeth") by the reemergence of an archaic image accompanying the sensation of pain ("the bitter, galling stream of ancient woe"). What is this "ancient woe" that the poetic subject feels rising to his mouth like a wave of nausea? This image points to a moment previous to castration because it is associated to "memories ever fresh"—memories of love with its pleasures and pains, all part of a delightful past. The poet evokes a past colored by a much different form of pain—*triturer,* "to knead," rather than *torturer,* "to torture"—a milder and more slowly moving pain motivated by an early moment of love: "I too felt all the beaks and all the jaws / Who once so loved to shred (*knead*) my shrinking flesh." In this strange evocation of ferocious animals gnawing at the poet's flesh, pleasure seems to manifest itself for both the animals lovingly tearing his body apart ("so loved"), and the poet whose flesh is being lacerated. The image of ravens and panthers delightfully inflicting pain on the poet's tender body brings to the surface of the poem a repressed masochistic tendency. The intricate notion of pleasure-in-pain felt by the poet is metaphorically articulated in the next two lines, in which he suggests the "charming" natural circumstances surrounding the "darkness" of his "bleeding" soul: "The sky was bright, the sea smooth as a table; // My future was a black and red-rimmed cloud."

Much has been written about Baudelaire's sadism,[14] and, in studying the poet's art of cutting the body, this study has also contributed to the debate.

Baudelaire's fascination with the torn female form, however, goes beyond his own demonic desire to control her beautiful and "gay" body as we witness the poet wounding and slashing the "joyous flesh" of the woman in "To One Too Gay" (1:156–57). In fact, Baudelaire often indulges in becoming victim of his own sadistic gestures, in "The Self-Torturer" for example, where he becomes at once the torturer and the victim. After acknowledging the dismembered condition of the dead man in "A Voyage to Cythera," the poet becomes the sole victim of the vicious attack by the beasts of prey slowly tearing his body apart. His slaying brings back memories of "ancient sufferings," which evoke two kinds of pains stemming on one hand from moral self-victimization and on the other from sexual transgression. As he reviews the fate of the hanged man punished for wallowing in sexual pleasures, the poet is reminded of his own lustful past rising from the depths of his soul. He knows the pain of castration and mutilation is the heavy price he must pay for his lewd abandonments. If castration, as I have shown, does not affect the poet whose body remains untouched by the observed scene (as confirmed in the last stanza in which the poet claims he "found nothing but a symbolic gibbet where hung [his] image" on Venus' island), pain, first perceived in its corporeal form and then transformed into a self-destructive moral force, imposes itself as the central metaphor of transfiguration bringing the poet closer to his phantasmatic Other. The feminine nature of this Other is sustained by his masochistic fantasy that Freud clearly referred to as a male fantasy touching upon the presumed female aspect of male sexuality.

In his 1924 essay "The Economic Problem of Masochism," Freud identifies three types of masochism: the erotogenic, the feminine and the moral. According to Freud, all three are related, or, rather, the feminine and the moral have roots in the erotogenic, they have dispersed origins in sexual behavior and eroticism. Freud asserts that masochism emanates from "situations of being copulated with and of giving birth"[15] that characterize femaleness and that there is a strong connection between guilt and erotism, a connection that dictates the behavior of the masochist who directs his punishment inward and thus becomes guilt-stricken. Freud's essay presents a number of remarkable issues on the implication of femaleness in the masochistic act. First, what he calls feminine masochism relates to the observation he makes of men's fantasies of being "forced into unconditional obedience." As is the case for castration, Freud examines a male phenomenon that can only be justified by unfounded claims based on the submissive nature of female sexuality. Freud evokes male masochism as man's secret fantasy to be "in some way maltreated" (286), a condition that he attributes to the female sex, or should we say, that he envies of the female body he imagines in a state of servitude. Having constructed a weak female sex for the purposes of male fantasy, the perverse male subject now desires its enslavement to male violence for which he becomes in turn the feminized victim. His becoming female necessitates the creation of her oppressed sex, either debased or mutilated. In fact, it is the debasement and the mutilation he inflicts on her body that he craves in his own masochistic fantasy.

The poet in "A Voyage to Cythera" endures the corporeal and moral pain of the hanged man in a strange substitution with an imaginary female Other that he secretly builds into the "symbolic" scene of horrible decay he sees on the Island of Love. The decomposing body of the hanged man recalls a similar situation in the poem "A Carion" (1:31–32) in which the poet and his lover come across the carcass of a rotting bird. While the carion is clearly identified with a woman of little virtue with "her legs in the air, like a lascivious woman," the decomposing body of the hanged man retains its male nature even though his sex has been mangled. The poet abandons any pursuit of the castrated other by abandoning his "symbolic" image of a body in pain on the island: "Venus, upon your isle I saw, upthrust, / Myself on a symbolic gallows-tree." In other words, the poet does not fully trade his place with his poetically constructed other. Therefore, he does not fully assume the pain of castration: he remains split between the two poles of the conversion.

"A Voyage to Cythera" has provided for Baudelaire a poetic field of experimentation for his split subject—split between the feminine and the masculine—through which he can assume both roles as observer and receiver of pain. His poetic identity can go in and out of the body in pain, in and out of femininity, in and out of masculinity. Thus, the poet defies sexual determination, and he harbors both genders in the construction of his identity. The undecidable nature of the poetic identity in (trans)formation throughout "A Voyage to Cythera" depends on the intermediate role played out by the figure of pain, the third element in the poetic configuration no longer restricted to representations of maleness and femaleness. Pain acts as a crucial signifier of transition; it determines the degree of mental and physical difficulty marking the moment of (ex)change from one subjective position to another, from masculinity to femininity. To go through any transitional phase does indeed imply a painful movement away from an original situation into an unknown future filled with new expectations, anticipated pleasures and/or pains. The relinquishing of the old and the expectation of the new meet for a brief but essential moment to create the full dramatic element of pain in which the poet of "A Voyage to Cythera" invests all his desires to become female, not castrated. For critic Robert Smadja it is in "Un Voyage à Cythère" that Baudelaire projects his complete meditation on the body by clearly identifying a second body, an imaginary body that enables the poet to play out all his fantasies of cutting without a scratch.[16]

My purpose in examining castration has been to demonstrate that Baudelaire, Truffaut, and Freud have in fact involuntarily disrupted its effects on their male subjects. Antoine Doinel, who became a man under the constant threat of castration, finally overcomes its effect in *Love on the Run*, when he finds himself projected back into a psychological time prior to the threat itself, a time of childhood relationships adapted to his masculine needs. His female companion, Sabine, presents no threat to him, on the contrary she provides him with the key for a happy return to a time of unproblematic love. While asserting the fact of woman's castration, Freud also admits to his limited knowledge of femininity. His vague speculation on female castration is in fact in complete contradiction with his assertion of the fact of her castration. He must, however, maintain his theory of her presumed castration in order to continue the examination of his thesis on the construction of male identity: man's fear of castration requires the presumed spectacle of the female castrated body, and fear of losing his penis soon translates into male anxiety of becoming (like) the female other.

Baudelaire's poem "A Voyage to Cythera" embodies the anxiety of castration, the pain associated with man's loss of virility, and his secret desire to become female. The castrated body of the hanged man, punished for giving in to bodily pleasures, offers the poet the image of a carefree hedonist whose disbelief in the threat of castration led him to his death and his emasculation. The poet, however, does not turn away from the hanged man's castrated body, facing, instead, the possibility of his own castration by assimilating the image of the hanged man to his own. Like Antoine in *Love on the Run*, he defies castration, its fear, its fact, and absorbs its pain by imagining himself in place of the castrated man, a place that Freud singularly and inaccurately assigns to woman. The complexity of the debate around the presumed castration of woman was felt by Freud, who, in order to symbolize the effectiveness of castration on the female body and its consequences on the male body displaced the site/sight of castration from her sex to her head: "to decapitate = to castrate" (*Sexuality and the Psychology of Love* 212). Having failed to prove female castration, does Freud secretly hope to be more successful in asserting her decapitation?

Decapitation

In his short note of 1922 on the Medusa's head, Freud restores a feminine figure to the cut inherent in the scene of castration, a cut that could not be represented as a direct expression of castration but which acts as a reminder of the missing penis on the woman's body and the threat it poses to the male body. For Freud, as well as for literary critics intrigued by the question of feminine castration, decapitation represents feminine castration more than castration itself. It is as if decapitation metaphorized castration in such a way that it became a more readily available illustration and a more viable representation of the questionable concept of castration. Indeed, the head of Medusa severed by Perseus presents the horrible sight of a mutilated feminine sex thus displaced from the woman's genitals to her head.

Focus on Medusa

In his attempt at finding a mythical figure to illustrate feminine castration, Freud briefly turns to a Greek female monster with dangerous powers to whomever looks at her directly: Medusa, the Gorgon.

> The terror of Medusa is thus a terror of castration linked to the sight of something. Numerous analyses have made us familiar with the occasion for this: it occurs when the boy, who has hitherto been unwilling to believe the threat of castration, catches sight of the female genitals, probably those of an adult, surrounded by hair, and essentially those of his mother. (212)

As far as the "anecdote" on Medusa is concerned, it is clear that Freud is not directly interested in the contextual events that resulted in her decapitation. Taken out of context by Freud, Medusa has the singularity of a frightful feminine figure and her decapitation comes to represent her "horrifying femininity" to whomever looks at the spectacle of this beheaded monster:

> The hair upon Medusa's head is frequently represented in works of art in the form of snakes, and these once again are derived from the castration complex. It is a remarkable fact that however frightening they may be in themselves, they nevertheless serve actually as a mitigation of the horror, for they replace the penis, the absence of which is the cause of the horror. This is a confirmation of the technical rule according to which a multiplication of penis symbols signifies castration. (212)

As a powerful female who is subsequently beheaded, Medusa is left devoid of her powerful head (and particularly, without the penises she has on her head in place of her hair). Freud translates the loss of the head into the loss of the penis for woman. As a monstrous representation of feminine sexuality, she offers the unbearable spectacle of her body cuts that Freud associates with castration—her mutilation.

However simple and literal this transcription of the myth of Medusa to the castration scenario seems, an unexpected twist soon develops as Freud interprets her petrifying look as a source of pleasure for the male-spectator whose hardened body he now reads as the representation of an erection:

> The sight of Medusa's head makes the spectator stiff with terror, turns him to stone. Observe that we have here once again the same origin from the castration complex and the same transformation of affect! For becoming stiff means an erection. Thus in the original situation it offers consolation to the spectator: he is still in possession of a penis, and the stiffening reassures him of the fact. (212)

The erect penis caused by the sight of the castrated/decapitated Medusa is as horrifying as it is pleasurable and reassuring for the man who knows that he has not lost the penis he felt to be stiff with pleasure. Among the horrified and delighted spectators present at the scene of Medusa's decapitation we must count Freud, himself petrified with excitement by his textual rediscovery of the Medusa. His textual "petrification" of the figure of Medusa may be the reason for which he exhibits no interest in the circumstances surrounding her decapitation.

What is the mythical episode from which Freud extracts and isolates Medusa? It involves Perseus, whose tragic life has to some extent the same odd beginning as Oedipus'. Both stories involve the birth of an unwanted male child—Oedipus and Perseus—unwanted by the father or the grandfather, each of whom is told by the oracle that the child could later kill them.[17]

It is interesting to observe the similarity between the episode of Perseus and Medusa, and the episode that brings together Oedipus and the Sphinx. Medusa is the feminine monster who kills with her eyes and the Sphinx is likewise a feminine monster who kills with her enigmatic language,[18] and devours those who cannot solve her riddle(s). Both Perseus and Oedipus must conquer these monsters by destroying their respective powers of sight and language in order to proceed with their male destinies. Although it could be argued that Freud's interest in mythical illustrations is aroused by the similarities between the two stories, it is also remarkable that he emphasizes different aspects of the two myths. In the Oedipus story Freud pays little attention to the Sphinx, who represents the riddle of femininity, which, unlike the riddle presented to Oedipus, remains unsolved, while the Oedipus complex is dramatized by Oedipus-like male subjects destined to kill their fathers and love their mothers. All of Freud's attention is given to Oedipus, who embodies the hero in a fictional scenario that forms the analytical foundation of the Oedipus complex. Of course, Freud has no need for a second mythical male hero, and he leaves Perseus totally unaccounted for. For her part Medusa captivates Freud more than the Sphinx because, while she embodies the same death threat as the Sphinx, she also promises pleasures worth the risk of exposing oneself to her danger. Like Medusa's victims, Freud enters what Jean-Pierre Vernant calls her "her field of fascination, with the risk of losing oneself there."[19]

Freud begins his short discussion on Medusa's head by freezing his own analytical language in a mathematical fashion requiring some comments. He represents the hypothetical conjunction between castration and decapitation by joining the verbs *to decapitate* and *to castrate* in an equation with an equal sign: "to decapitate = to castrate." The first remark that could be made about this mathematical formula is that it transcribes simply in shorthand a roughly taken note. It presents a preliminary, sketchy idea that is quickly jotted down by means of unconjugated verbs and the universal sign of equation. We must add that "Medusa's Head" is not a polished piece intended for publication or public communication. Although composed in 1922, it was only published for the first time in 1940, posthumously. The fact that Freud did not offer this piece of writing for publication when he was alive seems to substantiate the unreadiness of the note and the conceptual immaturity of the figure of Medusa, which does not then "officially"— or may never—represent symbolically the cutting of the body during castration.

Another possible explanation of the equation marking the beginning of "Medusa's Head" is based on the fundamental "scientific" nature of any mathematical equation. By imperatively equating castration and decapitation, all rhetorical arguments about the possibility of nonequivalence between the two terms is denied. It may be supposed that the scientific sign language of mathematics is being used here to reinforce the scientific legitimacy of psychoanalysis. Similarly, Lacan allows mathematical formulas to enter the field of psychoanalytical representations, since schemes and mathematical signs are a major part of his stylistic reformulation of Freudian psychoanalysis.

"Medusa's Head" belongs to Freud's private writings—those he has chosen not to publish—perhaps because it seems to describe a double phenomenon of fear and pleasure from which the writer has not distanced himself. It is in the privacy of his textual pleasure—a pleasure of petrification/erection provided by the figure of Medusa—that Freud places under mathematically rigorous rules the psychoanalytical language he uses to represent a feminine figure of destruction. Because Medusa points to the weakness of the analyst who should remain emotionally undisturbed in his scientific research, she has no place in publicized psychoanalytical discourse. It is precisely its private nature that has aroused great critical curiosity concerning "Medusa's Head."[20] For Freud these unformed ideas had not yet earned the right to emerge in the main text—the text focused on the discourse on castration. "Medusa's Head" is, to use a filmic analogy, a note "out of discursive focus," a note that remains unclearly demarcated in the background supporting the castration theory. Yet, paradoxically, the note has generated literary theoretical discourse from such notable critics as Neil Hertz and Hélène Cixous who have brought it back into focus. Freud's note on Medusa has risen from the psychoanalytical backdrop to occupy a prominent place in the foreground of criticism.

Neil Hertz has contributed to the refocusing on the Medusa's head, and in his book *The End of the Line*[21] he devotes a whole chapter to the decapitated figure: "Medusa's Head: Male Hysteria under Political Pressure." In this chapter Medusa's "horrifying decapitated Head"[22] becomes the major figure of threat in representations of political events such as the 1848 revolution, the Commune in 1870, and, indirectly, the French Revolution of 1789.

Hertz first recalls Hugo's literary chronicle of the events that took place in June 1848. Just like Freud's "Medusa's Head," this chronicle was published after the author's death. The particular passage analyzed by Hertz is entitled *Journées de juin,* but it is also accompanied by the following subtitle: "Miscellaneous notes." Just like "Medusa's Head," Hugo's note is not intended for publication, yet, after his death, it finds its way to the publishing house, which betrays its privacy while offering its intriguing and sketchy profile to literary critics. In fact, Hertz seems to have perfected the art of note reading as he reads Hugo's note against Freud's, thus bridging the figurative gap between the threat of historical upheavals and the threat of sexual disfiguration in the private folds of the two notes. Hertz certainly provides a fascinating critical "venue" where both notes seem to echo each other perfectly. Almost all aspects of Freud's Medusa are echoed in Hugo's text. Likewise, a near-complete Medusa appears in Hugo's text, except her reason for being Medusan, namely her decapitation. There are no actual decapitated women in Hugo's text—although there are apotropaic ones— no more than there is a castrated woman behind the representation of Medusa in Freud's text, although there is indeed a mythical story about the decapitated figure of Medusa and a Freudian belief that this figure impersonates feminine castration.

Before Hertz's Freudian reading of the historic representation of Medusa, Cixous proposes to deconstruct Freud's obscene Medusa into a laughing one in her article "The Laugh of the Medusa" (1975).[23] In her essay Cixous associates the laughing Medusa with femininity liberating its essence through laughter. Fighting psychoanalysis on all sides for having conditioned women to social and sexual roles of total servitude, Cixous is particularly enraged by the concept of the castrated woman. It is in order to demolish the most inconceivable image of femininity—Freud's invention of feminine castration—in order to undo a cut that is so detrimental to the symbolic place of woman in language and culture that Cixous restores beauty and laughter to Medusa:

> Too bad for them if they fall apart upon discovering that women aren't men, or that the mother doesn't have one. But isn't this fear convenient to them? Wouldn't the worst be, isn't the worst, in truth, that women aren't castrated, that they have only to stop listening to the Sirens (for the Sirens were men) for history to change its meaning? You only have to look at the Medusa straight on to see her. And she's not deadly. She's beautiful and she's laughing.[24]

In a later essay entitled "Castration or Decapitation?" Cixous effects a metonymic displacement from the Medusa's loss of her head to the woman's loss of her tongue. Cixous views women's silence with regard to their bodies as a result of the cultural, social, and political cutting effected on their bodies.

Freud knows better than anybody how to figuratively but effectively cut woman's body and how to theorize the cuts performed in the name of castration and decapitation. Cixous also refers to Freud's theory of hysteria as a continuation of his theory of castration and decapitation; to him hysteria becomes the symbolic severing of the tongue of his female patients—then, the female hysteric cannot speak about the traumatic scene that has caused her psychological disorder. Cixous accuses Freud not of having theorized silence but of having feminized hysteria to the point where the two signifiers—woman and hysteria—become one as they enter the discourse of psychoanalysis accompanied by all their signifieds: castration, decapitation, silence, body cuts.

> Silence: silence is the mark of hysteria. The great hysterics have lost speech, they are aphonic, and at times have lost more than speech: they are pushed to the point of choking, nothing gets through. They are decapitated, their tongues are cut off and what talks isn't heard because it's the body that talks, and man doesn't hear the body.[25]

In fact, Hertz's reading of the Medusa as a sign of male hysteria, a sign of male silence—of the cutting off of his tongue—in the political representations, presents a legitimate criticism of Freud's all-female hysteria. If the Medusa in Hertz's text is never decapitated, it could suggest that her uncut, unblemished body represents a threat to man's political power. An uncut female body destabilizes the laws of castration because the completeness of her beautiful body acts as a vision that silences men, provoking in them, as it does in Baudelaire and Truffaut, the desire/necessity to fragment them.

Hertz's and Cixous's rereadings of tales of female decapitation clearly indicate that Freud's formula "castration = decapitation" is a problematic equation with regard to a body cut that never occurred on the female body other than in symbolic terms in order to provide the backdrop of a trauma that affects the male subject exclusively.

Decapitation by Frame

Having already mentioned Truffaut's persistent aesthetic passion for women's faces, we must now emphasize the mode of (re)presentation characterizing each of these faces on the screen. They appear framed in various ways: photographs, slides, canvas, film frames. In *Jules and Jim* the first framed appearance of Catherine on the screen is that of a statue on a slide projected onto a portable screen rolled down against a wall. In *Day for Night* we are first introduced to Julie Baker through her various photographed portraits that Ferrand examines with great fascination; in *The Bride Wore Black* Julie Kohler's face becomes Fergus's artistic obsession while he paints her, first within the frame of the canvas and then, beyond the conventional frame, on the wall beside his bed.

Given Truffaut's constant use of framing techniques in conjunction with women's faces, it may be suggested that his passion for women's faces is mainly associated with the geometry of the frame. In analyzing the variety of frames used to delineate women's faces, we will find an explanation to the repeated motif of the framed face in his films. Why are most female figures in his films first captured inside a particular frame detached from the background provided by the whole screen? Why use an intermediate mode to frame these women's faces when the celluloid borders of the filmstrip provide a natural framing device? Why must their faces be framed twice, once in the stylized and visible frames of the slide, the photograph, and the painting and a second time by the natural frame of the screen?

The notion of framing becomes part of the history of filmmaking long before film evolves into the form of visual entertainment with which we are now so familiar. It is in the technical process of filmmaking that the frame's phenomenological presence becomes prominent. The material frame determined by four celluloid borders presents elements analogous to the negative of a photograph. Early on in the technical stages of filmmaking, before the film is projected, the frame contains a photographic moment. Each photographic frame presents minute changes from the preceding and the successive frames fixed on the celluloid of the filmstrip. The frames visually identifiable on the strip of film become paradoxically invisible when the film is being projected, as the movement of the film eliminates their borders. The rectangular celluloid frames of the filmstrip, when projected onto the screen, become the image framed by the screen. I will call these "screen-frames," large frames, while referring to the frames represented within the large frame and containing women's faces as small frames. The relationship between the large frame and the small frames in Truffaut's *Jules and Jim*, *The Bride Wore Black*, and *Day for Night* may be read in terms contrasting the general and the particular, the total and the partial, the background and the detail, in what Roland Barthes has termed the *studium* and the *punctum* in his study of photography.[26]

According to Barthes, the *studium* is the general interest one feels toward a photograph. It brings out "an average affect [an emotion relayed by Reason], almost a kind of training" (48).[27] Applied to the field of cinema, as is the case here, this term can designate the elements contained within the screen's frame. It indicates a sort of mise-en-scène in which all visual elements are arranged continuously and harmoniously and in which they appeal to the general interest—cultural, historical, political, psychological—of the onlooker. The *punctum*, on the other hand, is what breaks the continuity of the *studium*. It is "an arrow piercing me [. . .], a wound, a sting, a mark left by a sharp instrument [. . .] a small hole, a small stain, a small cut [. . .] it is this coincidence which bruises and daunts me" (49). Barthes insists here on the unexpectedness ("this coincidence") and the *punctum*'s traumatic effect on the body ("a wound, a sting"; "a cut"; "piercing me, bruising and daunting me"). According to Barthes, the *punctum* does not exist as much in cinema as it does in photography because the moving image does not allow the viewer to spend much time with the details of a single take. The *punctum* of photography is a supplement, something that the viewer finds and adds to the photograph as he looks at it longer and in more detail. In fact, the photograph is an image that does not go anywhere and that offers its details to me / the viewer "who stands there in front of it [. . .] looking at it, scrutinizing as if I wanted to know more about the object or the person it represents" (154). Film, on the other hand, as it moves from one image to the next, leaves no time for the eye and the mind to rest.

Barthes locates the impossible *punctum* on the screen, the large frame: "In front of the screen, I am not free to close my eyes; otherwise, upon reopening them, I would not find the same image; I am constrained to an uninterrupted voracity". (89–90). But what about the small frames, those contained within the large frame and delineating women's faces in Truffaut's films? If the *punctum* is a traumatic and unexpected element in the immobile representation that, paradoxically—emotionally—*moves* the viewer standing outside of the representation, I propose that it could be what moves the men in Truffaut's films who are looking at the immobilized faces of these frame-bound women.

In *Jules and Jim* the protagonists are indeed moved by the mysterious woman's face they observe in a slide session in Albert's studio. The face is rich in various *puncta,* different points of potential trauma—the eyes, the lips, the hair, the nose. The camera focuses individually on the *puncta* affecting the two men; it also freezes the slide for a short while, thus giving Jules and Jim a chance to identify in the image at rest the different details of a beautiful face. At this moment the cinematic apparatus gives the illusion of a still representing Catherine's face, and, as a result, this particular image is closer to the photogram—the photographic unit—than it is to the filmic image. The camera seems to allow a moment of representation to the impossible *punctum* of cinema, to offer a commentary on the performances of the *punctum* in cinema.

We are nevertheless watching a film; *Jules and Jim* justifies its existence as a visual story in action, not a series of isolated photograms. In order to resume movement, the film must break the immobility of the slide. In the next shot, the photogramic representation of the woman's face is repeated while we see another slide of the statue, another representation of the same face, but this time shown in a profile position. The camera movement must proceed with its visual narrative. Before resuming movement, the camera gives Jules and Jim a second chance to contemplate Catherine's face. They ask Albert to go back to the slide representing her face. This demand for a second viewing of the woman's face on the slide is a confirmation of their aesthetic desire to be "punctumed," punctured by the details of Catherine's face. It is also a demand for love, that is, a staging of the moment of desire, its eruption on the screen that Barthes calls "le *Kaïros* du désir" (95), the moment of impact between the desire to see and the object of desire—the moment in which the forces of desire gather around a particularly acute visual detail that promises satisfaction, so reminiscent of the lyrical moment I have analyzed in Petrarch's poetry.[28] This moment has just erupted in the lives of Jules and Jim. Desire has peaked. Their photographic demand for love has exceeded their repressed sexual selves, and they confront the object of their unleashed sexual desire when they ask to see the statue's face again. Indeed, as they look directly into her eyes, they willingly allow her Medusan powers to exert their pleasurable yet dangerous effects on their bodies. In fact, as a way to confirm how spellbound they are by the Medusan woman, the camera gives us two brief shots of Jules and Jim as they look at the slide of the statue's face. They are motionless, as if turned to stone, "hardened" by the mere look cast on them by the beautiful framed apparition. The face on the slide is the Medusa of pleasure, which makes their bodies "stiff" with delight and thus reassures their masculinity by verifying that castration has not been performed.

The immobile face on the slide sets the lives of Jules and Jim into motion as they undertake a search for the woman it depicts. The photogramic component of the slide points to the greater magnitude of the aesthetic experience of photography in comparison with the aesthetic experience of cinema. The slide is the point of departure for the film's actual narrative, which takes off from the moment of encounter between the two men and the woman on the slide, the slide establishing the film's dramatic knot. From this point on, the two young men's easy lifestyle is deeply disturbed and reorganized around the mysterious *puncta* of Catherine's face and its details, her dissected face. These *puncta* will reappear individually in subsequent shots of the woman's face—the actual statue on the island—as the two men get closer and closer to the perfect replica of the statue's face on the slide, the real Catherine.

Truffaut's representation of Medusa would not be complete—that is, would not be completely Freudian—if the Medusa of pleasure who holds Jules and Jim under her fascinating powers and makes them "stiff" with pleasure was not doubled by the Medusa of pain. We know from Freud's "Medusa's Head" that pleasure does not come alone, and, however pleasurable the Medusan face on the slide may be, it also contains the danger of femininity that Freud resists by endorsing the full decapitation of the dangerous Medusa—a symbolic castrating gesture—and that Truffaut also resists by using frames as instruments of decapitation to cut the woman's head from her body. I have already proposed that the frame of the slide could also be a *punctum* (a small cut) in relation to the large frame, the screen. The small frame of the slide is a disturbance in the visual continuity of the large frame; its geometry breaks the visual field on the screen into two dimensions, two spaces: the immobile space of the decapitated woman separated from the mobile space of the effects of pleasure and pain regulating the level of desire of Jules and Jim in the narrative.

In *Day for Night* Truffaut repeats the decapitation of the main female character, Julie Baker. Her first appearance on the screen is also as an immobilized face in a still. As I have already stated, *Day for Night* is Truffaut's personal filmic statement on the art of filmmaking. Ferrand, played by Truffaut himself, is a film director who is in the process of shooting on location. The personal lives of his team of technicians and actors, the technical difficulties, Ferrand's own dreams, in short everything contributes to the making of his film, *Meet Pamela*. Everything is related to the cinematic enterprise as if private lives were subordinate to the "whims" of cinema, as if life on screen was the only life worth living, as if representations of people were superior to people themselves.

Truffaut often claims that cinema is more important than life itself. To him representations of women are certainly superior to real women. Julie Baker represents this perfection of beauty as she appears in the photographs that introduce her for the first time on the screen. Her framed beauty surpasses the beautiful woman she may be in actual life. None of the personal comments offered by the assistant about her personal life, her psychological problems, and her resemblance to her mother, have any effect on Ferrand, who remains totally absorbed and fascinated by her photographs. To him she is "pretty"; "she has very beautiful green eyes"; "crystal eyes"; "a very pretty and pleasant facial shape"; "she looks sad, slightly sexy." What Ferrand is looking at in Julie's photos is not her identity but her soul, in the hope that he might capture on film the truth of her beauty and the depth of her femininity behind her sad and sexy appearance. Indeed, her sadness and sexiness seem to traverse the thickness of her body and of her inner female self to endow her face with "un air," "an appearance/expression," a shadow of femininity. Her expression of sadness tinted with a certain sex appeal may be read as an expression of photographic truth. Barthes places this truth of representation in something that is unspeakable and undividable: the "air," the look on one's face. The air is without object, but it expresses the subject better than the face itself. Julie *moves* Ferrand with her sad and sexy look. This look is the indivisible quality of her femininity which transgresses the borders of the photograph by conveying the feminine nature of her entire body to her decapitated head. Barthes calls the transgression of the body on the face a "luminous shadow": "the expression is thus the luminous shadow emanating from the body" (169). Julie's face bears the look inspired by the "truth" originating from below her face, from her feminine body, which radiates sadness and sex appeal. In other words, her face is overshadowed by what Truffaut perceives as the sad condition of her feminine sexuality: the condition of female sexuality that Freud has identified as the "fact" of her castration, and that continues to mark the manner in which male artists construct their vision of the beautiful female. Her framed face carries all the repressed elements of her sexuality, and it is only as a castrated woman / a Medusa that she appeals to Ferrand's sexual desire and to Truffaut's male desire feasting on an ephemeral moment of pure pleasure.

The ideal cinematic woman for Truffaut may very well be Medusa and all her doubles. In his films she seems less cinematic than she is photographic, as we apprehend her image almost exclusively caught in the frames of slides, photographs and paintings. Immobilized by photography/painting and decapitated by their frames, women in small frames operate inside the large frame of the films as enclosed units, set apart from the motion, the life, the action of the film. Yet, because they are contained but not subdued representations of Medusa, these women also radiate pain when they transgress the borders of the small frames and inevitably invade the movement operating within the large frame. In the large frame they affect men's sexual desire and consequently change the course of their lives. The representations of women in small frames are, however, more effectively fulfilling than their direct representations, since they offer a distinct visual enclosure in which men's sexual desire is safely allowed to run wild, while representations of women in large frames have disrupting effects on the men sharing the large frame with them. Within the large frame women are not mere victims of decapitation by framing, for they also display their female bodies the minute they step out of the small frames, and become part of the motion that governs the screen. In fact, they perform on Truffaut's screen what Freud speculates they might perform on the body of the little boy, that is, they create the fear of castration for all male viewers, be it the actor in the film or the spectator in the theater. Frames contain and release Medusan figures throughout Truffaut's films, and their presence indicates the possibility for represented women to perform visual acts of sexual transgression, even acts of bodily violence.

Truffaut often uses the large frame to display the danger associated with the Medusan female characters. As they invade the full visual space of the screen, they affect the men around them with an almost organic reality. Without the protection of the small frame, male characters come in close contact with Medusan females ready to unleash their punishment on them. The male bodies then become vulnerable to corporeal acts of female aggression applied indirectly by means of textual injunctions such as letters, thus illustrating the metaphor that language hurts and that words have a way to reach not only the deepest layers of the soul but also the very surface of the body, which translates and carries signs of the inner suffering. Letters become an important metaphorical conveyor of violence, a spelling board for the chilling acts of violence performed on screen by women on men whose fear to become victims of Medusa seems to have materialized.

In Truffaut's cinema woman's body often enters the realm of images through the artifice of the letter. Letters in many of Truffaut's films hold an important transitional role between the vocal and the visual, between the voice-over and the image it narrates, between the thought of cutting or marking the body and its expression or action. They also actively participate in the development of the plot. They stimulate the forces of the past, as in *The Man Who Loved Women,* in which Bertrand Morane finds a drawer full of old letters and photographs, which incite him to write about his tumultuous past love affairs; in turn, writing becomes for Morane a way to express his adoration for women's legs.

In *Jules and Jim* letters bring confusion to the relationships between Catherine and her lovers. In one instance Catherine announces in a letter to Jim that she is pregnant with their baby: "Your love is part of my life. You live inside me. Believe me, Jim, believe me. This paper is your skin, the ink my blood. I press hard to make it cut in." The letter becomes more than just a piece of paper announcing Catherine's pregnancy; it turns into Jim's skin upon which Catherine's blood-ink seals unerasable words printed on his skin like a painful tattoo. The physicality generated by Catherine's letter touches the spectator's sensations; his imagination becomes doubled with a corporeal reaction carried out by Jim's immediate reaction to the letter: he jumps out of bed as if he had felt the sharp nib of Catherine's pen cutting deep into his skin. Even though Catherine's letter is in Jim's hands, it is Catherine who is reading the actual letter; it is her voice we hear. On the screen we see her face superimposed on a background representing a forest. The double exposure of Catherine's face on a wooded landscape produces the visual effect achieved by the ink-blood pressed upon the paper-skin. The "body" marks the entire scene. It marks the scene by presenting the visual transcription of the letter as a physical act claiming love as its motivation but manifests itself like a torture inflicted on Jim's body.

Truffaut's crucial rapport with the physicality of the "letter scene" goes beyond his desire to be truly original. To him the scene was so powerful that, in 1971, he repeated it in *The Two English Girls:* Muriel is desperately in love with Claude, and she writes him a series of passionate letters. In one of her letters, visually represented by the superimposition of her face on a wooded landscape, the sentence "this paper is your skin, the ink my blood. I press hard to make it cut in" is repeated from *Jules and Jim.* Here, again, these words represent the same type of physical violence applied on the body of the male reader, here Claude, a young man whose love is not as fully committed as the female writer's, Muriel, the young English woman. In both *Jules and Jim* and *The Two English Girls* the visual effects used to render the physical inscription of the female love letter on the body of the male reader detach the woman's face from the rest of her body and, as if bleeding on screen after her symbolic decapitation, her face penetrates the forest appearing in the background. This superimposition carries out on the screen the force generated by the physical inscription left on the imag(e)ination of the spectator by the blood-writing of the woman.

In comparison to the danger presented by the female body on the large frame, small frames assume a paradoxical position. They visually set apart and immobilize women, yet, at the same time, they prefigure women's active participation in the narrative, standing in for their momentary absence. Women in small frames also have an inherently disturbing quality later set to motion in the lives of the men who contemplate and fear their bodies evolving in, invading the large frame. From the small frames through which they already unleash signs of their dangerous femininity upon the male figures spatially separated from them, the female figures create a sexual tension that triggers the film's action. Framing women is a way of punctuating their presence, of focusing on their (perceived) untamable female sexuality. In fact, women are paradoxically more menacing within frames than they are out of them, as if the quick pleasure they bring to the men examining the stillness of their faces harbored a dormant but portentous form of turmoil.

As he concludes his book on photography, Barthes suggests that what is contained in the photograph is a form of madness "threatening unceaselessly to blow up in the onlooker's face" (180). According to him, cinema is a way of trimming the "wild edges" of photography. We could apply this claim to Truffaut's representations of women. Feminine sexuality, unknown and fearsome to men in the film, becomes a monstrous fantasy and thus presents a potentially more unruly woman when contained within the framed representation of her face than when women are allowed to participate directly in the action of the film, to be fully present, whole, on the screen. Outside the small frames they merely act out the version of femininity as misconceived by Freudian decapitation theory, a theory that male characters in Truffaut's films seem to have totally internalized. Within the artificially constructed small frames, however, they suggest a form of madness expected to burst at any time, thus destabilizing male identity built on the Freudian expectation that the beautiful face in the frame possesses the quality of a decapitated Medusa, rendered docile, or at least manageable, by her photographic representation.

In *The Bride Wore Black* the character of Julie Kohler helps us put into perspective the paradoxical effects of the two frames. In the frame of Fergus's painting Julie displays an almost too intense surplus of tension that must be liberated by the action taking place in the large frame. She steps out of the small frame and becomes a human Diana, who kills Fergus. The uncontainable femininity she evokes in the frame of the painting is so difficult to represent that she has to step down into the real world and do her "Freudian thing"—that is, her impersonation of the castrated and castrating female, castrated by frame-decapitation and castrating by killing all the men she fascinates. From the very beginning of the film we know that the problematics of frames are related to feminine sexuality as we see a collection of photographs representing an expressionless woman—Julie herself—accompanying the credits. The scene in which Julie-Diana the huntress slays Fergus is a logical manifestation of this latency in the big frame.

As she is painted by Fergus, Julie becomes his ideal woman, immobilized by his canvas. Fergus paints Julie's face several times, and each time she appears on a different canvas. Can we assign the agency of castration to all the frames? It could even be argued that decapitation by frame does not actually take place because her painted face is free of the conventional frame represented by the actual wooden structure placed around the canvas. Here the frameless canvas is set on an easel, and its natural borders are the only borders separating her painted face from her human face. These natural borders are indeed fragile borders and certainly raise questions about the definition of the frame and its ability to represent a contained and concentrated fantasy of decapitation.

In *Truth in Painting*[29] Jacques Derrida expressed the difficulty of defining the frame in the discourse of aesthetics. He became interested in the frame through his reading of Kant's concept of the *parergon* in the *Critique of Judgement*. Kant defines the parergon as an ornament, an adjunct, a supplement to the work of art itself. It is not only the frame of the painting, but also draperies on the bodies of statues, or the decorated columns of a building. Kant also poses the question of the parergon's relationship to the work it ends up supplementing: is the parergon inside or outside the ergon, inside or outside the work itself? To this question concerning the limits of the represented object, Derrida adds the unlimited space outside of the parergon, thus making it impossible to define a stable and localizable frame in aesthetic space. The resulting indeterminacy of the frame, its participation inside the work it frames as well as outside that same work, makes the frame an uncertain border between inside and outside: "*Parerga* have a thickness, a surface that separates them not only, as Kant would have it, from the inside, from the body of the *ergon* itself, but also from the outside, from the wall on which the painting is hung" (24). If we apply Derrida's argument on the impossibility of establishing solid determined margins around artistic representations to framed faces of women in Truffaut's films, those women's faces no longer appear as so strictly separated from their background. Derrida thus offers additional support to the previous argument that small frames provide women with a fragile enclosure that is unable to restrain the turmoil of their femaleness ready to explode into the "reality" represented within the large frame.

It may be said that the permeability of the frame is responsible for shattering the classical male fantasy by which the photographed woman represents the ideal woman. In *The Mississippi Mermaid* (1969), for example, Louis Mahé's future bride, a woman he only knows through letters and a photograph, turns out to be a con artist. About the film Truffaut admits to the treachery of the photograph when he comments: "*The Mermaid* is in fact the story of a man who marries a woman who is the complete opposite of what he wanted."[30] Thus, it appears that small frames become the breaking point of male fantasies, marking the impossibility of sustaining their idealistic projection. What Derridean theory adds to the problematics of frames posed by this analysis is a philosophical dimension located beyond the dichotomized representation of the frames. Small frames and large frames have to make room for "the framing," which becomes a third contender in the representational game played by the filmmaker. Indeed, what I have called the small frames—the frames inside the screen frame, that is, the slide, the photograph, and the painting—cut a space of detachment for the faces but also for the background against which they appear. In Derridean terms, by allowing the inside to be outside and the outside to be inside, the small frames present the arbitrariness of their border.

In *The Bride Wore Black,* if Julie appears somehow contained by the fragile borders of the canvas, she also defies their power of separating inside from outside: she invades the inside of her framed face when she cuts out her own painted face from the canvas with Fergus's razor. She symbolically enters the space of her decapitated image with a cutting, castrating gesture, a male gesture creating an even smaller frame as if smaller meant safer. For Julie cutting out the canvas is a means of preserving her anonymity, of eliminating her face from the scene of the crime, of denying the small frame its status as clue (which would provide the police with the means of identifying her). She thus mutilates her own image.

This gesture of self-effacement is as much a gesture of self-mutilation as it is a gesture set to prove the inability of frames to fully contain femininity.

If the frame cannot keep within its borders what it is representing (ideal femininity for Fergus) this may be because, as suggested by Derrida, the frame does not exist in and of itself.[31] According to Derrida, however, "there is framing" (39), whereby objects and people seem detached from a context in which they are in fact still participating. The frame does not detach itself from the inside and/or the outside; rather, it participates in both and offers no determinate boundary between them: "the *parergon* is nevertheless a form that has traditionally been defined not as setting itself off but as disappearing, sinking in, effacing itself" (25–26).

Further on in the film we see Julie's face painted on the wall beside Fergus's bed. Except for the rough limits set by the dark background colors against the white wall, no borders are clearly demarcated, and her face seems to blend gradually into the wall. The actual canvas frame has disappeared. The safety of the frame has been replaced by a loose framing of her face. There, by Fergus's bed, hidden behind the pillows, she not only illustrates Derrida's frame under erasure, she also calls into question the castrating function of the frame, its Freudian power. By casting away the frame around the decapitated women in *The Bride Wore Black,* Truffaut may be shifting the Freudian value he usually assigns to framing; what initially appeared as the castrating function of the frame is doubled with the possibility that the represented female can indeed escape the cutting fate of the frame, thus endangering the artist who framed her in the first place.

Frames may first appear on screen as means to decapitate women, however, as I have demonstrated in my analysis of the small frames, no frame ever rigorously isolates the object it intends to represent. Decapitated by frames, women in Truffaut's films express the classical male desire to contain her (dangerous) beauty, to admire and love her like a museum piece. Beyond and in spite of the director's intention, however, the framed woman has proved that she can descend from her represented status and unleash her transgressive femininity, thus blurring the clearly drawn separation between inner frame and outer frame. Although the primary function of the artificial frames—slides, photographs, paintings—is to satisfy Truffaut's artistic gesture of decapitation, frames still remain fragile borders only partially containing woman who *can* break free from what falsely appears to be the unyielding law(s) of framing. For Truffaut decapitation by frame problematizes the concept of castration because at the same time as the frame's power to confine weakens, the male primacy to cut the female body diminishes. This tendency is dramatized in *The Bride Wore Black,* in which Fergus dies after losing the frame around Julie-Diana the Huntress, after cutting her . . . loose.

Poetic Decapitation: "A Martyr"

In *Flowers of Evil* there is only one poem that deals directly with feminine decapitation: "A Martyr." Here Baudelaire describes a drawing that represents a beheaded woman and imagines the circumstances that might have led to her decapitation. His fascination for the decapitated woman parallels his obsession with the castrated hanged man of Cythera in "A Voyage to Cythera"; in both poems Baudelaire seems to be under the sign of both Sade and Sacher Masoch.

The subtitle to "A Martyr," "drawing by an unknown Master," indicates that the author of this picture is a respected artist, a "Master," but he remains unidentified, "unknown." As an unknown Master, the only evidence of his artistic talents may be found in his drawing and assigned to his nameless self. It is inside the natural frame of the drawing that Baudelaire is able to identify the hidden artist while locating his talents behind the representation of the decapitated woman. There is no evidence that this drawing ever existed as described, and Baudelaire may have devised the artifice of the framed decapitated woman to provide his poetic self with the fragile safety of the frame. Protected by the frame, this self is able to express its sexual desire as if it were someone else's. As he borrows an unknown artist's sexual identity, as he finds his voice in contact with the visual scene of castration created by this Other, the poet is able to liberate his poetic imagination as well as his "poetic" libido. But the frame in which the female martyr is enclosed does not provide him with the safe distance that a separate work of art would classically establish between painting and admirer. The martyr stirs the poetic subject so deeply that by the end of the poem Baudelaire describes her as a "a frightful face" whose hair is arranged in "hard plaits" and whose mouth displays "cold teeth." Her "frightful face" recalls that of the fearful Medusa. The elongated shape of the martyr's plaits evokes the snakes on Medusa's head while their hard consistency recalls Freud's interpretation of Medusa's hair as penises. The cold teeth, although not directly related to the Medusa's representation, add a feeling of vampiric monstrosity to the portrait. From this description alone the martyr emerges as a Medusan and vampiric figure with destructive forces transgressing the enclosed space provided by the drawing's limits.

Once again, the framed Medusa steps out of her frame and becomes a real danger for the male poetic subject exposed to her frightful body. Derrida's concept of framing, which claims an indeterminate space of representation despite the presence of the frame, may be applied to the indeterminate frame of the drawing representing the martyr. The representation of the martyr may be cut out and contained by the frame of the drawing, but her Medusan features extend beyond this frame and cast a terrifying visual impression on the poet. In order to protect himself against her, the poet decapitates her by way of the unknown painter whose identity he has borrowed, and by way of the poetic form, which detaches *the head* at the beginning of the sixteenth line: "Like a ranunculus beside the bed, // Rests on the table, empty of all thoughts." This rhetorical decapitation is soon followed by another one on the nineteenth line where the verb *rests* related—in a subject-verb group—to the severed head of the sixteenth line is isolated at the beginning of the line.

By rhetorically, textually, and symbolically decapitating the female martyr, the poet is free of his fear of femininity, having thus conquered the terrifying Medusa. The decapitated body of the woman becomes a body of pleasure, part of a poetic sexual fantasy unfolding in the first twelve stanzas of the poem. There the poet enjoys the sight provided by her dead body bathing in its own blood: "Hot, living blood, that soaks, with crimson stain a pillow." His pleasure grows stronger while examining her nude and indiscreetly unveiled erotic body: "the carcass, unabashed, shows, in complete abandon, without shift, the secret splendour." The nude and provocative body lets go of its "secret splendour" in the imagination of the poet for whom the framed decapitated woman offers a private and intimate scene of pleasure. In contrast to the terrifying face of the Medusa, the decapitated and therefore docile woman of pleasure remains within the privacy of the frame, which provides the poet with the enclosed space his phantasmatic self requires to unleash its morbid enjoyment.

For Georges Blin, the poem is yet another example of Baudelaire's consistent attraction to sadism, a perversion that he examines in his study *Le Sadisme de Baudelaire.* Blin comments on the necro-sadism of this poem, in which "Baudelaire accentuates the carnal aspect of the scene in an unbearable manner."[32] Indeed, every aspect of the carnal scene, the bedroom, the body of the martyr, the clothes and items of toiletry seems so erotically charged that they all appear untenable in considering their relationship with the murdered female body. Nevertheless, death and erotic pleasure are intrinsically bound throughout the poem: the voluptuous bedroom where the crime took place is first noticed for its "gilt fabrics," "flasks of scent and wine," its "rich furniture," and "perfumed robes;" the recently decapitated body is caught in the indecency of its pleasure, the remaining traces of past guilty pleasures as indicated in the phrases "guilty joy" (*coupable joie*),[33] "feasts of strange delight," "infernal kisses," the possibility of her *jouis-*

sance amid her death seems an extreme association of love and/in crime ("her senses, were they bayed / by packs of wandering, lost desires, and hunted, / and finally betrayed?"). Yet, despite the mad fantasy mingled with erotic pleasure and criminal acts, the poem's greatest transgression is achieved by the poet's persistent and pleasurable observation of the scene. His eyes are riveted to the drawing, and they find visual delight in the immobile representation of a sexual fantasy. It is the lifeless scene represented in the drawing, "a languorous portrait," that paradoxically moves the poet's imagination into the realm of the Real, where necrophiliac fantasies are activated.

The languid nature of the drawing appears in opposition to the upbeat metropolitan scene of "To a Passer-by," in which a woman disappears into the crowd long before the poet has been able to use his fleeting vision to satisfy his desire to see more. In "A Martyr" there is something constantly erotic in the woman's body represented in the drawing, something that can be enjoyed at leisure, something "languid" and static, something that invites the subject's desire to venture inside the privacy of the frame, closer to the experience of forbidden pleasure. But, as mentioned earlier, the body of the decapitated woman does not allow the poetic subject to get too close to her femininity, to her *jouissance*. The poem suggests that his desire to capture her erotic body within the privacy of his poetry may not suffice to satisfy his perverted fantasy. Decapitated, the martyr seems more likely to satiate his desire than when she was alive, yet the poet expresses doubts about the worth of her decapitation when he asks the question:

> The vengeful man, whose lust you could not sate,
> (In spite of much love) nor quench his fire,
> Did he on your dead flesh then consummate
> His last, monstrous desire?

Man's desire, although immense, is punctuated by a question mark, just as is woman's desire in the preceding stanza. Dead or alive, the martyr, a double figure of pleasure and fear, exhibits an unusually excessive sexuality, but she also leaves male and female desire unfulfilled and the poetic subject unsatiated.

The questions asked by the poet about these desires remain unanswered, even when he demands an answer from the decapitated martyr: "Answer me, corpse impure!" But the poet's desire to know about feminine sexuality remains unsatisfied and, in the end, the woman's sexuality remains her own. In another effort to break open the mystery of her feminine body, the poet examines, in a fetishistic mode, selective parts of the martyr's sexual body and of her intimate clothing. After having symbolically detached her head from her body and from the poem, he demarcates her trunk, stocking, leg, garter, shoulder, hip, and waist. To each new fetishistic detail of the martyr corresponds the poet's repeated intention to cut the female body where it is most likely to surrender some of its femininity.

Despite the fetishization of her body and her symbolic decapitation, however, the woman's femininity remains enclosed in her body. As she dies, caught in the privacy of her lovemaking, as her head is severed from her body, her femininity does not pour out of her body like her blood. Instead of giving the poet the satisfaction of knowing her pleasure, her *jouissance*, her femininity, she will display her threatening Medusa's face, her "grim visage." Only then, in the third stanza before the end, does the poet let go of her body. In the last two stanzas he will let her body return to the privacy of its sleep ("sleep peacefully, strange creature") and to the faithful mind of her lawful companion: "Your lover roams the world. Your deathless shape watches his sleep." The sexual scene evoked by the drawing of the decapitated woman has passed, and the poetic subject separates himself from his morbid fantasy: "Far from inquiring magistrates that sneer, / far from this world of raillery and riot." The distance between him and his fantasy is suggested by the repetition of the preposition *far*. Free from the poet's fantasy, the martyr keeps the secrets of femininity sealed off in her "bier of mystery and quiet," and resumes her peaceful role as an immortal love figure ("your deathless shape") watching over her absent husband. After cutting her body in the hope of penetrating the mystery of her femininity, the poet returns her body to a more conventional lover, her husband (*époux* in French, meaning "spouse"). He no longer has any use for it. Yet he has acquired a taste for the pleasure involved in the dissection of the female body, and he will reactivate this pleasure on other female bodies by becoming an expert in the art of fetishistic representations.

Fetishism

Against the fear of castration, the child builds a protection for himself. Indeed, prior to castration, having established that all bodies are equal, and that his body was not different from his mother's, except that his mother's was bigger in size, having thus fixed his understanding of bodily forms to a single pattern, it comes as a shock for him to discover that his mother does not have a penis. In spite of the reality that she does not have a penis, the boy continues to believe in the existence of a maternal penis. She must have a penis, either a small one or one that is not fully developed: "They [little boys] deny its absence, and believe they do see a penis all the same; the discrepancy between what they see and what they imagine is glossed over by the idea that the penis is still small and will grow."[34] His belief that his mother must have a penis is so strong that the boy denies the reality that she does not have one. The belief that she has one and the knowledge of her not having one converge (while yet remaining distinct from one another) under the sign of the fetish. In other words, the fetish, chosen on the woman's body or among its attributes, brings together belief and knowledge as the two main conditions of fetishism. The appearance of the fetish in man's sexual development coincides with the appearance of doubt in the development of his logical thinking. Doubt, as we are reminded by Guy Rosolato, "helps maintain the status quo, and avoid making choices,"[35] and the little boy experiences doubt when, to avoid choosing between his belief and his knowledge, he somehow maintains them both under the sign of the fetish.

There is a measure of undecidability in Freud's understanding of the fetish. A fetishist—and not every man is a fetishist—is a man of doubt who abandons trying to make a final decision. He adopts a fetish to maintain all his beliefs, and to be able to make them re-appear whenever his desire calls upon them. His first desire to maintain sexual pleasure and its dearest provider, the penis, turns him into a castrator of his mother's body upon which he cuts out fetishes of all sorts.

The Freudian fetish is a substitute for the penis that the mother does not have. Rhetorically, it coincides with metonymy insofar as it is contiguous with the object of castration, and it also coincides with metaphor, insofar as it hides the effect of castration. In Christian Metz's words, it "signifies the penis as absent, it is its negative signifier."[36] The common elements of the fetish with the figures of speech in language become clear as we examine the similar functions assumed by both. The function of the fetish is to give an acceptable substitute figure to an unacceptable perversion. By way of metaphors and metonymies the poetic and filmic text reveals images— repressed or not—translated from the world of unacceptable perversions into poetic and cinematic language, a language of substitution. The fetish is a substituted form of the dismembered body of the woman that in turn becomes acceptable to language in its fetishized form, cut into figurative pieces. We must now examine these pieces of women activated poetically and filmically by words and images representing dismembered women: Baudelaire's "To a Passer-by" and Truffaut's female legs.

Cutting Out the Passer-by

TO A PASSER-BY

> The street about me roared with a deafening sound.
> Tall, slender, in heavy mourning, majestic grief,
> A woman passed, with a glittering hand
> Raising, swinging the hem and flounces of her skirt;
>
> Agile and graceful, her leg was like a statue's.
> Tense as in a delirium, I drank
> From her eyes, pale sky where tempests germinate,
> The sweetness that enthralls and the pleasure that kills.
>
> A lightning flash . . . then night! Fleeting beauty
> By whose glance I was suddenly reborn,
> Will I see you no more before eternity?
>
> Elsewhere, far, far from here! Too late! never perhaps!
> For I know not where you fled, you know not where I go,
> O you whom I would have loved, O you who knew it!

The *moi,* the self opening up the poem, appears isolated from the crowd around it but is nevertheless attached to it by the howling noise it hears: "The street about me roared with a deafening sound." The relations between the poetic self and the rest of the world appear to exist exclusively through the sounding of an atrocious and inhuman scream, a bestial howling ("roared"). Indeed, the intensity of this cry is such that it renders the poet's *moi* deaf ("deafening sound"), thus achieving at the outset of the poem a separation of the self from the material and sensual world to which it was so lightly attached. The deafened poet becomes a foreclosed ego, a prisoner of its own "psychosis," which brings a new set of noises to the subject primarily turned inward. Yet, although the poet is separated from the outside material and sensual world, the poem makes it possible to meander in the psychotic world the poetic subject has built for himself. Deafened by Parisian uproar, the poet turns his attention inward, as if the scream that cut him off from the outer world in the first place had traversed his senses and was now resounding in the depths of his inner poetic world.

The howling noise coming from the street is the last evidence of the street life surrounding the poet before the passerby comes into poetic focus. This howling sound is in fact the point at which the poet's sensory perception becomes disconnected from the new poetic vision of the passerby, which turns his senses inward, toward his poetic pathos. The howling is not in and of itself a pleasurable vocal effect, as it is more the expression of urban mur-

mur impairing the poet's senses thus creating a feeling of anxiety plunging him in a "spleen" mood. The scream does not have the pleasurable quality of the voice as we studied it in chapter two. It evokes pain only, and it is accompanied by an image of separation, a severing of the poetic subject from the familiar noises of the city. Immediately after this roaring, the poet constitutes his subject from inside his poetic vision, like a mother creating a baby from inside her maternal womb. In the process of detaching himself from the exterior world, he receives the powerful image of the passerby.

The passage from the exterior world to the inner vision of the poet is not an easy transition, and the uproar at the end of the first line can be perceived as the symbolic sonorous representation of the difficulty of this transition. The scream becomes a frontier separating the exterior from the interior, and it places the rest of the poem inside its enlarged limits. For the subject to penetrate the interior world of poetic creation (a place where the poetic subject is being constructed) it must override the prosodic challenge presented by the only punctuation mark of the line, the period, which grammatically marks the completion of a sentence and prosodically indicates the configuration of a poetic idea. The real function of the period is to demarcate an idea within a grammatical mold. In the poem the period puts a "classical" end to the invasion of the crowd on the psyche of the poet by stopping the phrase after the twelfth syllable, the alexandrine. According to French versification, each verse must contain one idea, and run-on lines would be considered a violation in the classical rhythmical pattern governing French poetry. The first line of the poem stands harmoniously in agreement with proper formal poetic patterns, and the period accentuates such a demonstration on Baudelaire's part of his true attachment to the lyric tradition. Yet his fidelity to tradition brings his poetic subject into a psychic disorder, the result of a traumatic scream caused by the poet's separation from the outside world.

The scream in this first line is a long and continuous howling sound expressed in the imperfect tense, the past of unlimited duration. The passage from the street to the poet's vision is measured by the grammatical tense of the verb *to howl* while also evoking the long suffering involved in the transition. Both ideas of length and suffering are transposed into the second line: "tall" "majestic grief." The long scream in the first line traverses the line break and the world of the poet from his outer to his inner senses and now resonates in the second line, thus providing a way to penetrate the poet's private vision, which at first seemed so hermetically sealed off. "Tall, slender, in heavy mourning, majestic grief," these four adjectives and adjectival phrases present a line split into four distinct rhythmical groups, each separated by a punctuation mark, a comma representing the end of a "breath group" between the four sections of the line. The textual cutting of the line has not yet developed into a more comprehensive imagery of dissection, but it has already expressed in the form of the poem the idea of a repeated breaking up of the poem's textual body. The four adjectives also retroactively give voice to the scream of the first line, a scream identified here as a scream of pain—a majestic grief.

The pain evoked here is the pain of "heavy mourning." Even though the poet has not yet revealed the identity of the apparition, the feminine ending of the adjective *longue* (tall) indicates that it is a woman. The female apparition entering the poet's vision strikes his imagination because of the deep pain and mourning accompanying her appearance. She bears (and wears) the sign of a painful separation with which the poet identifies for having himself been separated from the exterior world not by death but by the deafening sounds in the howling street. Pain and separation seem to conjoin the female apparition and the male subject in a poetic moment so sudden and yet so powerful that the poet will want to keep it alive throughout the sonnet even though the woman is long gone: "A woman passed, with a glittering hand / Raising, swinging the hem and flounces of her skirt; // Agile and graceful, her leg was like a statue's."

The woman expected in the second line enters and leaves the poet's world in three words: *une femme passa* (a woman passed). This flashing moment of appearance and disappearance is confirmed by the grammatical tense of the verb *to pass* conjugated in the literary past (*passé simple*), a past indicating the definite completion of the act of passing in the space of these three words and therefore giving to the rest of the poem the value of a memory, a simple trace left in the wake of this brief passage. Everything after this verb *passed* can only be a recollection of the original scene of the unknown woman's passage. More to the point, the poem presents itself as a double remembrance of the woman. On the one hand, the poem as remembrance suggests the effort of the poet to draw back into his memory, and, on the other hand, it suggests his desire to restore her dismembered body into fetishes like her "glittering hand" or her "statuesque leg." Thus, to remember the passerby is an attempt to put her together again. The poet, at this point, focuses on two parts of her body: her hand and her leg. By focusing on these two parts of the woman's body, the poet presents his "narrator" as a fetishist who fights the effects of the textual cuts or textual castration, by giving himself the protection of fetishes. In "Fetishism" Freud attributes the maintaining of the fetish in the fetishist's life to the protective qualities of the fetish. He says: "it [the fetish] remains a token of the triumph over the threat of castration and a safeguard against it" (216).

The first fetish in the poem is the "main fastueuse," a hand easily imagined covered with "sober" jewels (since she is in mourning) and playing with a certain indifference with the edge of her skirt—a hand in motion, as is the poet's desire. The hand, the jewels, and the skirt all invite the poet's desire to manifest itself. Indeed, these three fetishes tease the eroticism of his writing as well as his memory. For Baudelaire, as well as for Freud, fetishes like jewelry and pieces of clothing have the qualities of flesh, because of the cloth and the stones they are made of. Similarly, in *The Painter of Modern Life* Baudelaire clearly expresses his fascination with the irresistible world of feminine apparel that he calls "mundus muliebris":

> What poet, in sitting down to paint the pleasure caused by the sight of a beautiful woman, would venture to separate her from her costume? Where is the man, who, in the street, at the theater, or in the park, has not in the most disinterested of ways enjoyed a skilfully composed toilette, and has not taken away with him a picture of it which is inseparable from the beauty of her to whom it belonged, making thus of the two things—the woman and her dress—an indivisible unity? (31)

In "To a Passer-by" the fetish of the cloth ("le feston et l'ourlet" [the flounce/furbelow and the hem])[37] is as powerful and erotically charged as the flesh it is attached to: the hand and the leg.

Having thus escaped his own castration by creating fetishes for the protection of his own masculine body, the poetic subject finds its erotic and poetic force preserved in the following line: "Tense as in a delirium, I drank" ("*Moi*, je buvais, crispé comme un extravagant"). This *moi*, "I," isolated at the beginning of the French line, indicates two complementary and paradoxical positions of the poet's psyche: first the presence of the two commas indicates the *moi*'s detachment from the danger of the outside world, a symptom of its psychotic state, while recalling its similar state in the first line, then this presence indicates the self's return to a narcissistic condition from which it defies castration by closing itself off from any exterior threat.

The only part of the outside world that the poet wishes to integrate with himself is the fetishized woman passerby, a woman eroticized both by this fetishization and by her fleeting, inaccessible quality. Both erotic and fleeting agents leave unfulfilled the poet's desire to possess her.[38] In isolating his self from the world, the poet also isolates it from his body, which assumes a petrified position ("crispé comme un extravagant" [tense as in a delirium]), as if numbed by the alcohol he is drinking ("Je buvais" [I was drinking]) or sexually aroused by the beautiful apparition. In opposition to his numbed or rigid body, his self seems to be taking a fluid form, in the erotic flow of softness and pleasure in her eye: "From her eyes, pale sky where tempests germinate, / The sweetness that enthralls and the pleasure that kills." Here the fetish of the eye (if an eye can be fetishized) confirms the presence of narcissistic pleasure in the self. However, the woman's eye also suggests a vision of danger ("où germe l'ouragan" / "plaisir qui tue" [where tempests germinate / the pleasure that kills]) revealing a flaw in the narcissistic state's protective capacity. This vision of danger inscribed in the brewing storm finally materializes in the next stanza: "A lightning flash . . . then night! Fleeting beauty / By whose glance I was suddenly reborn, / Will I see you no more before eternity?" This streak of lightning violently releases the imminent danger that was lurking in the fetishized eye of the preceding lines in which female danger was associated to a storm germinating inside her eyes, an imminent squall putting the poet's heart at risk. Here the lightning, as a violent tear in the dreary and ominous sky of the poet (*ciel livide* [pale sky]), suggests that the previous danger located in her eye was also an anticipation of the tearing of the poet's self whose assumption of safety in the narcissistic world turns out to be false.

In the first tercet the actual wrath of the fetishized woman finally descends on the poet. It applies to "the skin of the poem," a deep wound that takes the form of an ellipsis, a blank expanse, a dotted area, suspending time and space for a brief instant, as the French name for this elliptical punctuation mark indicates: *point de suspension*, literally meaning "suspension marks." This ellipsis is also the most significant graphic form of separation indicated in the poem. It is as if the separation were even more intensified when recalled than it was when it actually happened in line 3, directly after the passing of the woman. The unerasable image of the moment of falling instantaneously in love with the unknown woman finds its painful way back into the poem within the mystery of the three dots of the ellipsis. The ellipsis is the trace of this brief love affair ("fugitive beauté" [fleeting beauty]) in which, for a second, the poetic body and the feminine body merged in a state of *jouissance* never to be found again. The ellipsis marks separation and merging at once. It performs a rhythmic halt as well as a graphic one in terms of the poetic form and also suggests the brief pleasurable union between the poet and the woman. Lastly, the ellipsis fulfills the same function as the crowd in the first line, it brings together the woman's body and the poet's body, puts them in contact, only to tear them apart. The ellipsis may be said to be the punctuation mark figuring the symbolic cut present from the very first image of the poem.

Besides the ellipsis, various punctuation marks continue to figure body cuts in the remainder of the poem. In the final stanza the unusually large number of punctuation marks indicates an increase in rhythmic pauses, which effects a chopping in the fluidity of the lines. Like the ellipsis, these marks break the figurative representation of the poetic body as well as the rhythm of the line. The body in the poem and the form of the poem are equally affected by the cutting nature of the punctuation marks. Commas and exclamation marks present themselves as compulsive repetitions employed by the poet to inflict the grief of separation on the body of his poem: "Elsewhere, far, far from here! Too late! Never perhaps! / For I know not where you fled, you know not where I go, / O you whom I would have loved, O you who knew it!" The first line of this last stanza is cut in four different places, once (twice in the English translation) by a comma and three times by an exclamation mark. The cut represented by the comma is less sharp than the one made by the exclamation mark; it is a mild pause in contrast with the strong interruption created by the exclamation mark. As a result, it seems that the pain inflicted by the "punctuating poet" intensifies from the soft comma to the sharp exclamation mark, from the possibility of meeting the woman "elsewhere" to the realization by the end of the line that the poet will "never" see her again.

It is through these four cuts that the impossibility for past love to repeat itself is marked. The use of the pluperfect subjunctive, in reality a literary past conditional of the verb *to love* indicates the speaker's regrets for being unable to ever love the mysterious woman. The love encounter with the passerby is built on the impossibility of ever representing its reality in the poetic text. In fact, we wonder if this moment ever happened in reality or if it arose as an illusory vision of the inebriated poet whose inhibitions and repressions were weakened by his intoxication. The shock received by the poet at the time of seeing the woman may have resulted from a combination of some unspecified woman passing through the poet's field of vision with the poet's particular repressed desire to cut her body. The sight of the woman prompts a repressed psychological event buried in the poet's mind, a scene in which the female body is dismembered in order to satisfy the subject's fetishistic perversion to possess her in bits and pieces. If the actual occurrence of their encounter is questionable, its deep inscription as a powerful image in the poet's psyche makes it a legitimate poetical event that can only be reproduced as it presents itself to the poet, that is, in a fragmented form adapted from its mode and object of remembering: the cut up body.

In this analysis of "To a Passer-by" I have tried to show the importance of the cut on the body of the poem, as well as on the body of the woman. We have seen that the body of the woman provides a place of exchange for the poet and that this exchange takes place under the symbolic cut performed by the poet. It is on the fragmented and fetishized body of the woman that the poet finds his double place as castrator and castrated. The fragmented woman in Baudelaire's poetry, this hybrid woman who is both ideal and modern, can only be found in the cut, in this space where the mutilated and reconstructed body lives in pain, a pain that no language can ever capture except for the bestial sound opening up the poem. The howling resonates in the first line of the poem and echoes throughout the rhythmical pauses provided by the poem's punctuation, which we have read in terms of painful cuts in the fluidity of the poetic form as well as on the fetishized body of the imaginary woman. Represented by punctuation marks, pain escapes traditional linguistic categories. Indeed, pain has no linguistic object, as Elaine Scarry remarks: "it is itself alone. This objectlessness, the complete absence of referential content, almost prevents it from being rendered in language: objectless, it cannot be objectified in any form, material or verbal."[39]

The materiality of the punctuation marks gives pain an objectified form in the poem, but the marks are not, strictly speaking, linguistic objects. Nor are they exclusively verbal symbols of pain that could express the poet's inner suffering. Rather, they belong to the internal rhythms of the poem, just as the suffering of the poetic subject is internal. The poet's suffering prompted by the traumatic vision of the beautiful woman whom he will never possess has no direct linguistic representation other than the arbitrary use of the punctuation marks cutting the poetic lines. Such cuts are the versified form of the poet's figuration of the fetishized woman. For the poet there is no traditional language that could represent his painful fragmentation of the woman's body because the unspeakable nature of his mutilating gesture has no place on the poetic scene. As for the mutilated woman, the poet can only claim that she escapes description as a totality because every part of her beautiful body must be thoroughly and reverently adored. Thus, the body of the fragmented woman represented by poetic language can only be revealed in details and fetishes, in other words, in a displaced and fragmentary form invested with a linguistic and libidinal force but always in a position of difference from the idealized and unified body.

The Man Who Loved Legs

Women's legs are compasses which measure the globe in all directions, giving it its balance and harmony.
—Bertrand Morane, in *The Man Who Loved Women*

In "To a Passer-by" we have seen how Baudelaire expresses the devastating moment of the sudden appearance and disappearance of a woman passing in the street. The movement of her skirt on her statuesque leg imprints on his mind the snapshot of a brief moment of love that is born and dies in the same instant. In Truffaut's *Man Who Loved Women* this episode repeats itself each time Bertand Morane catches sight of a floating skirt on a beautiful pair of legs. Bertand Morane is "the man who loved women," and more particularly, women's legs.

Here, like Baudelaire, Truffaut performs a symbolic act of cutting on the bodies of his female characters. The first instance of this act of cutting occurs at the beginning of the film when the protagonist, Bertrand Morane, a renowned skirt-chaser when he was alive, lies lifeless in his grave, where he is in the perfect position to observe a procession of women's legs passing above him. During this procession the legs occupy most of the frames. Each frame—and particularly its top edge—acts as a cinematographic device that Truffaut uses to cut each pair of legs from the rest of the woman's body not appearing on screen. The function assumed by the cutting frame is that of suggesting a feminine bodily presence whose total sexuality must be censured and cut off from the visual field of the onlooker. Thus, the frames in this scene perform a cut on the sexual body of the woman, and they isolate their fetishized legs—the only remainder of their censured sexuality.

These women's legs are Bertand Morane's fetishes, that is, the mark of undecidability that always begins with a moment of conflict subverting the logic of thinking and the logic of viewing. This moment of conflict is inscribed in a double movement performed by the legs, a dual dimension contained in the metaphor of the "leg-compasses" that Bertrand has devised in order to express the geometric motion of women's legs tracing the globe like the compass a page: "women's legs are compasses which measure the globe in all directions, giving it its balance and harmony." The first movement is horizontal, and it engages the legs in a passing and pleasurable motion controlled by the male gaze. Indeed, these women's legs move on and off the screen, displaying one by one the detached individuality of their beauty. Second, the movement of these legs is vertical, as each pair of legs, shaped like a compass or a pair of scissors in motion, slowly opens and closes as if they were cutting right into the erotic gaze both of the camera and of the protagonist. Indeed, the camera and the protagonist lie together in the same grave, since the whole scene is shot from below.[40] The vertical motion of the legs/scissors can thus be read as the countereffect to the horizontal motion of the parade of legs. The camera constructs the protagonist's (and viewer's) pleasure in looking at the horizontal movement of the women's legs, but it also evokes the possibility of castration for him (them) through the vertical movement of the legs. Vertical and horizontal movements are not separable in the filming of this scene, for they establish an interdependence in the pleasure of seeing and the pain of castration. For Bertrand Morane and the sutured spectators visual pleasure also bears the danger of castration represented in the first scene by the fact of death— Morane's death, for relentlessly pursuing his insatiable pleasure in eyeing women's legs. The filming of this first scene is analogous to the content of the scene because the double movement of pleasure and pain emanating from the act of filming these legs in motion is also inherent to the fetishized legs themselves.

In this first scene the women's legs figure the fetishistic representation of the women in pieces, women whose remaining bodies are somewhere off-screen. At the same time, these legs are the representation of the castrating female, whose "scissoring" legs cut right into male desire that yearns for visual pleasure. The feminine is established from this first scene both as being subjected to the editing cut severing her legs from her body—thus responding to the camera/protagonist's scopophilic desire to isolate the pleasure provided by female legs—and as the agent of the cut slicing through the protagonist's visual enjoyment with legs/scissors. In fact, Bertrand Morane is dead, killed by an accidental pair of legs, as we learn by the end of the film. It is through the fetishization of the legs that this double moment of cinematic representation in *The Man Who Loved Women* is made possible.

If Truffaut's cinematic fetishes are a mise-en-scène of the double and conflictual nature of the sign whereby legs signify both cutting and being cut, they are also clearly related to a mise-en-scène of the literary. It is Bertrand's fetishistic interest in women's legs that incites him to write the story of his perversion. In order to transcribe onto paper the details of all the women in his life, Bertrand Morane brings out a hidden typewriter, and, in an instant, becomes a writer. His book is nothing but the story of his leg fetish that he needs to write down as a therapeutic measure against his obsession, thus using writing as an ideal place of transference. The book-in-progress becomes a kind of silent analyst for Bertrand, but nevertheless an analyst whose ability to record his repeated leg obsession places it symbolically in the position of the crucial receiver of all affects, and consequently in the position of resolving Bertrand's fetishistic tendency. Through transference the book also becomes the fetishized object of Bertrand's obsessive love. In fact, it is thanks to his book, the only remnant, after his death, of his life as a fetishist, that the film is made possible and the understanding of

Bertrand's fetishism made accessible to the spectators. Thus, the film, as it opens up Bertrand's book in order to retell his story of fetishism, adopts the narrator's perspective and makes this film Bertrand's film. The film is not critical of Bertrand's fetishism as it places itself behind his written confession. In fact, the film could not be critical of Bertrand, since it finds in his fetishism the ideal place to echo its own fetishistic production and structure. While it creates a filmic space for Bertrand's story, the film finds the space for the telling of its own story, the story of its own fetishistic art of representation—an art that deals with fetishism through its own use of fetishistic styles and techniques.

The coherence of a film depends paradoxically on its editing process, by which a story becomes a scenario after being mutilated and reconstructed by the director. In a 1962 interview with the French newspaper *Le Monde* François Truffaut confirms that to create a film he first works the written text "with scissors and glue."[41] The simplicity of this statement is nevertheless very meaningful as far as the understanding of the basic principles of cinematography are concerned. Indeed, the formative process of cinema— from scenario writing to actual shooting—involves two essential gestures: cutting and pasting. *Cutting* in cinema is more than just a technical term theorized for the sake of discourse and emptied of its fundamental active meaning. Cinema has a strong claim to the term *cutting* and particularly to its performative aspect. As Truffaut's statement indicates, *cutting* is to be taken literally as a signifier for all the scissors and blades that have participated in the creation of a film.

From the fragmented text of the screenplay the film is produced as a body of discontinuous scenes related to each other by cuts and separations. The body of a film is in fact a collage of cut out pieces, each invested with enough signifying stimuli so as to easily produce the illusionary effect of a continuum for the spectators. On the subject of collage, Tom Conley rightly remarks that its principles were never better suited than to the techniques of cinema "where cuts and junctures of editing would be the medium closest to the objects fashioned by the very name which collage brings to mind."[42] Conley defines the collage artist as a master of composition able to render on screen phantasms of the body with gestures that he qualifies as acts of "cutting and decapitation" (154), followed by the "glueing and binding" of the sliced pieces through montage. The double movement of cutting out and pasting together contributes to the fundamental filmic creation, and as he composes his shots and his scenes the filmmaker resembles the modern painter when he brings together the familiar and the uncanny, figures of everyday life shot in unusual angles. Conley's theory of collage is a compelling one that specifically addresses the filmmaker's work. Another form of collage occurs, however, when the spectator is put to work, when the film imposes on him to fill in the gap left by the cuts of montage.

In fact, films can only make sense when each shot, each scene, is related to the next by the suturing spectator, who uses his/her own set of values and opinions to stand in where shots and scenes left an absence that must be filled for cohesion's sake. The spectator is not entirely free to suture as he/she pleases, however, and he/she remains skillfully manipulated by the camera, while constructing a process of identification between the dismantled images of the movie and his/her desire to create a unity of fragments. In *The Man Who Loved Women* the camera goes from the first scene in the cemetery where women's legs are walking by Bertrand Morane's grave, to the next scene taken from Bertrand's past, in which he catches sight of a pair of woman's legs walking by the basement-laundromat where he is doing his laundry. Bertrand Morane immediately feels a magnetic pull toward the anonymous legs and rushes outside, only to catch the plate number on the car that is carrying away the beautiful female apparition he must find again at all costs. In the previous scene in the cemetery the viewer is made aware of the important role that the legs may have played in Bertrand's death; the second scene confirms the danger involved in the apparition of the legs for Bertrand, who goes to extremes in order to satisfy his desire to reexperience the short-lived thrill he felt when he first saw the legs. The focus on the legs allows for the smooth transition from the first to the second scene, and the camerawork creates an illusion of continuity for the viewer who unconsciously bridges the gap between the two scenes.

Yet the illusionary effect remains a delusion behind which lies the reality of the broken pieces. The art of the cinema is that of attached/detached pieces—an art of suture—always pointing to a primal gesture of cutting as its inherent principle of fabricated continuity. As such, it coincides with the way in which Roland Barthes characterizes the work of the artist who " 'detaches' a feature, a shadow, if need be enlarges it, reverses it and makes it into work."[43] Regarding film as an art of detachment is "always perverse and fetishistic" (68). Thus, when the fetishistic process of filmmaking exercises its technique of representing a story about fetishism, it first creates a narrative space for the representation of a particular obsession with women's body parts—that is, legs for Bertrand Morane. At the same time, however, it offers a commentary about its own technical identity. The technical identity of Truffaut's film *The Man Who Loved Women* depends on its multiple cuts, which isolate first story parts, then film parts, and finally body parts in a fetishistic mode. Thus, we must read *The Man Who Loved*

Women as a film with a double intention, narrative and technical. Its first intention is narrative as it hopes to present the screen adaptation of Bertrand's book and its fetishistic content. Its second intention is technical, as it unfolds the fetishistic process of going from book to film, from written text to image text. And it is a reading of the fetish that reveals the double intention of *The Man Who Loved Women.*

We must then return to the reading of the leg fetish in *The Man Who Loved Women* to confirm its double play in the written text and the image text. Bertrand's obsession with women's legs reveals itself, in the book and in the film, through a succession of unhappy relationships that always fail when, at one point, the woman's identity replaces the legs' anonymity. The film is generous in giving the spectator clues to understanding Bertrand's obsession with women's legs. These clues are provided by three flashback scenes that stage the adolescent Bertrand and his mother. In one of these scenes his mother appears to force her nudity upon him, when she nonchalantly undresses in front of him as if to prove to herself that he does not exist, thus choosing to ignore her son's natural curiosity for the female body. While she parades in front of him in her lingerie, he sits quietly on a chair silently flipping the pages of a book.

This scene sheds light on the association of fetishism and "early" erotic relations with the mother's body; it also sheds light on the emergence of eroticism in relation to reading. In this scene Truffaut creates a visual critique of Freud's theory of castration while simultaneously preserving the association between the mother's body and fetishism. When the mother's body imprints the reality of its eroticism on her teenaged son, she is in direct opposition to the Freudian mother, who *accidently* makes visible her symbolic castrated sex to her shocked child. Truffaut seems to underline the grotesque nature of this scene, the unthinkable act of symbolic striptease of a mother for her son. Truffaut clearly offers this scene, however disturbing, as a possible explanation for Bertrand's fetishism, defining the moment as the "sexual" event that projected Bertrand's sexuality into a full dependency, first on the fragmented female body and then on the eroticism invested in the act of reading.

As a critical variegation of Freud's symbolic castration scenario, Truffaut transposes the scenario of Freud's castration theory onto Bertrand, who, as an adolescent, develops pleasurable sexual fantasy, not fear of castration, after seeing his mother undressing in front of him. This fantasy is presented in relation to Bertrand's reading pleasure, thus giving the book the status of a fetishistic object associated with the erotic body of the mother, not with her monstrous castrated body, as Freud proposes in his thesis. Truffaut remains painfully aware that Bertrand, like a majority of children in his films—Antoine in *The 400 Blows,* Julien in *Small Change,* Jeanine in *The Little Thief*—was an unhappy child neglected by his mother. He represents Bertrand's missing out on early maternal love in a scene in which Bertrand lures a young woman looking for a babysitting position into coming to his apartment for an interview. When she asks to see the baby, Bertrand declares: "I am the baby!" thus humoristically indicating his desire to be loved like a baby by his mother, as a way of counterweighing his lack of maternal love.

What I propose is that in the opening funeral scene Bertrand has resumed his child's position vis-à-vis his mother's body. These women's legs are the fetishistic representations of Bertrand's love for his mother, as Truffaut confirms in another scene, in which we see Bertrand as an adolescent captivated by the movement of his mother's legs as she passes by. In this scene the camera juxtaposes two moments, that of the clever streetwalker, whose brisk and determined walk misleads men about the nature of her profession, and that of Bertrand's mother walking by as he flirts with a girl his age. The bridges between these two scenes and these two women are the legs that we see and hear passing by. From this scene we are able to understand Bertrand's fetishistic habits in relation to his mother's body, which, like the prostitute's, provides pleasure.

Similarly, it is also the mother's body that creates the fetishistic situation for the child in Freud's account of fetishism. In "Fetishism" Freud also attributes the likelihood of the leg fetish to "the circumstance that the inquisitive boy used to peer up the woman's legs towards the genitals."[44] This circumstance is a spatial one. From below the little boy in Freud's theory has a frightful visual perspective on his mother's body. He then replaces the vision of his mother's "castrated" sex by her legs, the last part of her body that he saw before focusing on her sex. Although in placing the moment of fetishistic formation at the time of Bertrand's adolescence Truffaut casts away the traditional concept of castration fear, he still retains Freud's spatial understanding of the onset of fetishism acted out in the funeral scene of *The Man Who Loved Women,* as Bertrand's dead body, from the bottom of the grave, peers up between the women's legs walking above him.

During the funeral scene Bertrand's repressed love for his mother, embodied in the fetishized legs of the anonymous women, approaches spatial perfection in Bertrand's desire, as the voice-over of his literary agent confirms: "From there, Bertrand was in the perfect position to observe what he loved best about women." From there, that is, from this lower position,

Bertrand is more likely to come closest to his mother's body and, by extension, to this mother's love. The spatial mise-en-scène of Bertrand's funeral must be read as a mise-en-scène of his desire. And his desire is that of recapturing in these legs his mother's love, which appears in the flashbacks as an impossible love, given the mother's severity and indifference toward her son. What the funeral scene does is to confirm the impossibility of ever recapturing maternal love. Indeed, for Bertrand maternal love is an unseizable concept, graspable only in a conflict of differences between love and hatred. The place for such a conflict is the dismembered feminine body, the fetishized legs of the women in his life.

It is thus only through death that Bertrand Morane reconciles himself with his (lack of) mother's love. If he has spent his life under the tragic and magnetizing effects of women's legs, symptoms of his mother's indifference to him, he is now spending his death satisfying his mother's desire to "break a leg" instead of having a son: "I would have been better off breaking my leg the day I bore this little idiot." Now that he is dead, he is finally worthy of his mother's love. Her desire for a broken leg in place of his birth is metaphorically fulfilled by these bodiless legs—these legs broken from their bodies—gathered around his grave to pay their last and loving respects to him. In fact, this burial scene captures the essence of the poetic moment, not so different from Baudelaire's tragic encounter with the passerby. Through Truffaut's camera, these disembodied women actually embody a moment of love, albeit a love at last sight.

Chapter 4

Men, Babies, and Fantasies

I am the baby.
  —Bertrand Morane, in *The Man Who Loved Women* (1977)

I am pregnant.
  —Arnold Schwarzenegger, in *Junior* (1994)

Three Men and a Baby

For fathers of the 1980s and 1990s willing to do so, it has become part of the childbirth experience to cut the umbilical cord of their newborn baby. By taking on this symbolic gesture of initial separation between mother and child, fathers have felt more involved in the birth of their children, a moment from which they had traditionally been excluded, by cultural habit or personal choice. This "cutting" gesture has become significant in rethinking fathers' roles throughout the entire childbearing and child-rearing process. At birth the medical shears have come to replace the congratulatory cigars, and delivery rooms have superseded waiting rooms. Fathers have thus begun to expand their paternal role by becoming more actively nurturing than in the past. This is the past in which the maternal experience was often denied, even rejected or ignored, as apparent in Baudelaire's, Truffaut's, and Freud's representations of the mother.

However harshly the "three men" in our study may have expelled the mother from their texts, they have nonetheless become, even *obliquely*, involved with maternal fantasies. In doing so, they have replaced their repressed desire to participate in acts of "maternal" creations by "nurturing" gestures of textual formation in their respective works. I will argue that our "three men" have taken on a mother's role both in shaping and caring for their own creation, "their baby," as it arises from poetic metaphors, filmic images, and psychoanalytical analyses. In order to focus on maternal fantasies in Baudelaire, Truffaut, and Freud, I have chosen to use the metaphor of the nurturing father depicted in a recent film, *Three Men and a Baby*.

This section's title is inspired by Coline Serreau's 1985 film *Trois hommes et un couffin*,[1] about three bachelors suddenly facing the responsibility of taking care of a little baby girl left on their doorstep by the ex-girlfriend of one of the three men, the baby's father. The film is a comic portrayal of the awkward relationship between the three men, unprepared for fatherhood, and the little girl, whose demanding daily needs go far beyond anything that they had (or had not) imagined about life outside their exclusive love/work circle. Their situation is first presented as unsurmountable and totally chaotic but gradually changes as the three men become impromptu but very competent paternal mothers / maternal fathers, mastering the art of diaper changing and bottle feeding. The situation seems to have settled into a routine, when the mother comes to take her little girl back to live with her. Once the baby has left, the three men fall into a deeply melancholic state, unable to cope with the loss of the baby. They become plagued by an array of maternal fantasies, and the biological father, particularly affected by the separation, acts out a phantasmatic pregnancy by walking around his apartment, haggard and disheveled, his shirt stuffed up with a pillow, thus creating for himself the illusion of a pregnant body. The fantasy of male pregnancy portrayed in Serreau's *Trois hommes et un couffin* is not an isolated case[2] created for farcical purposes in a film in which nothing is to be taken seriously except for the little girl's well-being. I would like to suggest that it is this same fantasy—a fantasy derived from the impossibility to know/to be the mother—which is the source of Baudelaire, Freud, and Truffaut's depiction of maternal situations in their work.

For Baudelaire, Freud, and Truffaut, whose works depend a great deal on the presence of women in the dynamics of their text, motherhood is an unavoidable subject addressed with some uneasiness but which nevertheless occupies at times a substantial space. Like the three men in Serreau's film, they are, so to speak, "bachelors," textual bachelors whose interest in women focuses primarily on their beauty, sensuality and sexuality. Yet, when the beautiful, mysterious, and sexual female characters of their dreams[3] inevitably express maternal desires or even become mothers, the male subject in their text is caught unprepared for this maternal moment. The first reaction to the unexpected but inevitable appearance of the mother figure in their text manifests itself in a disparaging form. Within their respective context mothers seem to be unhesitatingly and foolishly rejected, as if the surprise created by their sudden appearance took the male subject by surprise, leading him to react irrationally and negatively to the unexpected presence. I will argue, however, that this sudden denial is symptomatic of a dormant but active desire to reproduce like a mother, or as Tania

Modleski debates in her analysis of the American version of the film *Three Men and a Baby* that "envy of woman can coexist with castration anxiety and with the profoundest misogyny."[4] In spite of themselves and beyond the vigilance of their essential manhood, the male subjects in Baudelaire's poetry, Freud's psychoanalysis, and Truffaut's cinema let genuine fantasies about becoming mothers surface out. Beyond the apparent contradiction of this proposal, I will show that male maternal desire is in fact as Modleski ascertains "concomitant with fear of feminization" (78). It is this fear and denial of motherhood that I will examine in the following section of this chapter, while in the last five parts, I will outline its latent side, the paradoxical desire to (re)produce like a mother underlying Baudelaire's, Freud's, and Truffaut's ostensible invalidation of the mother.

No Mothers Allowed

For Baudelaire, Freud, and Truffaut, negating maternal figures is a way to deny their role as birth givers and first love providers, and thus to protect the ideal female figure constructed in their text for the pleasure of the male subject. The ideality of this female figure resides in the representation of her untouched and untouchable body, a body barred from reproduction. A mother can conceivably be a figure of ideality as long as her reproductive functions have no place in the text. In the case of Baudelaire, Freud, and Truffaut, the rejected mother is the reproductive mother, the mother whose body is perceived as it gestates, gives birth and nurtures, the mother whose body is in parturition. In their work the reproductive mother is contrasted with the ideal mother, the virginal figure inherited from the Christian tale of the immaculate conception.[5] In contrast with the reproductive mother, the virginal mother figure, the ideal mother presents to those who love and respect her an unviolated body dissociated from the sexual and "birthing" body of the reproductive mother. With the unexpected figuration of the reproductive mother in Baudelaire's, Freud's, and Truffaut's text it is the mystery of her gestating body, the repressed horror of flesh separating at birth and the uneasiness associated with early nurturing that dominates the feeling of maternal rejection expressed by the male subject.

Once Baudelaire, Truffaut, and Freud, our three bachelors, have mitigated in their own terms the initial shock of motherhood, once they have reluctantly learned to accept the facts of pregnancy and birth and their effects on the female body, their ideal image of the dream-woman seems tainted forever. In other words, the ideal woman steps out of their male dream of femininity when she becomes the pregnant woman whose fertile body is perceived and transcribed in direct opposition to the pleasurable body of the barren but beautiful woman.

Despite the male subject's effort to discredit the gestating female body, the femininity of motherhood nevertheless appears to represent a crucial component in the poetic, analytic and filmic construction under examination. In the process of de-idealizing the initial image of the pregnant woman, the male artist/analyst must first reject her aesthetically and analytically, thus turning her into a tainted and unfit female for poetic, analytical and filmic composition. The mother continues to appear in texts and films, but she becomes evil as in Baudelaire's "Blessing" (1:7–9), or maternally forbidding as in "The Moon Offended" (1:142), untrustworthy like Stacey in Truffaut's *Day for Night,* and unhealthfully fertile as in Freud's "cloaca theory." In each one of these cases the representation of the insensitive mother is imposed on texts and films by the consistent reappearance of unappealing images of motherhood centered around the disturbances affecting the mother's fecundity and her nurturing qualities.

The poem "The Moon Offended," one of Baudelaire's earliest compositions, provides a first valuable account of the repressed figure of the reproductive mother. Here Baudelaire creates a dramatic setting in which Cynthia,[6] the moon, is given the role of the voice of a divinity exhorted by the poetic speaker. The poet's questions to the divinity concern love, poetry, Satanism, and finally Cynthia's own nocturnal wanderings. His questioning, however, finds a seemingly unrelated answer in the last tercet when Cynthia, overlooking the poet's specific questions, chooses instead to inform him about his own mother: "I see your mother, by her mirror, buckled / By weight of years, poor child of death and harm! / Patching with art the breast at which you suckled!" Here the symbolic denial of the mother's first and precious love for her child finds its expression through the powerful figure of the mother's patching her nurturing breast. Cynthia disregards the poet's desire to know about the mysteries of the night, and instead presents him with a painful image of maternal alienation whereby the sensual mother disappears of her own will behind a shell of plaster, and her maternal breast becomes a sculptured object that belongs to the arts, to an aesthetic conception of womanhood: "Patching with art the breast at which you suckled." Thus, she becomes a fixed/sculptured work of art totally severed from her past, that of a nurturing mother. This final artistic gesture by which the poet's mother becomes an ennobled representation of his past, a representation of maternal beauty cast in eternal lapidary style may also be read in opposite terms for it also characterizes a gesture of self destruction by which the mother condemns her old and empty breast to its final immobilization by means of "cementing" the breast that satisfied the poet's primal sensual pleasures associated with suckling. By confining her breast to its final cast, the poet's mother appears to assert her inability to remain the mother of his past. Her gesture clearly indicates her decision to break apart their mother/son relationship, and it may be even interpreted as a form of physical and emotional abandonment.

We must understand Cynthia's harsh words about the poet's painful abandonment by his mother as the result of an unspoken offense alluded to in the title "The Moon Offended." Indeed, it seems that the poet's apparently innocuous questioning offends Cynthia so deeply that she exercises her godly rights in order to reciprocate by striking him deep within the unsettled privacy of his emotions for his cherished mother.[7] Cynthia's words disclose the de-idealized image of an aging and unloving mother to the poet who is unprepared for such an intimate and personal intrusion. The moon's unexpected response has a paralyzing effect on the poet who will remain speechless, unable to respond to the verbal trauma inflicted upon him by the angered divinity. The composition of this poem allows for such an interpretation of the speechlessness of the poet who is bound to silence by the actual frame of the sonnet, which imposes its rigid form—two quatrains and two tercets—and thus figures the impossibility to go beyond the second tercet bearing the moon's offensive words. Indeed, after the moon has spoken her bitter words in the second tercet, there is no further lyric space for Baudelaire's poetic voice to respond, and the ending sonnet imposes a formal poetic silence on the disheartened poet.[8] The moon's sour remarks on the poet's mother, the poet's inability to retort, constrained as he is by the limits of his own poetic format, all of this remains part of Baudelaire's formal plan in this particular poem. The poet's staging of his mother's aggression and his own dumbfoundedness, are symptomatic of Baudelaire's inability to deal with the nurturing mother, of his unwillingness to allow the return of the repressed mother from his early days as an infant.

Freud's cloaca theory appears to be a psychoanalytical counterpart to Baudelaire's lyrical expression of shock at the unexpected appearance of the mother figure. Freud believed that children spontaneously produced sexual theories of their own, one of which takes shape at the time when a child is under the influence of anal eroticism, and owes its name—the cloaca theory—to its excremental site of development. Freud believes that for the child, it is the expulsion and the detachment of fecal matter that comes to signify the separation of the baby from the body of the mother in human birth.[9] The child imagines that babies are born from the anus like excrement, and because feces passing through the body of the child repeat the pleasure principle first experienced in the oral stage, birth is associated with bodily pleasure.

The pleasure of giving birth to feces/babies becomes a psychological pleasure whereby the expelled matter is given the role of a gift presented by the child to the mother. Feces "were the first gift that an infant could make, something he could part with out of love for whoever was looking after him."[10] The child—the male child in Freud's theory—intends his feces to be a gift of love for his mother, and with each one of his excremental gifts he repeats the birth of a baby: "Defaecation is the model of the act of birth" (100). With every bowel movement the child also re-enacts his own birth, and each time he carries out three possible phantasmatic roles; that of a mother, that of a father giving birth through the anus, and that of the son expulsing his anal baby like his parents while also being the excremental baby born from his own bowels. Thus, through his birth fantasy the child assumes both roles as birth giver and gift of birth, he is the creator and the creation. This double function of the child in the cloaca theory can be explained as a natural development of the narcissistic stage during which the child has a monopoly on his mother's love. From his perspective—the only perspective for the narcissistic child—the mother loves him for two reasons: first in return for his presenting her with the absolute gift of love, an excremental baby, and second for being himself the love object inside the "gift box."

According to this theory, the child confirms in his mind that women do not have the exclusivity of bringing babies into the world and also believes that both men and women, provided they have an anus, could give birth: "It was only logical that the child should refuse to grant women the painful monopoly of giving birth to children. If babies are born through the anus then a man can give birth just as well as a woman" (34).

As soon as Freud has put into analytical language the child's theory of birth and the sexual ambiguity it contains concerning the identity of the birth giver, he also seems to realize that this ambiguity may be counterproductive to his other theory on the prominent male model of sexual development, a theory that he gradually pieces together from his personal observations of children as well as from his psychoanalytical investigations of neurotic adults. In order to fight the possible feminine component of male subjectivity that may be derived from the cloaca theory where both men and women are believed to give birth, Freud asserts that the boy will not come out of his anal stage altered in his masculinity: "A boy can therefore fancy that he too has children of his own without our needing to accuse him of feminine inclination. It is only his still active anal erotism at work" (34). It is the maternal/feminine involvement in the act of birth that becomes the threatening factor emerging from the cloaca theory where, according to the child, there is no specific gender claim toward birth. Where the child sees no sexual differences, however, Freud seems unusually aware of the feminine aspect undercutting the supposedly "ungendered" act of birth.

If we read Freud's narrative closely, the feminine appears as a disturbing agent within the child's understanding of the birth process. The feminine component of the cloaca theory comes to disrupt the male narrative voice of the essay, and whereas throughout most of the essay the child is given the persona of the analyst in charge of translating his own infantile sexual theories into analytical coherence, at one point Freud transgresses the child's narration by forcing on it his own point of view, clearly a male one: "My remarks apply chiefly to the sexual development of one sex only, namely, the male" (27). He feels a possible female intruder could threaten the male subjectivity that he claims as the basis/reference for recognizing and interpreting all gender specifications.

In examining Freud's rhetorical strategy in this essay, the first question that comes to mind is: who are "we"? Who are those of us who would "need to accuse the boy of feminine inclinations"? Is Freud here referring to the psychoanalytical society of his time, including himself, and is he predicting (in order to defuse it) the criticism that the moment of gender undifferentiation in the cloaca theory may raise among his skeptical colleagues? Or is he simply referring to himself, playing devil's advocate, and hiding grammatically behind the first-person plural? In the latter case Freud's cloaca theory would not be received negatively by his colleagues, it would appear to appeal to their senses. Here the connotation of the "we/(our)" is not one of dissension between Freud and his colleagues but, on the contrary, one of support for the full argument presented in Freud's text. In this case the argument appears to be a rhetorical example for an indirect critical dialogue, Hegelian style, in which an argument (the boy thinks that both men and women can give birth) is brought forth in conjunction with its possible critique (doesn't this theory make the boy into a feminine subject?) but is finally resolved by a synthetic remark confirming Freud's previous research on anal eroticism—such a theory only confirms the working of anal eroticism—and does not alter the boy's masculinity. In the final analysis Freud's clear assertion of his presence behind the boy's conception of how babies are born, confirms that the cloaca theory is Freud's very own creation forced upon the little boy. Freud's cloaca theory simply expresses his own desire to create an "excremental" theory that establishes the site of birth at the anus and which presents the baby as a fecal-like object. Such symbolic association between birth and defecation indicates Freud's own psychological refusal in dealing with birth beyond the scenario he creates to address its occurrence.

If the enlarged body of the mother-to-be has a meaning in the masculine theory of sexuality pursued in the cloaca theory, it is dictated by male fear and denial of her womb confused with the fecal chamber. The metonymic operation by which the womb becomes associated with the anal cavity relies on the phantasmatic creation of the male child observed by the analyst who, in turn transforms the phantasmatic vision of the child into an analytical system set to undo the mother figure, and more specifically to deny her reproductive interiority. The denial of maternal interiority is symptomatic of the difficulty Freud has in dealing with the initial shock triggered by the emergence of the image of the pregnant or birthing mother in the course of his theoretical development of male sexuality. Freud will end the paragraph on the cloaca theory by giving the example of one of his adult patients, a "maniac," a woman, reliving the infantile birth theory as she leads a visiting physician into her cell to show him a pile of feces on the floor that she describes to him in these terms: "That is the child I bore today" (34). The maniac woman is laughing while pointing to her "fecal baby," a detail that adds a touch of Medusan diabolism to the maternal figure she presents. Faced with the horror of such birth textually reported as a disgusting act of defecation, the analyst is led to think of the mother with utmost fear of her reproductive power: in the final analysis he sees what she delivers as nothing else but a repulsive offspring, an undesirable bodily "reject." It thus clearly appears that Freud expresses a form of masculine anxiety toward motherhood that becomes the site for abject reproduction.

In *Day for Night* François Truffaut playing the role of Ferrand directing a film, *Je vous présente Paméla,* is also shocked by the pregnancy of Stacey, an actress playing one of the minor roles. While shooting the swimming pool scene already referred to, a scene in which Stacey reluctantly appears in a bathing suit, Joëlle, Ferrand's assistant, notices Stacey's altered figure. Ferrand needed the eyes of a woman to bring out in the open an aspect of femininity unfamiliar to his masculine gaze. In fact, Stacey's pregnancy could only be perceived by Joëlle's expert bespectacled eyes: Joëlle's competency in feminine matters seems to exceed that of any expert as she notices the unnoticeable. Here Truffaut must have confused feminine intuition with some "supernatural," not to say "magical," gift of vision with which Joëlle is endowed.

Stacey is only three months' pregnant, and her pregnancy is barely visible. Joëlle enigmatically shares the visual detail of Stacey's pregnancy with Ferrand—she never actually says that what she sees is a pregnant body, but she merely points to it as if the pregnancy were so obviously visible that it did not need to be named. He is amazingly quick to interpret her intuition correctly and identify the unapparent signs of pregnancy on Stacey's body. Here is their exchange about Stacey's invisible and unspeakable pregnancy:

> *Joëlle:* Well, I understand why she would not put on a bathing suit . . . Look at her!
> *Ferrand:* She is very beautiful.
> *Joëlle:* You don't get it . . . look closely!
> *Ferrand:* My god!

Ferrand is shocked, and he feels cheated by Stacey: "Stacey fooled all of us: she is three months' pregnant and kept the secret to herself . . . I personally think that we ought to break her contract." His first impulse is to reject her by breaking her contract despite the producer's arguments in favor of keeping Stacey on the set. The anticipated image of Stacey's pregnant and heavy body brings out the worst in Ferrand, whose sudden outburst of temper clashes with the apparent mildness of his character.

For Ferrand there is no doubt—the pregnant woman must be replaced immediately, her swollen body must be eradicated from the set where only dreams of feminine ideality are pursued. It is his dream of feminine beauty that Ferrand clearly enunciates when he declares: "she is very beautiful" as he is first invited by Joëlle to look attentively at Stacey's body. He can only see feminine beauty as he looks with pleasure at a woman's ideal body.[11] He accordingly suggests that she be replaced immediately by another actress: "It's easy. We will replace her right away, then we'll call the agents . . . Here are some girls . . . lots of girls." Ferrand is not looking for a good actress to replace Stacey, and he is surprisingly even less interested in replacing her with a "woman"—*une femme*; rather, he flips through his photo-catalog of available actresses as he repeats the word *girls:* "des filles . . . des filles" and not "des femmes," women. The term *filles,* girls, first refers to immature and budding young girls with no interest in motherhood, and it also bears the connotation of virginity, innocence, and naïveté generally associated with *filles,* girlishness. As a result of his shock regarding Stacey's pregnancy, Ferrand appears to redirect his professional interest for female actresses to girls, young girls representing yet-unreproductive figures of femininity. He momentarily erases woman from his disenchanted mind because he feels threatened by her maternal potentiality. Second, the word *des filles* also quite paradoxically refers to prostitutes—*filles de joies, filles des rues*—debauched and lewd women to be disposed of at men's leisure, women procured by pandering impresarios as Ferrand mentions: "we'll call the agents." From one minute to the next Stacey embodies the beautiful muse and the unacceptable mother who must be replaced by an unreproductive whore. Ferrand initial rejection[12] of her pregnancy confirms his/Truffaut's inability to deal with motherhood.

The scenario of maternal fantasy informing Truffaut's filmic imagination seems incomplete, however, when the only reference to the maternal stands at the pre-natal stage under the metaphor of pregnancy. The image of creation being constructed in *Day for Night* is an image inspired from the pregnant body, but what about images of birth and child rearing? Can Truffaut undo the magic realm to which he confines all of his female figures by entering the realm of motherhood from pregnancy to birth and child rearing?

The idea of motherhood (here the pregnant actress) becomes a threat to his construction of dreamlike (magic) female characters: to him, an ideal woman is a barren woman, and "his" mothers are either disenchanted with motherhood, disinterested in children, or deprived of their children. In *The 400 Blows* Antoine Doinel is the product of an unwanted pregnancy, barely escaping the abortion that his mother had planned. In his posthumously produced film *The Little Thief* Jeanine is abandoned by her mother and when, in turn, she finds herself pregnant, she first goes to the local abortionist before finally deciding to keep her child. In these two films the major theme revolves around the question of unwanted children. Often, Truffaut's response is to spare the unborn child from abortion, while in other cases the mothers-to-be in his films have miscarriages. In *Jules and Jim* Catherine loses the child that could have saved her relationship with Jim, and following her miscarriage she falls into a depression that will eventually bring her to kill herself and Jim. In *The Little Thief* Séverine, Jeanine's boss, a happily married woman loses the child she wanted so much. Because Séverine is the picture of moral and physical perfection (she is young, beautiful, generous, kind, and intelligent), she is also the perfect target for Truffaut's personal revenge against all the other unfit and "bad" mothers in his films: Antoine's indifferent mother in *The 400 Blows;* Julien's abusive mother in *Small Change;* also in *Small Change,* another mother's negligence leading her son to fall off the ninth floor of their apartment building. These examples represent a minimal sampling of Truffaut's repeated concern with the character of the "bad mother."

Nevertheless, the following question remains both valid and crucial: does the mother figure in Truffaut's movies redeem itself through the physical suffering of birth? Does the mother become a more esteemed figure once she has suffered in parturition? In his 1970 *Bed and Board,* the fourth installment in the Antoine Doinel cycle, Antoine becomes the father of a little boy, Alphonse. His new paternity corresponds, however, to his estrangement from the mother of his child, his wife Christine. For a while they grow apart, until they eventually stop communicating, and until Antoine begins an affair with a Japanese woman with whom he is also unable to communicate because of the language barrier. Since communication—matrimonial or linguistic—has stopped producing positive relationships with women, Antoine feels that his paternity may save him from being completely isolated from the world around him. But once out in the streets of Paris he realizes that he cannot communicate his joy at being a father to anyone.

His wife's pregnancy did not interest him much, and the birth of his son creates a surge of paternal feelings that will bring no improvement to his relationship with his wife. Christine's role as a new mother is overshadowed by Antoine's full endorsement of his paternal role at birth as the picture of his newborn son and himself seems to indicate: Christine is not invited to pose for the family picture, as if Antoine had already put aside her maternal part, as if she counted even less as a mother than she did as a wife. Truffaut's camera participates technically in Antoine's indifference to Christine's maternal experience: on her hospital bed, Christine is left out of focus rather than out of frame, while Antoine, in full focus, holds his son in the foreground. In this shot Christine's presence is defined by her weak and grainy contours, by her position in the background in contrast with the well defined paternal Antoine proudly posing for the picture. With the composition of the frame and the lens work the film makes a statement in favor of Antoine's paternity and to the detriment of Christine's maternal role. In a single cinematographic instant, Truffaut erases the mother whose recent delivery has had no place in Antoine's life, a natural continuation of his indifference to Christine's pregnancy.

Truffaut skips the actual birth in *Bed and Board* because for him, nothing seems less desirable than representing the very moment when the baby is thrown into a world of deceiving mothers, also a moment when the beautiful body of the woman becomes the painful site of motherhood. He manages, however, to capture this moment in one of his other films, and his camera follows the expectant father inside the delivery room where his child is being born. In *Small Change,* Truffaut offers a paternal perspective on the actual birth of a child. In the film, Jean-François Richet, a schoolteacher at an elementary school in a small provincial town, is about to become a father. His unhappy personal experience as a child places him among other characters like Antoine Doinel in *The 400 Blows* and Jeanine Castang in *The Little Thief.* In his final lecture to his pupils before they leave for summer vacation he says: "I also wanted to tell you that it is because I have bad memories of my childhood and because I do not like the way children are cared for, that I have chosen this profession: to be a teacher." Like Antoine and Jeanine, he was an unwanted and unloved child, and as a grown-up he represents an aspect of the maturing effects of early unhappiness: "By a kind of strange balance, those who have had a tough childhood are often better equipped to face adulthood." Richet has just faced an adult moment of his own: the birth of his first child, and, paradoxically, he has lived through it with the perspective of a child. He has relived the traumatic moment of birth separation while visually exposed to the birth of his own son.

What are the visual symptomatic elements of his trauma during the scene of his son's birth? First, Richet, finding himself in the delivery room at the time of birth is so paralyzed by what he sees happening on the delivery bed that he is unable to take any pictures of the birth, despite the constant reminder by the nurse that he will not have another chance to capture the moment on photographic paper; she says: "Go on, if you want to take pictures, it is now or never." The moment in question is shot by Truffaut from a completely masculine perspective since the camera does not move away from Richet whose eyes remain wide open as if he had just seen a ghost, the ghost of femininity and motherhood. It is Richet's stupefied attitude, petrified as if under the spell of Medusa's gaze, that Truffaut examines while his wife is delivering a baby. Richet is in shock, witnessing the spectacle of birth taking place in front of him. While he appears to be a man of great confidence throughout the film, he suddenly becomes silent and totally disarmed by the event of birth that Truffaut chooses not to show. Truffaut feels as incapable of shooting a birth scene as Richet is unable to take pictures of it. The two men conjoin in this scene and their stupor reduces them to the level of children confronted by an impressive and intimidating human spectacle. Their bodies freeze (Truffaut's camera is immobile while shooting Richet's frozen body), and the only sense of movement in that scene is provided by the female nurse passing in front of Richet and reminding him that he ought to take his pictures.

The next scene gives some indication of the infantile nature of Richet's temporary paralysis. While waiting for Richet who is late the morning after the birth, the pupils explain in their own spontaneous terms how they view their teacher's photo session in the delivery room. To them he is a sort of pervert ("The teacher is a dirty pig") taking dirty pictures, perhaps in order to sell them on the pornography market ("Is he going to sell them?"). From this infantile conception of the pornographic significance of the birth pictures, we may confer a childish attitude to Richet as he remains incapable of taking pictures of his son's birth. Richet feels uncomfortable with the spectacle of his wife's opening body almost as if he were in the presence of a pornographic representation of her body. He feels like a pervert looking at a forbidden scene in which the woman's body would display the utmost secrecy of its interiority. He cannot possibly capture with his camera this unthinkable exhibit of the female body, and similarly Truffaut cannot capture what he regards as the indecent "opening" of the female body. While her body is being torn by the child being born, Truffaut gives no visual or even aural perspective of her suffering body. The mother's body that we are left to imagine is itself silent since no cry is heard from the delivering mother. In this scene of birth, the mother has completely disappeared from the field of representation, visually and orally absent, she is completely erased. Her absence may be the result of the unconscious threat her pregnant and laboring body may represent for Richet and, by extension for Truffaut reacting to the sudden appearance of the object of repression. Her body thus qualifies as the Real body, Lacan's "frightening apparition."[13] In Rankian terms it is the very moment of separation of mother and child that creates such anxiety, and in Lacanian terms it is the site/sight of female bodily disclosure that prompts a fear of the mother, of her reproductive body.

Creation and Procreation

Is it the shape of the pregnant female bodies, the feelings of pregnancy, the thought of birthing bodies, the unique experience of motherhood, that touch male sensibility somewhere so deep that mothers become the least appealing yet necessary figures in the dynamics of their text? Can we read Baudelaire's, Freud's, and Truffaut's treatment of motherhood as a form of negation by which they strangely and unwittingly assume the figure they seem to deny? Is there a profound phantasmatic desire on their part to become mothers by way of textual identification? As we unpack the various aspects of the mother figure in their texts, we will see how the unappealing mother is in fact symptomatic of a male desire to retrieve the lost union between mother and child and thus to become a perfect mother and a perfect child. The male desire to return to maternal times springs from two different and paradoxical positions. First, this desire materializes in fantasies of reproduction whereby the male subject envisions his ability to conceive like a mother; second, it revives repressed images from the inferred memory of a time both prior to and after birth, a time of pure bliss either as an unborn or a nurturing child.

The study of the dual male desire implicated in the folds of the maternal metaphor will lead us to a better understanding of the mechanism at work in the sublimated male fantasy of pregnancy whereby the artist and the analyst take the place and the role of the fertile body of the mother and/or return to its bountiful pleasures. Such fantasies transmute into creative modes of thinking for the poet, the filmmaker and the analyst who paradoxically create destructive mothers as if to deny them their ability to procreate, an ability of which male subjects often feel deprived and envious. As analyst F. Boehm writes, boys are preoccupied by and jealous of the female ability to procreate: "Boys have great difficulty accepting this inexorable decree of nature. Wishing death and castration for the pregnant mother are not just rage against the rival, but also a desire for the maternal condition."[14] Male jealousy for maternal attributes becomes a source of aggressiveness often realized through the symbolic castration of the mother. In Boehm's theory it appears that the male subject perceives conception as an unfair natural casting among the sexes, and his repressed feelings against the maternal advantage manifest themselves through the creative and scientific processes. In short, what the male's body cannot produce, his maternally invested text/film can.

Susan Stanford Friedman demonstrates how easily the childbirth metaphor has slipped into language as a way to write about "creativity," about the "maternal" approach taken by the artist giving birth to new concepts and compositions. Although the childbirth metaphor has been used extensively by both men and women, Friedman remarks how differently it has affected the works of male and female artists. She argues that the birth metaphor bears the marks of the artist's own stance on gender differences: male childbirth metaphors focus on the separation of mind and body, they "intensify difference and collision,"[15] while female metaphors unite "word and flesh" (93), thus allowing women to regain literary control over their fragmented bodies. We are reminded of the fertile bodies of the cats in Baudelaire's "Cats," in which we witness the perfect example of a metaphor of childbirth in which the pregnant body of the cat is filled with electric and cosmic sparkles thus evoking the concept of collision and even shock perceived as the inner workings of (pro)creation in the last tercet:

Their fertile loins are full of magic fires;
as in fine sand, gold scintillations [parcels] gleam
vaguely within their mystic eyes like stars.

The fertile body of the cat will give birth to "gold parcels," a myriad of bright constellations suggesting that the fecund feline body has engendered a cosmic explosion, a burst of fragments in place of a complete and united body. In the poem the literal absence of women is compensated by a strong metaphoric presence of the parturient mother superimposed on the poetic text where procreation becomes part of a creative process generated by collision and fragmentation.

As for Truffaut, the omnipresence of the maternal figure in his films has been commented on by several critics, among them Anne Gillain who writes, "Each one of his films represents an unconscious inquiry on a distant, ambiguous and unreachable maternal figure."[16] The creative dynamic constituting the foundation of each film is informed by a maternal metaphor often as destructive as the mothers in his films. In *The 400 Blows,* for example, Paris becomes Antoine Doinel's surrogate mother after he runs away from home and his insensitive real mother. Gillain notes the nurturing qualities of the city, which provides food, shelter, and water to the fugitive child. It is, however, a sad and tearful Antoine who is driven away from the city he loves so much by the police taking him to reform school in the provinces. Gillain remarks that it is at this particular moment that Antoine is truly "separated from the giant maternal body" (37) of the city. Again the childbirth metaphor signals a tragic moment of separation between the mother figure and the shortly adopted child.

From the birth experience psychoanalysts have principally retained the trauma of separation that they have variously adopted and adapted into the language of a theory of birth. Although Freud recognizes the potential traumatic aspects of birth, he refuses to believe in its long lasting effects on the individual's identity and sexual development. Lacan is also swift in eliminating the experience of birth, which he characterizes entirely as an initial separation dominated by the loss of the placenta, the prototypical *object a*. According to him, the body at birth separates from the placenta symbolizing the lost part of the individual that can never be retrieved. After the separation from the placenta the individual experiences other losses that cut her or him from bodily pleasures experienced in contact with bodily parts such as breasts, and feces. Placenta, breasts, and feces become the lost bodily objects that Lacan calls *objects a*. Each one of these objects originates from the body and is subsequently cut off from it, thereby becoming the child's impossible objects of desire. In Lacanian theory the mother's body is nothing more than an object destined to be dissected into irretrievable parts causing the emergence of human desire.

Yet in other theories of subjectivity, such as Melanie Klein's, the subjective split analyzed by Lacan is recentered around the body upon which it first took place. Indeed, long before his or her coming into full subjectivity, the infant feels like an "unfinished" body with a nervous system that has not yet fully matured. During this period of premature condition the infant perceives his or her body in bits and pieces, isolating body parts associated with his or her needs for survival, pleasure, and comfort: breast, mouth, and skin. In fact, during this period of early development the baby makes no difference between his or her body parts and the mother's. According to Melanie Klein, in the baby's Imaginary, body parts seem to float freely from him or her to the mother until the child is able to identify the particular contours of their separate bodies. Klein claims that the infant's primal fantasies of dismemberment are built around a central object of love and hatred: the mother's breast, "good" when it feeds him and gives him pleasure, "bad" when it pulls away too early leaving him or her unsatiated. When the breast is good it projects the baby inside the plenitude of the mother's body, his body and hers merge their different parts, while when the breast is bad, the baby also transports his aggressiveness inside her body violently carving it from inside. These fantasies associated with the activity of the maternal breast produce the idea of the dismembered body although the child and mother's bodies are not yet distinct from one another: "In such phantasies, products of the body and parts of the self are felt to have been split off, projected into the mother, and to be continuing their existence within her."[17]

Completely dependent on his mother for all his needs, the infant lives in symbiotic unity with her until he is able to recognize his own image and establish a clear demarcation between his body and the mother's. As we have seen, for Lacan the young child begins to establish his subjectivity with an initial separation from the mother, her body, her image, her language at the time when the infant recognizes his or her image in the mirror. Although both Klein and Lacan agree on the fragmented apprehension of his or her body image by the infant, Klein places the terms of this fragmentation in the contextual relation established between the interacting bodies of mother and child. Lacan points to the initial loss involved at the time of birth, then bypasses the early period of infancy as one with no bearing over the child's identity that he sees emerging during the mirror stage. To him birth is separation. Indeed, revealing the genealogical aspect of these two instances, he reminds us of the etymological similarities existing between birth and separation in the verb *to separate:*

> *Separare,* to separate—I would point out at once the equivocation of the *se parare,* of the *se parer,* in all the fluctuating meanings it has in French. It means not only to dress oneself, but also to defend oneself, to provide oneself with what one needs to be on one's guard, and I will go further still, and Latinists will bear me out, to the *se parere,* the *s'engendrer,* the *to be engendered,* which is involved here.[18]

Like the poetic and filmic language of creativity expressed in male metaphors of childbirth focusing on the principle of conflict and separation, the male language and theory of psychoanalysis addresses issues of identity in terms of separation and loss introduced to the subject at the time of his or her birth, while the female counterpart views the constitution of subjectivity in terms of separation and retrieval.

The poetic, filmic, and psychoanalytical kinship of the two notions of birth and separation in the language used by the poet, the filmmaker and the analyst contributes to my argument regarding the inevitable gesture of cutting performed by the artist and the analyst as the essential marks of separation applied on the body of woman and similarly on the body of the poem, the film and the text in which she appears fragmented. Yet, because birth often appears as a repressed moment of separation in the works of Baudelaire, Truffaut, and Freud, its metaphoric presence in their text also indicates a repressed site of origin, a denial and rejection of the bad mother, and a sublimated desire to become the good mother and thus to create the perfectly conceived poem, film, and theory.

Birth Theory

The good mother in psychoanalysis is construed from the desire to produce a theory of birth accounting for a crucial emotional and psychological bond between mother and child, a bond that physical separation cannot eliminate. Birth, then, appears as the point of eternal return for the individual troubled with difficult separations, it becomes the model separation demonstrating the successful parting of mother and child, while their emotional union remains untouched by the natal break.

On the subject of birth, Freud remains virtually silent but other psychoanalysts write about its role in transference during the analytical treatment, as well as its crucial role in the creative process. Otto Rank, for example, brought to light the importance of the birth event and the marks it leaves on the individual's body and mind. While keeping in mind that Rank's primary interest in birth is in understanding the child's identity, not the mother's, we nevertheless still benefit from Rank's insight on the trauma of birth because it confirms the notion that a male perspective on the subject of the mother is limited to secondary views on her body emanating principally from the child's point of view. At best Rank's theory on birth brings us closer to understanding why psychoanalysis cannot engender a positive concept of motherhood. His theory represents another frustrated effort to overcome the bad mother, but it creates a propitious background of investigation into male maternal fantasies at work inside poetic, filmic, and psychoanalytical texts. Although *The Trauma of Birth* is not specifically a book about birth but, rather, a book about the trauma occurring at the time of birth, it nevertheless makes birth the focal point of the study.

In *La Maternité et le féminin* French psychoanalyst Danielle Brun recalls that birth was a subject suspiciously avoided by Freudian psychoanalysis.[19] She retraces Freud's steps in his refusal to understand positively the deep implications of woman in the psychical development of all human beings from birth to adulthood. According to Brun, the primal scenes and fantasies that inform human desire have their sources in archaic representations of the maternal. In her hypothesis she relies on the unbreakable emotional and structural ties that characterize the relationship between mother and child, and she argues that, in turn, such strong ties emerge as the feminine component of human desire.

In her chapter on "The Maternity of a Man," she specifically deals with man's desire to give birth, to become the mother of a fictitious child that would provide a peaceful mental solution to constant masculine awareness of sexual differences and fixed sexual roles. In this chapter she expresses some (ironic?) surprise at Freud's silence on male desire to give birth, particularly because of the many occurrences of such a desire in male dreams and fantasies, and also because of Freud's persistent interest in the question of desire and its relation to the unconscious. According to Brun, a man can only endorse his paternity after he has phantasmatically experienced the motions of maternity: "If we consider that the boy and the girl's wish to have a baby dates back to early infancy, it does not automatically bring the grown-up man to accept his paternity without any difficulty. It may be that a passage into maternity becomes necessary" (69).

Such a detour inside the body of the mother represents too great a deviation from the father-dominated theory developed by Freud and may explain the too few references to birth in Freud's own writings. In fact, his rare comments on birth are either inspired by Rank's work, or, when opening in broader contexts, they seem "almost" irrelevant to the main argument. As the great advocate of the Oedipus complex, Freud could not open his theory to the maternal outlook promoted by Rank in *The Trauma of Birth,* in which the father figure had no important place in the psychological configuration supporting the theory that the newborn child experienced birth anxiety. The absence of the father in Rank's theory represents an unthinkable demotion of the father's crucial role in the Oedipus complex. For Freud the father is the dynamic figure of authority behind the threat of castration. He creates fear of losing the penis, and such fear represents the most influential element for making a man out of the little boy. In other words, Freud, father of psychoanalysis and symbolic father of Rank,[20] reacts against his fear of losing his psychoanalytically constructed "baby"— the father in the Oedipus complex—by choosing to separate from his adopted son, Rank, who threatened the happy life of his "castrated child."

In 1924, at the time of the publication of Rank's *Trauma of Birth,* Freud ceases to be Rank's symbolic father but Rank remains attached to the precepts of psychoanalysis, while developing his own psychology in which the role of the ego predominates as the active element of the psyche, in opposition to Freud's concept of an ego that remains the vulnerable element in his "topique," always under the influence of the id while also being limited by the intervention of the superego.

Rank is a psychologist whose position is ambivalent inasmuch as it depends greatly on Freud's theories while carrying forward its own developments. The duality of his position is amply illustrated by his thesis in *The Trauma of Birth.* This work theorizes the subject's primal moment of fear of separation from the body of the mother and its desire to remain/return inside the comfort of her womb. Rank understands the birth of any individual—male or female—as the very first instance of anxiety whereby the child experiences a necessary but undesirable separation from the womb. The thesis of the book, although relying heavily on the biological aspect of birth, has strong Freudian overtones in its formulation of the concept of anxiety. In 1910 Freud addresses the question of anxiety in "A Special Type of Object Choice Made by Men," in which he claims that in order to repay his mother for giving him his life, a little boy elaborates "a rescue" fantasy where he visualizes himself putting his life at stake to save his mother from all dangers: "The experience of birth itself is the danger from which he was saved by the mother's efforts. Birth is in fact the first of all dangers to life, as well as the prototype of all the later ones we fear; and this experience has probably left its mark behind it on that expression of emotion which we call anxiety."[21] This 1910 textual evidence of Freud's favorable opinion about the idea of a possible trauma of birth is probably a crucial source for Rank's theory on birth. In fact, throughout his book, Rank continuously praises the discoveries of psychoanalysis and the influence of Freud's theory on his work.

It is generally agreed upon by psychoanalysts that there is no recollection of the moment of birth, but Rank believes that the neurotic patient in therapy does in fact psychologically relive a moment similar to that of his own birth. This time, the analyst plays the role of the mother from whom the patient must detach himself in order to be cured, that is, in order to be emotionally independent of the analyst:

> The Patient's "rebirth phantasy" is simply a repetition in the analysis of his own birth. The freeing of the libido from its object, the analyst, seems to correspond to an exact reproduction of the first separation from the first libido object, namely of the new-born child from the mother. [. . .] It is proved then, without doubt that the essential part of the work of analysis, the solving and freeing of the libido "neurotically" fixed on the analyst, is really neither more nor less than allowing the patient to repeat with better success in the analysis the separation from the mother. (4–5)

Rank acknowledges that nothing about the actual act of birth is remembered by the patient, but the undeniable occurrence of birth gives the analyst an irrefutable reference by which he understands the process of primal separation as a reality with multiple effects on psychological development. On the subject of memory Rank seems to be much inspired by Freud's theory on screen-memories when he claims

> In this sense all memories of infancy must to a certain extent, be considered as "cover-memories;" and the whole capacity for reproduction in general would be due to the fact that the "primal scene" can never be remembered, because the most painful of all "memories," namely the birth trauma, is linked to it by "association." (8)

During the process of analytical transference the patient unconsciously repeats his own birth and she or he is "reborn" from the analysis, detached from the analyst as she or he was physically from his mother's body.[22]

In *Vocabulaire de la psychanalyse*, Laplanche and Pontalis remind us that, etymologically, the word *trauma* means "wound" in Greek and, more precisely, that it is a violating wound. The wound in question could apply to the body and mind of the child but also to the body and mind of the mother. After all, it is her body that tears when giving birth. When Rank retraces some infantile fantasies of origins, he accounts for the "wounded" body of the mother in the following terms:

The later theory moreover, to which many people cling for a long time, that the child is born by cutting the mother open (generally around the navel), is based on the denial of one's own pains at birth which are then completely imposed on the mother.[23]

In Rank's terms, the patient displaces the concept of birth pain from the body of the child onto the body of the mother. The consequence of his denial of pain is a transmutation of the painful birth on the mother, who then appears as the sole victim and sufferer in her mission to bring the baby to life. Feminist poet and theorist Adrienne Rich reminds us that it is our patriarchal culture that has often determined that the image of the sufferer is/ought to be reserved to the mother, and that she seems to become a more valuable social being once she has suffered labor and birth pains: "Patriarchy has told the woman in labor that her suffering was purposive—was the purpose of her existence; that the new life she was bringing forth was of value and that her own value depended on bringing it forth."[24] Pain almost always appears strongly connoted with the aspect of femininity related to pregnancy and birth. A sampling from Freud, Baudelaire, and Truffaut's texts will reinforce the association between motherhood and pain.

In "Morning Twilight," Baudelaire metaphorizes the difficulty of going from dark to light in terms of a painful birth: "It was the hour which between cold and dearth/increases the woes of women in childbirth." "Morning Twilight" is the last poem of *The Parisian Tableaux,* and it seems to summarize the difficult poetic moment experienced by the poet troubled by his own transition from lyric to modern poetry. Every day the poet living in the ever changing Paris of the nineteenth century faces the spectacle of human suffering while walking in the streets of the capital. Baudelaire finds himself imbued with anxiety and pain when he reaches the "transitional"— neither lyric, nor modern—phase of *The Parisian Tableaux.* Most of the poems in this section deal at some level with the difficulty for the poetic subject to adjust to changes, the difficulty to be born to a new day, a difficulty contained in the idea of "morning twilight," during which dusk meets dawn, as if the absolute darkness of night had melted with the remaining traces of the day before and the breaking of a new day.

In the poem "Morning Twilight," night has passed and day is just about to come. Like the vampiric figure often mentioned in his poems, Baudelaire feels death coming as the first rays of sun appear on the horizon. Yet day and death will not come in the poem because the poetic subject lingers in a state of limbo, a moment of pure transition recalling the second title Baudelaire had intended for *Flowers of Evil:* "Limbo." The entire poem maintains a sense of inconclusiveness against the finality of death threatening the poet as he witnesses sunrise. As Paris wakes up and daylight slowly breaks, the poetic subject is caught between two overlapping limits in a poetic space of uncertainty and anxiety. In this poem all the characters—adolescents, writers, prostitutes, women in labor, the dying, and night revelers—experiencing the morning twilight show signs of weariness as they feel the threat of the approaching light. Before the new day comes, their tired bodies must withstand the painful test of passage. It is therefore no coincidence to find women in labor among the weary characters of "Morning Twilight": "It was the hour which between cold and dearth/increases the woes of women in childbirth." The poet, himself a night wanderer, may well identify with the worsening pain of the women in labor. Like them, he is undergoing the painful process of "delivering" a poetic creation. He is progressing painfully toward the creation of a poetic body that could account for the many hours of labor preceding its coming to existence. Like the women in labor of his poem, he knows the price his own *pregnant* poetic body must pay to reach the end of the night. The day announced by the rooster's crow also announces the end of the transitional morning twilight, the end of a painful uncertainty, but it also announces images of death accompanying the newborn day.

The violence of daybreak is reflected by the metaphoric tearing of the sky: "The cockcrow song tore through the fog," the pulling apart of the last misty and opaque veil covering night, allowing the new light of the day to pierce through. With such suggestive metaphoric undertones the poem appears to represent daybreak as a body at birth, a body tearing and bleeding from the passage of its creation: the poetic child that will finally see the light and breathe freely with the new dawn while dying to the warmth of the womb. Further on, daybreak is compared to "un sanglot coupé par un sang écumeux" (as blood-flecked foam through the choking sobs is gasped), a stream of blood (*sang*) gushing from a tear (*sang*lot) in the sky. Although it is true that the immediate image the poet wishes to convey in this verse expresses the violence of daybreak that he perceives in terms of a bleeding body, it could also be argued that the violence of the metaphor proposes a continuation to the preceding image of the women in labor. The poet seizes the violence of daybreak through language often employed to describe birth scenes because no other lexicon can construe more accurately the feeling of the pain associated with birth, a moment of feared and unwanted separation. The poet expresses his terror of the coming daylight as if witnessing a difficult birth and confronting directly a woman's body slowly engaged in labor. A prisoner of his fear, he is not yet ready to accept the full implication of the metaphor of birth; he is still in poetic transition between the mother inside the text and the mother inside his fantasy. To reconcile the two mothers, to become creator and (pro)creator, he must allow his creative writing to take him back to the womb of creation, he must allow his fantasy to bring him closer to the imaginary world of a poetically reconstructed intra-uterine life. For example, the poem "Music" appears to represent such an attempt to return to the womb via the maritime world organized around poetic harmonies and playful images perceived from within the oceanlike womb: "Within me I feel quivering all the passions of a ship in distress."

In *Jokes and Their Relation to the Unconscious*, Freud illustrates his point about the effectiveness of a joke by relating the comical anecdote about a pregnant Jewish baroness. In the last stages of labor, she expresses her pain three times and in three different languages, while the doctor and her husband are playing cards in the next room: "Ah! Mon dieu que je souffre," "Mein Gott, mein Gott, was für Scherzen," "Oï waïh, waïh." "Now, it's time," says the doctor, wisely recognizing the last cry of the pregnant woman as the actual onset of birth, and they both rush to the patient's side. According to Freud, this joke is "successful" in two different ways: it shows the primal side behind the aristocratic facade, and it indicates that details are often catalysts to important decisions. About the first humorous component of the joke Freud writes: "It shows how pain causes primitive nature to break through all layers of education."[25]

In this case the baroness is an aristocrat who, while experiencing pain, lets her most primitive self, her true Jewish identity hidden behind her noble attitude, overcome her refined and cultured self represented by her expressing pain in French, the adopted language of gentility. German acts as the happy medium, the language of everyday life yet another acquired language for the baroness who can only be herself when she speaks Yiddish, her mother tongue. Her use of homebred language perceived as uncouth utterance for a lady of her rank unmasks her true station, thus contributing to the funny defrocking of her aristocratic status. Yet, beyond Freud's intention to point to the class-conscious nature of the joke, Sarah Kofman rightly remarks his spontaneous act of "unmasking and covering with ridicule"[26] the woman behind the baroness, and specifically the parturient mother. If, as Freud claims, pain experienced by aristocrats is the actual issue of the joke, we might question his choice of a comical situation in which pain is so intrinsically associated with parturition, thus eliminating the male aristocrat from becoming the object of derision. The situation picked for the joke offers no possibility of exchange between the two sexes, and it leaves the woman, the mother, as the only possible object for men's scoffing pleasures. Her body in pain is the comical material upon which the joke is conceived, as if riddling about maternal pain was a means to escape the seriousness of the subject at hand. The association of maternal pain and comedy indicates Freud's wariness at relating in a serious and "scientific" manner to the maternal body.

Freud believes that the second winning component of the joke is that it shows "how an important decision can be properly made to depend on an apparently trivial phenomenon" (81). Here, again, what Freud calls the trivial phenomenon of the joke is the expression of pain by the parturient mother. In the "trivial" expression of maternal pain the obstetrician is able to recognize the imminent birth of the child and the mother's actual need for his medical attention. By professional association the joke may be referring to Freud himself as the would-be "great obstetrician of the mind" whose medical knowledge of the female mind and body, although experimental and incomplete, still makes him defiant and almost indifferent to the understanding of maternal pain. Pain is not part of his medical competence, however, it remains symptomatic of the woman's imminent birth, one of Freud's most repressed subjects.

In Truffaut's posthumous *The Little Thief,* Séverine, a well-to-do young woman, is excited to be pregnant and shares her excitement with her young maid, Jeanine. Séverine is sorting out her maternity clothes and she gives them to Jeanine whose curiosity about motherhood initiates the following conversation between the two women:

Jeanine: Are you happy to expect a baby?
Séverine: Very happy! Of course I am terrified about delivery and all. I am afraid about being in pain.
Jeanine: You really think it is that painful?
Séverine: Oh yes! You ought to be careful when you are with your lover.

Séverine's happiness at becoming pregnant is soon overshadowed by the tragic circumstances of her miscarriage. In the miscarriage scene, we overhear Séverine's husband explaining to their doctor over the phone that Séverine is having a miscarriage. We also hear that her cramps began while she was coming out of the movies. It is Truffaut's directing presence that we may read behind the young couple's evening at the movies. Indeed, in all of his films, Truffaut sends his characters to the movies: it is his trademark as director, the sign of his presence. Truffaut may have become an unintentional agent in Séverine's miscarriage, because to him her deliberate intention to have a child is too incongruous with the repeated image of the unwilling mother punctuating his filmic representations of motherhood. Back from the theater, Séverine crashes on the sofa and remains speechless for a while. Her apparent suffering, both physical and psychological, transcends her inability to express pain and disappointment with words. Her desperate facial expression speaks silently the words that will finally come out of her mouth: "I am losing my baby." Séverine's intense suffering offers a tragic representation of maternal loss, emphasized by the fact that Séverine is really looking forward to having her baby. The loss of her baby echoes the long line of tragic instances afflicting mothers. For example, in *The 400 Blows* Antoine is sickened by the gory details of a conversation he overhears between two women outside the grocery store as they describe the bloody and difficult birth of a child, and in *Love on the Run* we learn that Colette's baby died in a car accident.

The common element in these three depictions of pregnant women is the way each pregnancy is associated with physical pain. It appears that for Baudelaire, Freud, and Truffaut, one of the least desirable aspects of pregnancy and birth is the pain, sometimes excruciating, suffered by the woman's body in labor. In addition, the dramatization of such pain has been reinforced by ancient tales and myths as well as by modern obstetrics. According to Adrienne Rich, a woman is culturally conditioned to fear the great pain of labor and birth,[27] while Emily Martin offers an analysis of how the medical field has dehumanized the pregnant body by reducing it to a machine, devoid of any sensitivity.[28] According to Martin, in the modern world of medicine, the discourse on pain has been rationalized into a language that offers no individual perspective, but assigns pain where it is expected to appear regardless of the individual; further, a mother has no identity until she has greatly suffered while giving birth. In terms sometimes recalling the Judeo-Christian tradition, Rich and Martin give a chilling account of the manner in which birth has been regarded as the plight of woman, and her pain as necessary to redeem herself from her female condition.

Throughout our cultural times masculine ideology appears to have counterbalanced the male impossibility to procreate with female painful birth. Indeed, if women have the secret/the advantage of (pro)creation, its value has been placed in the birth pain they endure. According to Nancy Huston,[29] birth pains are to women what the pains of war are to men. Huston describes how in mythology, history, and social contexts, men believe they know about birth pains because they know about war pains. Pain would be interchangeable and universal, and no pain would seem greater than any other pain: "every member of each sex pays his or her tithe of suffering: women are required to breed, just as men are required to brawl" (134). Despite the odd rapprochement between war and motherhood, a parallel established by means of the pain marking the passing of the two events, motherhood remains the unique domain of reproductive women. In fact, while a mother can become a soldier, a male soldier could never aspire to becoming a mother.

The terms of the impossibility of procreating have been captured by male artists who translate their impossible desire into maternal fantasies. For a male artist the phantasmatic desire to be a mother starts with his incorporation of maternal pain in childbirth: if nature has made it impossible for him to conceive like a mother, representation in general and language in particular have given him the possibility to take in the pain of childbirth and to transmute it within his creative realm. By addressing questions of birth pains, the male artist puts himself at the mother's level even if only by means of what Ludwig Wittgenstein calls language-games, a "primitive" process by which individuals learn how to recognize a sensation by associating manifestations of pain with the word *pain*. Pain itself remains private, gives no information about its content; it merely informs the individual observing "the subject of pain who is the person who gives it expression."[30] Birth pains, however, are only learned through language-games because the poet, the filmmaker, and the analyst can only report of their effects on the mother's body and translate them into language-sensations related to their own fantasies of birth, the only way for men to undergo parturition. Only in fantasies do the artist and the analyst learn to recognize and adapt maternal pain to their desire to understand and eventually stand in lieu of the parturient Other in the privacy of their work.

In her study of the psychological processes involved in men and women's desires to be the other sex, Joan Riviere attributes men's envy of women to the female ability to tolerate pain. She writes, "men envy women's capacity for passive experience, especially the capacity to bear and suffer. Suffering relieves guilt; especially is the pain that brings life into the world doubly enviable unconsciously to men."[31] Riviere implies that men develop a stronger sense of guilt than women for not suffering as much as birthing mothers do. In fact, Riviere also affirms that this sense of guilt diminishes for those men involved in creative endeavors: "Men's desire for female functions comes openly to expression in painters and writers, who feel they give birth to their works like a woman in labour after long pregnancy."[32]

The idea that a male artistic creation is linked to a repressed desire to achieve unconsciously what man cannot achieve in reality—to give birth to a child—has been quite familiar in Kleinian psychoanalytical circles. Karen Horney in particular has been the advocate of the theory that regards male creativity as a compensation for the impossibility to procreate. In order to create, the male artist incorporates a maternal figure, feeling that, while playing her reproductive role, he can also give birth to his sublimated creation, his work of art. French psychoanalyst Janine Chasseguet-Smirgel rightly remarks that the problem with such a theory is that it implies that women have little or no desire to create artistically because they hold the biological key to reproduction: "In fact, if creation was completely interchangeable with the power to give life, women with children would have no desire to create, a fact that is clinically incorrect."[33] In order to create, the mother consciously and unconsciously invests her maternal knowledge about pregnancy and birth into her creative work. But Chasseguet-Smirgel indicates that such knowledge, although crucial, remains insufficient for a woman to achieve her artistic endeavors. It is the conflict prompted by her oedipal situation that generates a fertile ground for creation. Freudian psychoanalysis regards woman as a subject left almost untouched by the oedipal phase because, as opposed to man, she has no castration to fight. In fact, Chasseguet-Smirgel reminds us of Freud's erroneous view on the peaceful oedipal journey that the little girl takes into womanhood, a journey that he calls "far simpler and less equivocal, than that of the little possessor of a penis."[34]

In contrast to Freud, Chasseguet-Smirgel indicates the difficulty of becoming a woman, since it implies a fight against two established psychoanalytical notions: the incorporation of the phallus as the ideal image and the rejection the mother as the rival for the father's love. Chasseguet-Smirgel explains that woman develops a great sense of guilt for her coerced detachment from the mother and her dependency on the phallus. To be a woman artist is to integrate this tension within the work as well as to identify with the feminine body and its power to reproduce like a mother, and, eventually, to reassess the position of woman in the oedipal situation as a conflictual one rather than a position of peaceful acceptance of the unconvincing facts of castration. Such reassessment revives the positive role of the mother in the formation of subjectivity for women as well as for men. Chasseguet-Smirgel invites us to reconsider maternity as the focal point for understanding the formation of subjectivity and the power of creativity.

Baudelaire's admiration for the poetry of Marceline Desbordes-Valmore, a nineteenth-century poet of motherhood, and Truffaut's respect for Agnès Varda whose films often revolve around questions of maternity and maternal love may be read as examples for the odd but sincere recognition by male artists that maternity has a place in poetry and film. Women artists whose work springs from a desire to represent motherhood may be providing admiring male artists like Baudelaire and Truffaut with the inspiration that informs their work with maternal overtones despite and beyond their representations of uncaring mothers. As they bring into their work the artistic legacy of women like Desbordes-Valmore and Varda, Baudelaire and Truffaut seem better prepared to construct a maternal text of their own thus counteracting the negative representation of mothers in their text/film. The form and construction of their work may be said to benefit from the maternal texts of Desbordes-Valmore and Varda, while the content paradoxically displays ruthless mothers.

This dichotomy may be characterized, following Melanie Klein's theory of the "good" and the "bad" breast, in terms of the double play of the good mother and the bad mother. On the one hand, the good mother, the mother Baudelaire and Truffaut have learned to love in their female counterpart's work, the mother they have incorporated in their techniques and in their metaphoric language is always an intricate part of their creative impulse: she appeals to the male artist as creator. On the other hand, the bad mother, the cruel and unloving mother often exposed in their narrative, remains part of their destructive, even sadistic impulse: she appeals to the artist's desire to represent and interpret the loss of maternal love as an explanation for their subject's tragic childhood.

For Baudelaire, Truffaut, and Freud the "successful creation" of a poem, a film, and a theory depends on what Brun identifies as a "brief but essential passage into the state of maternity," but this condition requires the male subject to come to terms with the bad mother, like the one in Baudelaire's "Blessing," in Truffaut's *The 400 Blows,* or in Freud's "cloaca theory." In order to downplay the role of this bad mother, however, the male creator must accept and incorporate into his work the "pains" of the good mother whose ultimate proof of virtue is to give birth to a child and to experience in a single moment the greatest pain and the greatest love.

Baudelaire's Fantasy of Motherhood: A Painful Subject

Baudelaire may be called a writer whose favorite literary subject is pain. "I know that grief is the only nobility" (1:9), claims the poet in "Blessing" after having been rejected by his mother and his wife. Elsewhere, expressing his elated anticipation of the moment of death, the expiring man in "A Curious Man's Dream" asks: "Do you know, as I do, the delight of pain" (1:128–29). In a long letter he wrote to his mother in May 1861, Baudelaire refers to the paradoxical concept of a delightful pain when he reminds his mother of a period of his childhood during which he "loved her passionately,"[35] a period of his life that he characterizes as the "best times of motherly love" (174) because he had his mother all to himself. He remains painfully aware, however, that during the same period—a period of fifteen months between 1927 and 1928 separating his father's death from his mother's marriage to his stepfather, General Aupick—his mother was still in mourning after the death of his father. His happiness at having his mother's love all to himself is colored by her sadness at being a lonely widow. Her pain becomes his pleasure. I will demonstrate here that for Baudelaire the figure of Pain is closely related to the figure of the mother, and that pain becomes the poetic figure that allows the poetic subject to act out a full fantasy of motherhood, that is a fantasy in which he is simultaneously the mother and the child, the figure of pain and the figure of pleasure joining forces in the (pro)creation of poetry.

Baudelaire may be characterized as a *Homo dolorosus,* an expression used by the psychiatrist Thomas Szasz to designate "a person whose humanity is intimately related to, or is wholly dependent upon, his being in pain and suffering."[36] For example, the manifold faces and figures of the Spleen presenting various states of suffering and depression affecting the poetic persona relentlessly emerge, somber and grimacing with pain in almost every poem. The old bell cracked like the soul of the poet left to die alone in "The Cracked Bell" (1:71–72), the sick and famished cat roaming in the gutter of "Spleen-Old January" (1:72), the feeble bat embodying the poet's Hope crashing against the decaying walls of the prison in "Spleen," "When a low and heavy sky" (1:74–75) are but a few of the numerous figures of pain encountered in *Flowers of Evil.* Baudelaire corresponds to the type of artist Susan Sontag calls "the exemplary sufferer" for whom "the making of art and the venture of love [are] the two most exquisite sources of suffering."[37]

If one accepts Sontag's premise that poetic creation and the pursuit of love become the two essential personal experiments for the artist, whose inspiration stems principally from the feeling of pain, then Baudelaire indeed appears to be the perfect type of sufferer, one whose lyric creation and personal yearning have bonded and flourished in a state of pure affliction. I propose to explore here the mental suffering through which Baudelaire associates the creation of poetry with the question of true love, an analysis that serves as a necessary preamble to understanding the representation of such pain as symptomatic to a different type of pain, one that is deeply repressed by the artist: the pain associated with the inevitable and troubling separation from his mother.

First, to sort out the question of true love immediately it is essential to recall the prose poem "The Rope" in *Paris Spleen* (1:328–31). Here Baudelaire unequivocally conflates true love and maternal love: "If there is one obvious, ordinary, never-changing phenomenon of a nature to make misapprehension impossible, it is surely motherly love. It is as difficult to imagine a mother without motherly love as light without heat" (1:328). As we have seen, this statement introduces in the poem the odd story of a mother who displays no emotion at the death of her son and then claims her maternal right to the rope with which he had hung himself, stating that it held some sentimental value for her, while her sole purpose was to sell it at the marketplace. Baudelaire's point is simple: only under extraordinary circumstances would a mother be devoid of natural maternal love. Having eliminated this extraneous possibility in the poem, he nevertheless remains convinced that no other form of love compares to a mother's love. We may now clarify that Baudelaire's illustration of Sontag's concept of the "exemplary sufferer" is that of the poet's most exquisite affliction emerging both from the desire to conceive a poem, the "making of art" writes Sontag, and the quest for maternal love, Baudelaire's approach of what Sontag calls "the venture of love."

Despite the natural gloom and bitterness typically associated with the figure of Pain, Baudelaire makes it his best friend. Throughout his writing, pain is embodied by numerous figures among which Woman appears to be the most prominent. It is in the late poem "Meditation" (1:140–41) that Baudelaire gives the most explicit account of the way in which Pain bonds poetically with its feminine spirit, thus becoming the allegorical representation of Woman. In "Meditation," the poetic subject speaks to a familiar and personified figure of Pain, "my Pain," with a capital P, as if it were an old friend, an old female friend, that he soon calls "my dear" and that he addresses like a tender mother would speak to her beloved child. The dialogue between the speaking subject and its dear and familiar Pain is filled with tenderness as he tries to comfort her by holding her hand: "My Grief, give me your hand; come near me," and by offering her the unthreatening darkness of the approaching night: "Hush, O my sorrow, and hold still. You called for evening, here it comes, it is here." What we recognize in the comforting language used by the poetic speaker are strong maternal resonances underscoring the phrases: "Hush"; "Hold still." The lyric subject feels a moral obligation doubled with a natural love instinct to protect and care for his figure of Pain like a mother compelled to protect and care for the child she loves. At this point, a comparison between Baudelaire's work and Marceline Desbordes-Valmore's poetry will further illuminate the association between Baudelaire's poetic creation and its maternal components.

These first lines of "Meditation" appear to echo a similar poetic injunction to go to bed, spoken by a mother to her playful baby boy who cannot settle down for his bedtime in Desbordes-Valmore's "A Little Boy's Bedtime,"[38] a poem she wrote some thirty-five years before Baudelaire's " Meditation." Desbordes-Valmore's own poem opens with the line: "Go to bed, little Paul! It is raining. It's night: it's time," while Baudelaire begins with: "Hush, o my Sorrow, and hold still. You wished for the evening, here it comes, here it is." Although Baudelaire's opening thought and mood extend over two lines while Desbordes-Valmore conveys the same feeling in a single line, one cannot miss the similarities in the rhythm, the tone, and the vocabulary that bond the two poems as if they were both expressing the maternal and poetic reassurance, respectively, for the boy and the pain facing that brief moment of anxiety represented by the passage from day to night and associated in the poems with the sun's last glow and the slow coming of night: Desbordes-Valmore entreats her little boy to go to bed "Go to bed, Little Paul," and Baudelaire asks his Pain to be still as night approaches "Hush, o my Sorrow, and be still." Both Desbordes-Valmore and Baudelaire, mother and poet of their respective children, Paul and Pain, remind their progeny that there is nothing more to fear now that night has come; night will bring peace to Paul's turmoil and Pain's distress: "It is night, it is time," says Desbordes-Valmore, and "Here it comes, here it is," announces Baudelaire.

Their short pronouncements on the coming of night suggest a paucity of language typical of the last soothing words that a mother whispers to her child before the silence of night finally envelops his resting soul. Here both poets try to soothe with their maternal language the last burst of energy displayed by Paul, who refuses to go to bed, and by Pain, who cannot stand still, displayed as a sublimated form or a response to the anxiety brought by the approaching night for Paul and by the dying daylight for Pain. In Desbordes-Valmore's poem the little boy prefers to engage in an imaginary fight with some childish foe he contains with the mere force of his toy sword, and in Baudelaire's poem Pain is described as still fighting the remains of the day represented by a dying sun while memories of past deaths have already begun to enter the field of darkness surrounding the poet. The mother and the poet both promise to their beloved "child" that night will eventually pacify their apprehension; by the end of her poem Desbordes-Valmore kisses her little boy who seems to have angelically fallen asleep, while Baudelaire's closing line in "Meditation" invites Pain to listen to or to be lulled by the sweetness of advancing night.

If Pain does not quite fall asleep in "Meditation," it does so in a poem of "The Parisian Tableaux" entitled "Fog and Rain" (1:100–101). In this poem Baudelaire speaks of the pleasure felt by the poet whose pain has finally sunk into sleep, even if dreams can in fact disturb the natural peace that sleep brings to his body and soul: "Nothing is sweeter than to put pain to sleep on a bed of chance." Although night may bring peace to the sleeping soul, it is also true that it plunges the sleeper into dreams often filled with fearful demons and monsters.

To illustrate the monstrous images populating the artist's oneiric voyage, we only need to point to Baudelaire's own fantastic dream, which he feels compelled to relate to his editor Charles Asselineau in a letter dated March 13, 1856.[39] Baudelaire recalls that in his dream he went to a brothel, which soon became an art gallery in which grotesque drawings and photographs of monstrous fetuses hung on the walls. The prostitutes living in the house had given birth to these fetuses, unfinished humans of which the framed representations seemed to remind these women of their inability to become mothers. Later in the evening of his dream, however, Baudelaire meets one of these monsters who had miraculously survived his birth and was now living within the confines of the brothel. Despite his repulsive looks, this grotesque character appears quite friendly to the poet—he still carries the long umbilical cord awkwardly wrapped around himself. The poet sees this abnormal character as part of the bizarre museum, a living oddity of the permanent collection, a constant reminder that he is the double product of the maternal body and the poetic unconscious—as it manifests itself in the dream. Poetic creation in the making may be as frightful as the gestating maternal body. The living aberration of the brothel becomes a painful reminder that the poet's dreams can also give birth to a poetic monster, a permanent reminder that, as he lays down his daily affliction to bed, his friend Pain, on his own "bed of chance," as he mentioned in "Fog and Rain," darkness may either dull his pain or revive it in the form of a Goyaesque miscreation.

In comparing Desbordes-Valmore's poem "A Little Boy's Bedtime" and Baudelaire's "Meditation" we see how the little boy and Pain have both been guided into peace by the soothing language of mother and poet, or, in a word, by the maternal poet, a phrase that may be used to evoke both Desbordes-Valmore and Baudelaire. Baudelaire, whose personal and lyrical perception of women remains primarily confined to the domains of idealization and condemnation, nevertheless praises Desbordes-Valmore's poetic endeavor in his art criticism; she is the only woman artist whose work he sincerely respects. He recognizes in particular the appeal behind her maternal lyricism: "Only in the poetry of the vibrant Marceline will you be able to feel the warm maternal embrace still lingering on in our memory" (2:147). Baudelaire also recalls that Marceline Desbordes-Valmore made the last corrections in her manuscript on her death bed, and that, despite the somber circumstances surrounding her final writings, her poetry radiates "a vitality more vibrant than ever as it rose from pain" (2:148).

Pain, maternal pain in particular, is a familiar feeling for Marceline who lost five of her children and transposed much of the pain associated with loss into her poetic language as she wrote numerous elegies and poems centered around the pure sadness of life; many of these are grouped in the 1833 collection entitled *Tears*. Baudelaire is also familiar with the pain of maternal loss as he absorbs the sadness surrounding the birth of his stillborn half-sister as if it were his own, as if he had himself died to his mother's love, a mother who had just remarried. As mentioned earlier, the fifteen months separating the death of his father from his mother's remarriage represented the "happy time" to which he refers in his 1861 letter to his mother. About the letter Sima Godfrey[40] rightly comments on the way in which Baudelaire imagines himself in place of the child inside his mother's body when the latter is in fact pregnant with Aupick's child: "but all the time, I was living inside you and you were mine alone."[41] Then, Baudelaire's "happy times" seem to designate more than simply the period of his childhood when he was his mother's exclusive love object; it also refers to that very early time when "he was living inside [her]," a time of intra-uterine life he imagines as the epitome of the subject's complete serenity with(in) the maternal world.

As a way to confirm the association I have drawn between creation and procreation in Baudelaire's poetry, I would like to quote a brief section of Baudelaire's letter to his mother dated March 27, 1852, in which he clearly enunciates the worthiness of mothers who have suffered in childbirth and as such have earned as respectable a status as that of men:

> To sum all my thoughts in one, and to give you some idea of the nature of my thoughts, I think forever and always that only the woman who has suffered and conceived a child can be man's equal. To conceive is the only thing which gives a female moral intelligence.[42]

Much needs to be said about Baudelaire's poor assessment of the female sex; here, however, he nevertheless confesses his admiration for the woman who has suffered in parturition. We have seen how much of the poet's suffering emerges from his idealized past and how it comes to replace a mother's love. Pain in place of maternal love, pain as a displaced figure of maternal love, this is what turns Baudelaire's poetry inward, cradled as it is by a dark and beautiful imagery of life and death.

The Birth of a Child and/or the Making of a Film

> Films are as fragile as babies.
> —François Truffaut, *The Films in My Life*

In August 1983 François Truffaut wrote to Annette Insdorf, a friend and critic: "I won't be coming to New York this year, mainly because I am expecting a baby; Fanny Ardant [his companion] won't be coming either and for the same reason!"[43] It is quite common to hear men speaking about their female partner's pregnancy as if it were their own, and it is even more common to hear them say, "we are expecting a baby," the use of the pronoun *we* signaling the mutual endorsement of pregnancy by both the father-to-be and the mother-to-be. In his letter, however, Truffaut is very explicit about his endorsing Ardant's pregnancy himself. The phrase "I'm expecting a baby" is not simply another unconscious production of language, an affectionate slip of the tongue used by modern fathers, an accepted idiom whereby the subject becomes the bearer of the action of the verb—here, the pregnant individual. The true resonance of this phrase comes from its apposition to the second phrase: "Fanny Ardant won't be coming either and for the same reason!" Although the second phrase is said in humoristic fashion, it is nonetheless revealing of Truffaut's particular relationship with pregnancy.

Truffaut places his participation in pregnancy ahead of Ardant's; he cannot travel to New York because his pregnancy requires him to stay put, and Ardant, his companion, is also staying in France for the same reason. Disguised under the comical effect produced by his rhetorical claim on pregnancy, Truffaut expresses his desire to be the pregnant individual. Had we been unaware of the respective genders of Truffaut and Ardant, and without the intervening of proper names to indicate grammatical gender, the whole sentence would have been easily understood by unfamiliar readers with Truffaut as the expecting mother and Ardant as the expecting father. Behind the surface of unequivocal badinage in Truffaut's phrase there may be an expression of indirect desire toward the culturally impertinent image of male pregnancy. Such an inappropriate "conception" can only survive in the nonchalance of its playful mode, disguised as it were in zany utterances.

As hypothesized by Freud in *Jokes and Their Relation to the Unconscious*, in which he draws a clever comparison between the dream-work and the joke-work, placing both phenomena under the same category of transformation, a joke, like a dream, is a linguistic manifestation of a latent wish that requires a translation. In Truffaut's case the joke has a rhetorical, chiasmatic form that consists of reversing the role of the mother and that of the father, to call attention to the possibility of an otherwise impossible and unexpected male pregnancy.

Two days later, on August 5, 1983, in a letter to his friend Jean Collet, Truffaut gives us the key to understanding his special relationship with pregnancy. He writes: "I'm returning to Normandy, since a baby (not a screenplay, a real baby) is due to be born at the beginning of October" (563). The oddity enunciated in these lines to Collet comes from Truffaut's need to add precision on what the phrase "to have a baby" means to him. Here he clearly separates two modes of conception as if, for him, they had always had the same meaning. The confusion may come from the fact that Truffaut's babies generally have the appearance of technically created images, illusions of reality, films, of which Truffaut himself says that they require an average of nine months before being brought into the world of cinema. He feels the need to emphasize the fact that his expected "human" baby is a *real* baby, thus expressing the desire to undo the fantasy that, all along his career as a filmmaker, had confused the making of films and the making of babies. "Films are as fragile as babies": Truffaut made and cared for his films like a mother her babies, filled with love, high expectations, investing his soul and body in the slow development of the filmic creation, and always seeking to become more "educated" about his progressing "child" by reading books and viewing other films.

In 1973, with *Day for Night,* he offered a cinematic perspective on the art of conceiving a film. As we have seen earlier, the film is a sincere attempt at portraying the life of a film director, played by Truffaut himself during filmmaking. We follow the intrigue not only from the director's busy, eventful days, but also from inside his conscious and unconscious mind translated into a voice-over constantly relating out loud his intimate thoughts, his dreams, and his personal worries. Many of these personal thoughts reveal a Truffaut engaged in a caring and *maternal* relationship with the film in which the main role is that of a personified cinema, a cinema whose technical and human complexity we now share openly. As his biographer Gilles Cahoreau recalls, in making *Day for Night,* Truffaut was aiming at "making cinema enter the film,"[44] thus confirming the crucial role played by cinema in the film. If the main character of the film is cinema, if its translator is

Ferrand, the director played by Truffaut, and if the story traces the many intrigues—human and technical—that constitute filmmaking, we might conclude that the actual actors in the film have a different function than they usually do in traditional films: in *Day for Night* they become the background information against which the main character, the film in the making, is being played. Each actor, each relationship, adds a new turn or another difficulty toward the completion of the film, toward the birth of the cinematic baby.

Day for Night is not essentially a film about relationships, but it is aptly a film about the conception, the slow development, and the birth of a film. Truffaut's emotional (*maternal*) involvement with *Day for Night* is so significant that he will not forgive Godard for mistaking the film for a sexy comedy. In one of his letters to Truffaut he writes: "One can't help wondering why the director is the only one who does not screw in *Day for Night*."[45] After seeing the film in 1973, Godard is one of the few critics to react negatively to it. He writes directly to his new wave friend and associate, but his letter is so offensive to Truffaut that it marks the official end to their personal and professional relationship. Expecting that a film about cinema would display the political reality of filmmaking or the working force behind filmmaking in general, Godard expresses his disappointment and accuses Truffaut of "being a liar" in the large sense: lying about male-female relationships, lying about the larger human and technical economy of filmmaking. Godard does not understand that the metaphoric content of the film claims the pregnant body of the mother-to-be as its field of reference; he does not understand that the film does not try to expose its modes of production but that it is actually involved in the representation of its reproduction, its own labor before giving birth to a fantasy: a creation so elusive that we shall never see it (*Meet Paméla*, the film being made in *Day for Night*, remains a virtual film that will never be seen in its entirety; it becomes a pretext to explore the inside of the director's head, a director whose desire—a maternal-like desire, since the director, like a pregnant mother, is constantly worried about and anxiously anticipating the slow formation of his unborn child—is put under the filmic microscope). Finally, Godard does not understand that in the film Ferrand embodies less the character of the director than that of the translating voice. As a translator of the inner workings of the pregnant body of the film, Ferrand's role is to provide an intelligible and imaginative commentary on how films are made. Because his role is to facilitate the comprehension of the metaphor of creation at work in the film, it is then not surprising that Ferrand does not become sexually involved with any one of his crew members. He belongs to a different signifying order from that of the other characters; he is the voice of synthesis telling us about the various human traits that often participate in the making of the film: love, sex, friendship, depression, knowledge, spontaneity, individual tastes, to name only a few.

Day for Night gives an indirect role to the metaphor of pregnancy applying its signifying images to the process of filmmaking, and this metaphor is opposed to the destructive impact made on Ferrand by the actual pregnancy of one of the actresses in the film. As previously suggested, Ferrand's rage at the actress's pregnancy may be read as the symptom of fear generated by motherhood, which can never be expressed outside its displaced form as a metaphor of filmic creation. Only as a sublimated visual expression does motherhood become the metaphor of productivity.

While repressing the figure of the mother, which appears to threaten male intelligence, sexuality, and psychological state with the terrifying force generated by her reproductive body, Truffaut still maintains a sense of fascination for the mother's power to reproduce. In his 1969–70 film, *The Wild Child,* he manages to put into filmic practice his fascination without his fear as he separates the process of birth/creation from traditional motherhood; paradoxically, despite the absence of the child's actual mother, it is the one film by Truffaut that contains the most impressive number of maternal metaphors.

The film is about an eight-year-old boy found living in the wild of the Aveyron forest, brought back to civilization, and educated by a male doctor, Jean Itard; it is also the story of a male fantasy of conception, a story in which man gives symbolic birth to a socially acceptable child without the mediation of the mother, without her frightful body. Here Truffaut, who could not give (would not give) the role of the doctor to anybody else but himself, thus works on two different levels. First, as Itard, the actor in the film, he brings a child into the world of social norms, and as such he may be seen as the epitome of a father figure disciplining and educating the wild child. Second, as Truffaut the film's director, he also brings a film to the screen, and is, as such, the symbolic mother of his own filmic creation. The film is about creation, human and filmic, a comparison that Truffaut attributes to his phantasmatic desire to create a film like a mother conceives a child: "Conceiving, directing and finishing a film usually takes nine months of our life. A comparison with childbearing comes immediately to mind; I admit it is a common one, some would say a cliché, yet I am convinced that this cliché is true, and as far as I am concerned I make films to experience the emotions of maternity and to apprehend the sense of plenitude it produces."[46]

A considerable number of directing activities contribute to the maternal treatment of *The Wild Child*. Maternal attributes are apparent in each of the major categories constituting the art of filmmaking: in the story and the mise-en-scène, in the cinematography, and finally in the soundtrack.

In 1966, Truffaut read the two medical reports written by Doctor Itard in 1801 and 1806 on his study of a wild child found by hunters in a forest of the Aveyron region. Truffaut is fascinated by the reports and, having decided to write a scenario out of them, he imagines that Doctor Itard writes a private journal documenting the child's development. Using this technique, Truffaut is able to keep almost exactly the actual text of Itard's reports. The story is therefore authentic, as announced at the beginning of the film, and it takes us back to 1798 in a forest where a young child is discovered by villagers. Believed to have grown up for the most part in the forest, that is, in complete isolation from society, the child is totally primitive, behaving and looking like a wild animal and unable to communicate with words. Doctor Itard is intrigued by the case of the wild child, and he decides to take personal care of him, to educate him, and to make a socially acceptable individual out of him. He brings the wild child to his house near Paris, calls him Victor, and, with the help of his housekeeper, Madame Guérin, provides the child with a rudimentary knowledge of language and manners. The child, however, does not bend easily to Itard's rules and retains a deep attachment and desire to return to his natural environment: the forest. At the end of the film he flees Itard's house to go back to the forest, but his few months under Itard's training have softened his animal instincts. Frustrated and saddened by his realization that he cannot live in complete instinctual harmony with the forest any longer, he halfheartedly returns to Itard's house.

Even this quick retelling of the plot presents us with two important symbolic births. The first occurs at the beginning of the film in the forest, or, more precisely, *through* the forest, since the forest may be read as a symbolic maternal body—just as Paris became Antoine's symbolic mother in *The 400 Blows*—providing protection (trees and holes to hide in); food (wild berries and mushrooms); and pleasure (soft cradling on the branches of trees) to the child who is totally dependent on her. When villagers finally track him down, the boy hides in a large foxhole. This extraction from the hole mirrors an actual birth: the baby extracted from the pleasurable environment provided by the mother's womb by a medical team may be compared to the wild child being pulled out of the nurturing ground of the "maternal forest" by a group of villagers. Hidden in his hole, the wild child feels protected from the villagers, until they throw down a branch on fire to force him out. The child comes out coughing, a physical reaction to fire that may be compared to the first cry of the child who has just emerged from the womb. It is time for the wild child to start his life outside the hole, outside the forest, his nurturing natural mother.

The actual directing of this extraction scene adopts the child's point of view, thus providing the spectators with an opportunity to identify with him, with his gaze at the moment of birth. Like him, we visually emerge from the hole in the ground, and the camera remains at ground level from where we can only see the legs of the villagers; we are spatially positioned at the site of birth by the camera-work. In addition, like the child born of the forest, we are unable to understand the language spoken by the villagers who are communicating in the Aveyron dialect, putting us in the same position as the emerging child, or any newborn unable to recognize "proper" language. Only the villagers' actions have a bearing on our understanding of the situation, not their incomprehensible language. During the entire scene in which the wild child is captured, Truffaut visually identifies with the child, as if he wished to understand the tragic separation from the maternal forest experienced by the wild child: his camera remains at ground level; the maternal forest represents the entire setting of the scene; and except for the unfathomable dialect of the villagers the world perceived by the child remains silent. Truffaut has fully dramatized the unavoidable and brutal separation of the wild child from the maternal forest. This separation of the child and the forest symbolizes a total tragedy for Victor who is brought out into the world against his will.

The second symbolic birth in the film is also a tragic one, this time from the point of view of the doctor whose role is similar to that of the birthing and nurturing mother. It occurs toward the end of the film after Victor's breakout. At that point Itard seems to have lost all hope of ever seeing him again and reacts to the loss as if he had lost his own child, or, rather, as if he had given Victor nine months to develop as a social being within the confines of his house to finally deliver a stillborn baby. In this final scene a despondent Itard is writing the following lines in his notebook: "This wild child had managed successfully in living in our quarters, and all these happy transformations had occurred within a nine-month period." Itard feels that he has conceived this child, given him nine months of his "scientific" knowledge but also of his nurturing love to grow into a human being, all of this within the confinement of his house. But he also knows that this symbolic pregnancy has come to a tragic end as Victor escapes one more time into the depths of the forest, his "real mother." In the next scene, however, Victor does come back to Itard's house. This time, in opposition to the feeling of loss lingering from the previous scene, Victor is finally born to the civilized world of Itard.

The ambivalence of the final outcome of his birth is transmuted onto the film as Victor's "torn" body still carries the marks of his difficult birth: "You are scratched all over, but at last you are here," and his sad face carries the marks of his unfulfilled desire to ever return to his maternal forest. The last image of the film freezes on Victor's sad face. Such sadness speaks about several other "gloomy" aspects of the film process. First, it speaks of Itard's bittersweet delivery of a semi-tamed child who may never become a completely active participant in the cultural world. It also points to the director's melancholic state in response to his strong emotional involvement with his conceiving of the film and his secret unwillingness to end it, to let it go free of his directorship while still "unfinished" in style and content. Then, it speaks of the film itself, of its unhappy yet inevitable conclusion, becoming an individual product whose future life no longer depends on the director who created it, but on the spectators. But, more directly, it reveals the wild child's heavy heart as he realizes that he cannot return to the maternal womb of the forest, which has now become, in its primary form, a strange and dangerous land from which he must find shelter in the "civilized world." Only through his new symbolic understanding of the forest will Victor be able to reconnect with some of the pleasures provided by the representations his lost infancy world, his maternal forest. Truffaut has again barred the good mother from the child's imaginary, having replaced her with his own phantasmic maternal self. Truffaut, however, plays the parthenogenetic role of father and mother, fatherly in his teaching and motherly in his loving. Victor reacts to the father figure with great frustration, while he abandons himself to the pleasures provided by his new maternal environment.

Throughout the film we witness Victor's coming into the civilized world in a succession of alternating images of frustration and pleasure. Frustration is associated with the blackboard and the dining room table, with the learning of language, manners, and moral values, while pleasure is found in the drinking of milk and water, in signifiers like the window, which provides him with visual longing for moments of fusion with nature. The first word that Victor learns is the word *lait*, "milk." His first word is correlative to the pleasure associated with the drinking of milk, and it is no coincidence that his first drink of milk is provided by the film's only mother, Madame Lemeri, one of Itard's neighbors. Madame Lemeri's maternal attributes are strongly connoted; among other things, she almost always appears on screen with her baby in her arms. She is the one who first gives Victor a bowl full of milk thus initiating a ritual that Victor will expect each time he goes to visit the Lemeri family. Itard adopts the maternal gesture from Madame Lemeri's milk ritual and bases his teaching method on Victor's pleasure in drinking milk by making him ask for it verbally before giving it to him. Victor's pleasure thus drives his progress into the world of language, and soon in Itard's pedagogy, drinking, formerly a source of pure pleasure, becomes a reward when Victor does well. The original bodily pleasures provided by the act of drinking have now become a moral reward, part of the learning process. This learning process, conducted by Itard as father figure but supplemented by a maternal component, complies with my theory of the double presence of mother and father behind the composite character represented by Itard/Truffaut.

The maternal elements of the story and the mise-en-scène are complemented by some aspects of the cinematography, also infused with the symbolic presence of the delivering mother. First, the film is shot in black-and-white at a time in the history of cinema when color enjoys tremendous commercial success. At that time, especially, black-and-white film is regarded as a regressive film, technically passé. Obviously, however, Truffaut's decision to use black-and-white is related to the fact that the story takes place in the past, in the year 1798. But the past depicted in the film in black-and-white is more than just a historical past; it is also related to an archaic stage in the psychology of early infancy, a time during which psychological evaluations of retarded children were either black or white without any nuances for individual cases, a time during which a singular diagnostic seemed to fit several patients with different form of mental afflictions. Psychology had not yet developed the sense of scientific flexibility built in the modern studies and research in psychoanalysis.

Thus, in the film the black-and-white may reflect the Manichaean practices of psychologists and psychiatrists of the period, while the grey may be said to reflect the scientific uncertainties surrounding the early period of research in psychiatry. In fact, the reason why the school of psychiatry Itard is professionally connected to is interested in educating the wild child is related to the fact that once educated Victor would probably provide the researchers with information about his past life in the forest, about the wonders (or horrors) of life before his symbolic birth. Before Itard's first meeting with the wild child, he reads the following passages of a report drafted by the society of psychiatrists who were the first to deal with the case of the wild child: "Let's hope that a quick education will allow him [the wild child] to give us the most exciting information on his life in the forest." It is clear that for the psychiatrists the wild child is nothing else but an object of research. For Itard, Victor is also a way to test his own ability as an educator, but, in addition, he becomes a real child, a son, as indicated in the last remarks Itard makes at the end of the film after Victor has returned from his breakout. While Madame Guérin calls him "my boy," Itard emphasizes the fact that Victor is now at home, his home: "You came back home. You are home." Victor's home is a black and white home, a home in which Itard, as scientist/father unsuccessfully attempts to explore the wild child's past, but a home in which Itard becomes a maternal figure whose concern and generosity toward Victor's emotional past finds its expression through the cinematography and in particular through the repeated use of the "iris shot."

By definition the iris shot is a masking shot generally in circular form that expands and shrinks recalling the dilating and closing movement of the iris in the human eye. With the iris shot the camera reminds the spectators of their dependency on the visual, and on the ability of the camera to direct the viewers' focus on important aspects of the film narrative. *The Wild Child* opens and closes with an iris shot thus setting the "tone," or, rather, setting the visual mode commanded by the camerawork. Throughout the film the iris shot returns and each time it aims at the main object of its focus: the wild child. Often the camera zooms in on the child, freezes on his facial expression for a brief instant, and shrinks the image to a black screen. The child's disappearance from and reappearing into the eye of the shot suggests that the child is not quite ready to become a full participant to the social world that adopted him; when the iris contracts he gradually recedes into the blankness of the dark screen, and when the iris dilates he returns to his tasks toward the accomplishment of his basic education, to the action of the film. With the iris shot he goes in and out of the film, as if Truffaut were still working on Victor's development as a fully—physically and mentally—constituted boy and did not want to release the boy from what may be perceived as the *caring* encirclement of the iris shot, the "maternal embrace" of the camera.

Annette Insdorf analyzes the iris shot as an element reinforcing the omnipresent inside/outside dichotomy. According to her, *The Wild Child* is a film that brings into contrast the forest as the figure of freedom and Itard's house as the figure of confinement.[47] It is the task of the wild child to find a happy medium between the outside (forest) and the inside (the house). Victor finds such a medium in the window. He spends much of his free time indoors by the window looking nostalgically at the spectacle of nature offered to him through the window's filtering glass. The iris shot is also the filtering eye through which Truffaut practices a form of cinematic nostalgia for the era of silent films during which the iris shot was a popular technique.

The iris shot gives him the opportunity to claim his desire for the purely visual, for the glorious past of the image when the director was a magician of the screen. Although with this particular film Truffaut remains turned toward a past aesthestics of the visual, he also problematizes sound by focusing our attention on the film's very few sounds. Throughout, our auditive relation to the film remains minimal: the natural noises of the forest, the foreign dialect used by the villagers, and then the music and the voice-over narration with very little spoken dialogue. For Insdorf this alternate use of music and narration also reflects the film's inside and outside dichotomy.

The inside/outside contrast that Insdorf identifies with the images and sounds related to freedom and confinement in the film can also be displaced to the field of motherhood, and may be understood as a contrast between the inside and the outside of the mother's womb. The dilating and contracting movement of the iris shot has its maternal counterpart in the uterus, which opens a little more with each contraction and closes again when the mother releases her contraction during birth. With its constant use of the iris shot the film technically replicates the long period of alternating contractions, "the pushing out of the baby," preceding birth. It could be said that *The Wild Child* proposes the technical form of a maternal experience, which reflects the director's avowed desire to conceive like a mother. The camera is no longer the phallic symbol characterized by its voyeuristic and fetishizing work, and becomes a maternal object using its techniques to put into perspective the development of a yet unidentified child, an unborn child, an unfinished and therefore uncivilized child who is born for the second time at the end of the film after nine months in Itard's care. In short, with his camera Truffaut becomes the mother of his film.

It remains important to notice that there are no beautiful women, no sexual scenes, no plots involving one perversion or another in the film, and, oddly enough, except for the peripheral Madame Lemeri and Itard's maid, Madame Guérin, there are no actual women and/or mothers. Despite the almost complete absence of women and mothers, love in this film is by nature maternal and fully invested in the camera work while the couple on the screen, Itard and Victor, fails to accomplish the expected father/son relationship. Victor will learn man's ways to operate in society, but the film remains ambivalent on how successful Itard will be in educating Victor. The last image indicates to a great extent the failure of paternal education as the camera closes in on Victor's somber look on Itard. But the failure of paternity is supplemented by the maternal technique of the iris shot, which finally gives birth to the tamed child of cinematography. The iris closes off; the *directing mother* has given birth to *The Wild Child*.

Freudian Womb Fantasies

In "Contributions to the Psychology of Love" Freud compares the unconscious and unbreakable libidinal attachment of a child to his mother to the actual marks of her pelvic cavity left on the skull of the newborn: "The comparison with the way in which the skull of the new-born child is shaped comes irresistibly to one's mind; after a protracted labour it always bears the form of a cast of the maternal pelvis."[48] The image of the child bearing the indelible marks of his or her birth, and particularly showing the mold of the mother's pelvis, seems the perfect illustration for the sporadic yet intriguing traces left by the whole question of birth on Freud's work. According to Freud in the preceding quote, birth marks on the child's skull are the result of a protracted labor, a lengthy period of toiling toward the final delivery of a child; this extended endeavor is comparable to Freud's own difficulty in recognizing some of the bare principles of the birth theory. This theory took a particularly long time to emerge from his "gestating" mind, as if he felt the need to postpone its final outcome for fear that it might problematize his understanding of his primary "other creation": the castration theory. In fact, Freud never quite gave the birth theory the respectable place it deserved in psychoanalysis. In 1924 he finally rejected the long awaited theory when he realized how destructive its principles could prove to be in relation to his theory of castration. Such a realization came up following the publication of Otto Rank's work *The Trauma of Birth,* which placed parturition at the center of all future cases of separation anxiety affecting the psychological well-being of all individuals. With *The Trauma of Birth* Rank severely undermined the problematic of sexual differences at the core of Freudian analysis.

According to Freud, Rank's biggest fallacy was to believe that birth was primarily an event of traumatic nature with long-lasting effects on the neurotic adults fighting the reemerging affective patterns originally set at the time of parturition. Rather than an omnipotent model for any future separation anxiety, Freud saw birth as a unique eruption and isolated case of anxiety, the outcome of which could potentially produce later emotions in the sensitive adult but not germane to the formation of his or her sexual identity. It is clear that for Freud the crucial trauma in any individual psyche emerges during the oedipal crisis. Although he grants Rank the fact that "a certain preparedness for anxiety is undoubtedly present in the infant in arms,"[49] Freud strongly opposes Rank's birth trauma as the prototypical event for all subsequent forms of anxiety, repeatedly asserting that "anxiety is the reaction to danger" (82) and that the fetus has no psychological awareness of the presence of any danger because it does not have a psyche to speak of: "the danger of birth has yet no psychical content" (64). According to Freud, the only danger forcing the individual into a situation of anxiety is the danger of castration. In this text he does not dismiss the potentiality for anxiety in the event of birth, but reads such anxiety as a retroactively constructed fear of separation from the mother equated with the fear of castration:

> Anxiety appears as a reaction to the felt loss of the object; and we are at once reminded of the fact that castration anxiety, too, is a fear of being separated from a highly valued object, and that the earliest anxiety of all—the "primal anxiety" of birth—is brought about on the occasion of a separation from the mother. (66)

The equation between the mother and the penis as both representing "the highly valued object" that the child is afraid to lose turns the event of birth into an early form of castration. The idea that birth may be a form of castration has gained popularity in psychoanalytical circles looking into an expansion of the sexually restricted concept of castration into a more accepted form of separation. In France, Françoise Dolto[50] has contributed to the widening of the concept of castration pluralized and defined as "symboligeneous castrations" or a series of radical prohibitions to pleasure and satisfaction already in place in the individual but that must be stopped—or sublimated—if the subject is to develop his or her individuality: "castrations in the psychoanalytical sense are patterns of symbolic separation [. . .] they are as important to the development of the child's individuation in relation to his mother, his father and his kin as the development of language" (82–83). Evidently, Dolto does not radically critique castration but envisions it as a necessary evil that eventually will bear its fruits by bringing the child out of the limited and somewhat regressive maternal/paternal realm into the sphere of language and communication.

Much of Dolto's formulation for the "symboligeneous" nature of castration is germane to Lacan's understanding of the phallus as the "universal" signifier orienting the subject out the oedipal crisis into his or her emancipation, into culture and language. Yet for Lacan, as for Freud, castration is essential to the question of sexual differences at the time when the subject is in the pangs of the Oedipus complex, and it has no place in the child's early life, his pre-oedipal days. For her part, and in conjunction with her formulation that castration is indeed similar to a crucial and difficult separation from early forms of pleasure, Dolto examines each stage of development from birth to maturation, as "a symboligeneous castration," a necessary rupture from the past. The first in the progression is the "umbilical castration," not merely the cut of the umbilical cord at birth, but along with this act the abrupt interruption from intra-uterine life, from the pleasures of the womb such as the soft cradling and symbiotic rhythms of the infant's and the mother's heartbeat. With the cut of the umbilical cord and the first gasp of air, the child is born to life *ex-utero*, renouncing *in-utero* pleasures. According to Dolto the "fruits" reaped by the newborn after this first castration are contained in an entirely new regime of perceptions in contact with "lights, smells, tactile sensations, feeling of pressure and gravity, and loud noises" (93). These new perceptions open up to new pleasures, oral pleasures in particular, which come to follow fetal bliss. Dolto continues her demonstration of the importance of each passage from one form of pleasure to another, sublimated form, claiming that each time the child must undergo the psychological pain associated with each castration, with each advanced order governing the late cut, which forces him to readjust his pursuit of pleasures to an acceptable form of social interaction.

For Freud to admit to the primal role played by the brutal and shocking separation occurring at birth represents a contradiction with his theory of genital castration, which marks the interdiction of the mother, of her body, and the successful entry of the subject into culture through compliance with paternal domination. Freud's dealings with the vague spirit of the mother remain scant, and throughout his writings she appears as what critic Madelon Sprengnether calls the "spectral mother" haunting the child's memory with images of her soft and pleasurable body and thus becoming in Freud's text a repressed figure occasionally reappearing in the child's psyche like a ghost.[51] Madelon Sprengnether defines the spectral mother as the phantasmatic and sporadic presence of the mother figure throughout Freud's texts, "never a major figure in Freud's theory, which revolves around the drama of the father-son relationship, she has a ghostlike function, creating a presence out of absence" (5).

Sprengnether also comments on Freud's quasi-silence on the subject of birth. Naturally, she then turns to the equivocal relationship (both professional and personal) existing between Freud and Rank with a long account of the theoretical dispute between them, attributing Freud's indecisive reaction to Rank's *Trauma of Birth*—his double feeling of fascination and dread for all pre-oedipal issues—to his own fear of opening the field of psychoanalysis to the question of the mother, and reading Freud's *Inhibitions, Symptoms and Anxiety* as a symptomatic text revealing through its unnecessary repetitions a compulsive fear of dealing with maternal issues. Sprengnether asserts the presence in Freud's text of a subject for whom "to return to mother [. . .] is to die" (153). It is Freud's belief that, in retrospect, birth is as much a moment of coming to life as it is a moment of death, a moment of return into the long lost maternal sphere that, from an adult's viewpoint, represents a regression into a phantasmatic world turning the subject inward as if "buried alive." In a footnote from *The Interpretation of Dreams* Freud mentions that fantasies of returning to the womb are connected to a fear of being buried alive and that such fear is resolved by interpreting life after death as a form of life before birth.[52]

Notwithstanding this somber connection established between death and birth, Freud continues his *labor* toward a possible acknowledgment of the birth theory, but, as remarked by Sprengnether, his prolonged confinement is represented by the almost exclusive mentioning of birth issues in margins or in footnotes (138). This marginalization of the birth theory is remarkable in itself because it creates a theoretical sub-place of advent for all forms of early psychological life, safely tucked away from the main text where, according to Freud, all important theoretical developments occur. For example, the following three remarks concerning birth find their way into Freud's *Interpretation of Dreams* only as footnotes to the main text, as if birth had to stand in a peripheral position because of its potentially disruptive consequences to the matrix of the text in which castration claims its status as main figure in the trauma of separation. Both the position of the footnotes—separated from the main text—and their content—the formulation of an embryonic birth theory—act as outsiders, partial objects cut off of the main body of the text and of the theory on dreams by the analyst who has (unwillingly?) raised questions but not quite accepted the argument they present.

The first footnote emerges while Freud is giving his own dream the benefit of his newly found scientific method in exploring unconscious manifestations. As mentioned before, this dream, known as "Irma's injection," is the specimen dream with which he hopes to verify his theory about the dreamwork. Beyond the scientific aim of his endeavor, however, Freud is also analyzing himself while analyzing the dream. Soon he encounters a point of resistance in his own interpretation that corresponds to the moment when Irma, the woman in his dream, refuses to open her mouth to let the doctor examine her. Why does not she want to open her mouth? What is she hiding from him? When Irma finally complies and allows the doctor to see inside her mouth, he seems shocked and uncomfortable with the unexpected shapes and forms facing his scientific eye as well as his male gaze. In fact, his shock justifies *après-coup* (after the fact) her resistance to let him look inside as if her knowledge of what was inside comprised her evaluation of his male reaction, not his medical one, to the spectacle of female interiority. She appears to have known in advance that the configuration of her inner throat would have propelled the male doctor into a state of confusion. In order to overcome the disarray provoked by her uncanny inside, the doctor calls upon his male colleagues and friends to help him bring Irma's case into a male perspective, that is, in an understanding that can momentarily reassure the man behind the doctor that the "ghost" of femininity, the spectral mother, who seemed so unfamiliar and fearful to him, can be controlled.

Such a reading of the dream reverses the roles of doctor and patient. Indeed, Irma's indirect speculation on the doctor's fear gives her the expertise of her own body for which he cannot provide a theory outside his own fear of the unknown female he is facing. Freud then appears as the patient, victim of a visual trauma prompted by his inspection of her oral opening. Both literary critics and psychoanalysts, Shoshana Felman and Jacques Lacan among them, have suggested that in the dream of Irma's injection Freud is faced with the horror of femininity displaced from the female sex to the mouth. As she resists Freud, Irma attempts to preserve the privacy of her femininity as well as his phantasmatic image of her. Because the dream must be interpreted, she cannot keep her privacy and he his (nightmarish) dream-woman. As he analyzes the part of his dream in which he speculates that Irma's refusal to "open up" may be related to her wearing false teeth, Freud asserts that Irma is a composite character made of a series of other women, a governess and a woman he never treated as a patient but whom he remembers at a time when she was "puffed up." The third *puffy* woman brings Freud to write a footnote, in which he identifies her as his own wife:

> The still unexplained complaint about pains in the abdomen could also be traced back to the third figure. The person in question was, of course, my wife; the pains in the abdomen reminded me of one of the occasions on which I had noticed her bashfulness. [. . .]
> [. . .] If I had pursued my comparison between the three women, it would have taken me far afield.—There is at least one spot in every dream at which it is unplumbable—a navel, as it were, that is its point of contact with the unknown. (143)

In her essay on the footnotes of the dream Shoshana Felman traces the "pains in the abdomen" to Martha Freud's pregnancy.[53] Freud himself identifies the third woman in the dream as his wife although he does not explicitly relate her abdominal pains to her pregnancy. The relation between Martha's pain and her pregnancy becomes clear, however, as we read the footnote a little closer. In the text of the dream Freud writes about the third woman's "puffiness," a detail that triggers the footnote in which he relates the bulging female body to his wife's abdominal pains. Freud does not specifically bridge the gap between the image of the swollen body and his wife's pregnancy, but the use of the expression *of course* while naming his wife places the episode of her pregnancy as the evidence behind the case of the puffy and bellyaching female of the dream. It is as if the obvious fact of his wife's pregnancy did not need to be spelled out, but simply signaled by the phrase *of course,* thus implying the following innuendo: "Of course, only my pregnant wife fits into the description of the woman with a big and painful belly. Who else?"

It may be said that the use of a footnote to reveal obliquely the presence of the pregnant woman in the dream-text is symptomatic of Freud's own resistance to the central position that the subject of childbearing could occupy in the interpretation of this crucial dream, the model dream for future dreams to come. In fact, with the thought of his wife Freud digresses from explaining the reason for her sufferings, observing that she is a "bashful" woman. This "bashfulness" may be read as a sign of her female reaction to his male desire to elucidate or lift the mystery of maternity that created his feeling of anxiety in the first place, or it could also be interpreted as his bashfulness transmuted upon her as a means to further dissociate his fear of pregnancy with the reality of his wife's pains. Her abdominal pains may have transformed him into a demure and humble man turning away from the experience of pregnancy. It is more likely a *bashful* Freud whose repressed memory of his wife's pregnancy enters the (con)text of his dream in a footnote.

In the second part of the footnote Freud gives the navel the status of a symbol representing a point of contact between the known and the unknown, the manifest and the latent, the conscious and the unconscious. In other words, the navel acts as a mediator, or, in linguistic terms, as the bar between signifier and signified, between the maternal reality expressed in the first part of the footnote as the pains associated with the bulging belly of the mother and the intra-uterine life that becomes in Freud's text the subject of his womb fantasies, fantasies so deeply repressed that they become "unplumbable," that is unfathomable, literally impossible to explore, impossible to expose in the main text and therefore always lurking at its periphery. As they appear beyond the perimeter of the text, these fantasies represent more a quick thought on the subject of birth than an extrapolation on the subject of dreaming. Freud's own free thought processes may point to a birth imagery, while his intentions are to elucidate the dream processes at hand. In fact, beyond the dream of "Irma's injection" Freud gives a long and extensively illustrated account of the different components constituting the dreamwork: condensation, displacement, and symbolization. Condensation is clearly the subject at hand as Freud delineates the different women who came to constitute the composite character of Irma. As he touches upon the "navel" of the dream, however, Freud feels that he cannot go beyond its "unplumbable" point, that the repressive nature of his unconscious does not permit him as a man to further infiltrate the realm of femininity.

It is at this particular point of impasse that the navel comes to represent what Felman calls "a cluster of women," "a knot of women" that cannot be untied any further because it has met with the outer limits of the analyst's own resistance: Freud is on the brink of the deepest layer of his own repression, that of the femininity of motherhood, Lacan's Real, unfathomable by (male) definition. Faced with the navel, Freud has met "the *nodal point* of the female pain and that which makes the nodal point of the female pain *unspeakable,* unspeakable in a male dream; unspeakable in the terms of a male solution" (Felman 67). Unable to go any further in the exploration of his unconscious, Freud involuntarily deflects his own repressive thoughts on birth upon other analysts while he continues to preserve his main text and his main theory from maternal incursions by keeping them far afield in the confine of footnotes.

In the chapter dedicated to the dreamwork, dreams involving the inside of the mouth reappear in the form of images related to painful dental operations such as the pulling of teeth. The dreams in question present scenes of brutal teeth extractions that Freud immediately interprets as sexual scenes related to masturbatory pleasures and therefore castration threats. While admitting to being unable to fully explain the dreams in question, in a footnote added in 1909 and completed in 1919, Freud recalls that Carl Jung and Ernest Jones interpreted dental dreams in women as birth dreams:

> A communication by C. G. Jung informs us that dreams with a dental stimulus occurring in women have the meaning of birth dreams. Ernest Jones [1914] has brought forward clear confirmation of this. The element in common between this interpretation and the one put forward above lies in the fact that in both cases (castration and birth) what is in question is the separation of a part of a body from the whole. (423)

By letting two other analysts occupy the space of the footnote and by giving them the opportunity to speak about the rapport between dreams about teeth and birth, Freud is twice, textually and theoretically, disengaging from the discourse on birth. It seems that the narrative technique by which another voice speaks about a taboo subject acts for Freud as a supplementary textual protection from the repressed topic of birth. Yet it is not so much the mention of birth that is remarkable—after all, birth does make a brief nominal appearance in the main body of the text—as the acknowledgment of the synecdochal structure of separation from the body during castration and birth. For the first time castration and birth are observed in the light of a similar act of separation; they are identified through the common cut that determined their place in psychoanalysis. As described indirectly by Freud, birth becomes a prototypical moment of castration, and more precisely a moment of fetishism when a part of the (mother's/child's) body becomes separated from the whole. Thus, Freud has brought the subject of birth on familiar territory by arranging its entry in the discourse on castration and fetishism. He is now able to let go of his resistance to birth and to engage in interpretations leading the subject back to the womb.

In fact, soon after the teeth dreams Freud becomes interested in water dreams that he interprets as womb fantasies. He is particularly fascinated by a woman's dream in which she leaps in the water of a dark lake partially lit up by the moon. Although in the dream the woman indicates her return to the water, Freud insists that the only way to interpret the dream is to reverse its movement from inside the water to outside. He feels that the woman's desire is in fact to emerge from the water, that is, to be born or even to give birth. Thus, the reversed direction of the dream indicates to him a desire for separation, an instinctual pulling of the subject outside the womb and not a desire to return to its aquatic symbiosis. In 1909 Freud adds a footnote to this dream revealing the basic principle of the birth theory that he will never fully develop but that Rank later pursued in *The Trauma of Birth*:

> It was not for a long time that I learned to appreciate the importance of phantasies and unconscious thoughts about life in the womb. They contain an explanation of the remarkable dread that many people have of being buried alive; and they also afford the deepest unconscious basis for the belief in survival after death, which merely represents a projection in the future of this uncanny life before birth. Moreover, the act of birth is the first experience of anxiety, and thus the source and prototype of the affect of anxiety. (436)

According to Freud's footnote, the fantasy of returning into the womb can be explained by the dread of life after death. In fact, birth and death are the two points of contact with the unknown life lying out there, beyond the first and last breath. Yet, because there is a knowledgeable medical discourse on the life of the embryo in the womb and no scientific knowledge of life after death, birth is in fact used here as a reassuring mirror reflecting the possible continuation of life beyond death. When the concept of birth could become the referential point that soothes the fear of death, the fear of not knowing what is beyond the cessation of life, Freud chooses the reversed proposition, which makes birth the reflection of death, the fearful arrival from the unknown.

Womb fantasies thus take on the appearance of a return to the unknown and therefore frightening body of the mother. Freud's formulation that the return to the womb takes on the appearance of death, of being buried alive, must be understood as an indirect formulation of his fear of the unknown for which woman and her body are responsible. For Freud, to face motherhood is to face death and in order to avoid the deadly mother, he places the parturient mother in footnotes where she resumes her role as a taboo subject that must be buried alive. Once buried in fantasies of the womb and separated from the life of the text in a subtextual grave, the mother figure has reached her final destination in Freudian psychoanalysis.

Freud's repression of the mother figure, her symbolic burial, is also a lyrical act not very different from Petrarch's immortalization of Laura, Baudelaire's memorialization/marmorealization of the female passerby, and Truffaut's idealization of Catherine in *Jules and Jim*. Like the poet and the filmmaker Freud is eternalizing woman, in his case the mother, by preserving her body in fragments. This act enables him, as it did for Petrarch, Baudelaire, and Truffaut, to keep his masculinity intact, to give him full access to "manhood." But it is precisely this same move that marks Baudelaire, Truffaut, and Freud's ultimate inability to confront the feminine and the maternal and prevents them from entering postmodernity, into a new definition of manhood.

Conclusion

"Cinema can and does fragment the body," claims Stephen Heath[1] as he comments on the "invention" of the close-up shot by D. W. Griffith, who was reprimanded by his producer claiming that the public expected to see actors in full human form rather than simply enlarged sections of their bodies. The producer's perception of the public's scopophilic desire for entirely represented subjects, for complete and thus visually satisfying bodies, is accurate. In addition to the necessity of representing individuals in full, however, Griffith had also realized that the slow satisfaction of this desire "to see it all" should be part and parcel of filmmaking strategy. In his mind, the fragmentation of the body was a way of teasing the public's desire to apprehend the whole body visually, and "teasing" becomes an essential feature in the unfolding of the visual narrative that reveals fragments of a whole bit by bit, that promises to show the full body each time it proffers a part of it. Heath calls this whole "the pay-off," by which he means the final presentation of the anticipated entire body: "the human person, the total image of the body seen is always the pay-off" (184).

The pay-off of this study of the fragmented female body in Baudelaire's poetry, Truffaut's cinema, and Freud's psychoanalysis is an understanding of the way in which woman's body has been transformed by acts of cutting and suturing directed by a complex male desire to carve, capture, and represent all of her, a task that proved difficult, if not impossible, as, for example, in Baudelaire's failed attempt to collect woman's fullness in his poem "All of Her." The second pay-off here is the affirmation that poetry, cinema, and psychoanalysis intersect, that their point of intersection can be formulated in terms of a common male desire to cut the body of the female subject in the text. However simple this proposition may appear, it has led us to a questioning of the traditional (oedipal) direction of male desire and to challenging the very premise of what constitutes the essence of masculinity. My claim that the study of the fragmented female body in Baudelaire's, Truffaut's, and Freud's work offers similar views on various manifestations of male desire emanating from three very different disciplines has made it possible to arrive at a notion of masculine identity that no longer exists separately from femininity and "mothering," two notions that Freudian psychoanalysis has consistently viewed as subordinate to masculinity and inessential to the oedipal development of male identity.

While the concept most repressed and misunderstood by psychoanalysis is that of the woman's body, it is precisely her physicality that is most represented in poetry and cinema. Psychoanalytical knowledge of woman's body remains minimal because it is a tributary of the larger concern with male castration; for their part poetry and cinema exercise the constant fetishization of the female body, thus offering a broad panorama of the dissected female body. For example, we have examined the ways in which women's bodies appear as dispersed written and visual manifestations in various poems such as "Beauty" and "To a Passer-by" and in films such as *Jules and Jim* and *The Man Who Loved Women*. We have established that woman's body in Baudelaire's poems and Truffaut's films was dissected by their male persona, motivated by his frustrated desire to apprehend the mystery of femininity, a mystery very familiar to Freud and also responsible for his frustration with concepts of female sexuality and femininity. Baudelaire composes poems such as "A Martyr," which discloses the vision of a decapitated female lover, and "A Beautiful Ship," in which the speaking subject fetishizes the body of the female passerby. Likewise, Truffaut is repeatedly attracted by glimpses of women's legs and faces, which he emphasizes in striking close-up shots throughout his films. Fragmentation and fetishization have become natural companions to close-up shots; each time bodies appear on screen they are inevitably broken down in pieces, often by way of the close-up. Not all bodies have shared an equal amount of time under the "dissecting" and enlarging eye of the camera; in filmic representations of the body the close-up shot has broken the gender neutrality that it may have enjoyed in Griffith's time, later becoming the technical process in which male desire found its ideal medium to "cut" the female body, to fragment and fetishize it unrestrictedly.

First, we have identified the way in which, in their attempts to capture aesthetically pleasing images of women, the poet and the filmmaker dissect the female body and luxuriate in the disclosing of her itemized body. In Baudelaire's poetry and Truffaut's cinema the incisions characterizing the female body lend themselves to understanding the common ground on which poem and film meet. By cutting the female body in bits and pieces, Baudelaire and Truffaut perform the lyrical ritual exemplified in Petrarch's *Canzoniere,* in which the subject, inspired by the vision of Laura, (re)mem-

bers her in its dismembered form. From our examination of Petrarch's fragmented form of poetry we have established that part of the lyric tradition
was based on the way in which the poet approaches and treats the female
body, that is, with great idealistic expectations but also with great fear that
within its unexplored territory may dwell a force capable of destroying him.
The lyric tradition (as it manifests itself in poetry and cinema) thus seems
intimately linked to the primordial act of cutting up the body. Baudelaire
attests to the act of cutting inherent in poetry in a letter to his publisher
Arsène Houssaye: "We can cut wherever we want, I my reverie, you the
manuscript, the reader his reading" (1:275). For Truffaut framing techniques become the crucial manner that attest to his cutting the female body,
which then appears in dismembered form in various photographs, slides,
paintings.

Cutting the female body is a deep-seated feature of Baudelaire's poetry
and Truffaut's cinema, an act that brings their respective works together
under the lyrical mode of disclosing fragmented images of woman. "Lyric
cinema" is a cinema depending on the representations of the dissected
woman, as, for example, the manner in which Truffaut focuses on women's
legs in his films and particularly in *The Man Who Loved Women*. The same
cinematic obsession for women's legs has caused the male subject in Baudelaire's "To a Passer-by" to restrict his apprehension of femininity to a patch-
work of various fetishes. For Baudelaire and Truffaut the female body manifests itself in a fetishized form not different from the one presented in
Freud's theoretical assumption that the female body does not exist in and of
itself except to present the male subject with the terrifying consequences of
castration on the body. Because castration theory by itself offers but limited
patterns of understanding for the female representations at hand, this study
took a "sharp" turn to consider the suture as a mode of reparation for bodies abused by the castrating cut and its analogues: decapitation, fetishization. We established that woman's fragmented body was then subsequently
repaired, sutured by the artist's and the analyst's desire in an unexpected
attempt to retrieve the lost plenitude with the mother's body and the eternal
maternal bond that remains untouched beyond and despite all cuts. Sur-
mounting their own repression of the mother's body, Baudelaire, Truffaut,
and Freud adopt maternal gestures to explore their deflected sense of motherhood and create textual bodies with renewed cutting practices inspired by
the birth cut, a paradoxical cut that is not alienating in the separation it naturally induces but satisfying in the psychological and emotional bonding
that occurs between mother and child. In this configuration the umbilical
cut comes to signify the possibility of a new and satisfying symbolic gesture

of bodily separation at birth, a cut not to be feared but repeated safely in all acts of creation: birth as the suturing model for an undisputable and necessary separation. Even though separation is always accompanied with some form of loss—what Lacan calls "object little a"—the primary mother and child nexus provides the last part of this study with a model for a new understanding of the cut, both tragic as it separates and gratifying as it is restored and sutured.

Yet, because "maternal" desire is not as openly represented as the desire to cut, its repressed nature forces the artists/analyst to deal with it in a continuous state of denial toward the mother's body. As they negate the mother's body, Baudelaire, Truffaut, and Freud disclose moments of textual repression that have affected their poems, films, and analyses: Baudelaire's denial of the mother in "Blessing"; Truffaut's constant and consistent representation of the appalling mother; Freud's theoretical indifference toward the mother. Whether negated or absent, the mother is nevertheless a "subtle" player in Baudelaire's, Truffaut's, and Freud's work in which she becomes the suturing agent, the healer of all cuts. We saw the way in which Baudelaire, through his assimilation of Marceline Desbordes-Valmore's maternal poetry, reunited himself with the repressed body of the mother in "Meditation"; the way Truffaut became a maternal father for the *Wild Child;* the way Freud allowed in spite of himself his repressed "womb fantasies" to seep through his main theory on dreams by way of footnotes.

Without denying the power of the Freudian cut, we have displaced it from the oedipal to the pre-oedipal stage, from a castration to a birth scenario, from a recognized discourse on sexual differences to a growing concern with the repressed yet active maternal confluence. Indeed, our work shares a growing interest evidenced in a number of studies that have been published on the maternal aspect of male identity, on its slow appearance in the masculine arena and on its power to transform men's established roles as fathers and leaders into "(post)modern" men rediscovering with pleasure their role as "mothers" and caregivers, a role that has allowed them also to share their psychological and social position with women. Some of these texts have greatly contributed to the theoretical framework in the final chapter on maternal fantasies—among others, feminist philosopher Sara Ruddick's *Maternal Thinking: Toward a Politics of Peace* (1989), in which she challenges traditional masculinity by singling out and recognizing the mothering potential at work in the male psyche: "A man does not, by becoming a mother, give up his male body or any part of it. To be sure, by becoming a mother he will, in many social groups, challenge the ideology of masculinity" (43); literary critic Madelon Sprengnether's *The Spectral*

Mother: Freud, Feminism, and Psychoanalysis (1990), in which she examines Freud's denial of the male (and female) subject's early maternal experience, his pre-oedipal relationship with the mother; French psychoanalyst Danièle Brun's *La Maternité et le féminin* (1990), in which, while examining femininity and maternity, she pursues a remarkable study of man's complex desire to (re)produce, a desire that Freud totally bypassed; French analyst Simone Bécache's *Le Désir et la maternité* (1993), in which she gives a full history of the psychoanalytical studies and interpretations of maternal desire as it affects both men and women; cultural analyst Elisabeth Badinter's *XY: de l'identité masculine* (1992), in which she offers a complete analysis of man's identity, his enigmas, his desires, his differences from and similarities with woman; finally, literary comparatist Ann Kaplan's *Motherhood and Representation: The Mother in Popular Culture and Melodrama* (1992), in which the author concludes her analysis of the "mother-paradigm" in modern culture on the increasing number of popular images (advertising, cinema) of the "nurturing" father.[2]

These studies constitute an important theoretical body of work, forceful and inspiring, which accounts for a new cultural phenomenon: that of the maternal, or mothering, man who has put aside his fears and has begun looking into his own repression of the maternal body, thus allowing him to familiarize himself with the mother "inside" without jeopardizing his masculine identity. However fragile, these recent discourses on masculinity have in fact evolved from and grown out of the denial of the mother faithfully and fearfully practiced by Baudelaire, Freud, and Truffaut. In the end this study of three "creative" men representing women in their respective fields by way of the cut represents another manifestation of a real and productive anxiety in the extended age of modernity during which what I have referred to as "lyricism" continued to be the main provider of images of women.

This study on Baudelaire, Freud, and Truffaut—three "old romantics" still attached to lyrical modes of representation while teetering on the edges of modernity, three innovators in their own field, three *painters* of bodies whose work, as I have shown, owes much of its originality to fantasies of motherhood—is also foreshadowing concerns of the postmodern age. In truth, for a collective late-romantic Imaginary to be nursing what Ann Kaplan qualifies as a postmodern desire to become maternal is historically unthinkable. Hence, naturally, Baudelaire, Freud, and Truffaut fail to symbolize the maternal fully, except when displaying this particular lack with unappealing representations of the mother. For them maternal fantasies remain a negation in the Freudian sense, that is, a latent desire that wishes for what it cannot have and therefore denies it and refutes it forcefully. It has been my purpose to highlight the latent but nonetheless active role of maternal fantasies in representations of women by late-romantic *authors* of "lyrical descent," to see the way in which their achievements already bear the traces of the early stirring of the postmodern concept of "becoming" maternal, despite and beyond their intention to keep woman docile, beautiful, and barren. Whether out of fear or fascination, when they cut the woman's body, Baudelaire, Freud, and Truffaut are less destructive that they are productive—even (re)productive—of a discourse on the mother that they could only historically symbolize through rejection.

Notes

Introduction

1. All quoted references to Baudelaire are from *Oeuvres complètes*, vols. 1–2 (Paris: Gallimard, Bibliothèque de la Pléiade, 1975, 1976); and *Correspondance*, vols. 1–2 (Paris: Gallimard, Bibliothèque de la Pléiade, 1973). Whenever possible and appropriate, published translations are used, and their references are indicated. English translations without publication references are my own.

2. All references to Truffaut's filmography, correspondence, and criticism are quoted from published translations when available and appropriate and followed by their references. English translations without references are my own.

3. To facilitate the reading of all quoted references to Freud I have opted to cite him from the readily available Collected Papers edition published by Collier Books and from the Norton Library; *The Interpretation of Dreams* is from Avon Books (see bibliography).

4. In his effort to establish the idea of the compelling dismemberment of the text, Derrida prescribes and performs a carving out of Philippe Sollers's *Nombres*, insisting on the nonoriginary and plural nature of his own performance, thus demonstrating the very terms of the disseminated text. *La Dissémination* (Paris: Seuil, 1972), 334.

5. Leo Bersani, *Baudelaire and Freud* (Berkeley and Los Angeles: University of California Press, 1977), 14.

6. Anne Gillain, *François Truffaut. Le secret perdu* (Paris: Hatier, 1991).

7. Naomi Schor, *Reading in Detail: Aesthetics and the Feminine* (New York: Methuen, 1987), 68.

8. Jacques-Alain Miller, "Suture (Elements of the Logic of the Signifier)," *Screen* 13, no. 4 (1977–78): 26.

9. François Baudry, *L'Intime: Études sur l'objet* (Montpellier: Editions de l'Eclat, 1988), 19.

10. Jacques Derrida, *La Dissémination* (Paris: Seuil, 1972), 336.

11. Roland Barthes, *Le Plaisir du texte* (Paris: Seuil, 1973), 19.

12. Jacques Derrida, *La Dissémination*, 337.

13. Didier Anzieu, *Le Corps de l'oeuvre* (Paris: Gallimard, 1981), 72.

14. Baudry, *L'Intime*, 21.

15. *Le Petit Robert, Dictionnaire de la langue française* (Paris: Robert, 1986); Ira

Konigsberg, *The Complete Film Dictionary* (New York: New American Library, 1987); Henri Morier, *Dictionnaire de poétique et de rhétorique* (Paris: PUF, 1961); TVF Brogan, ed., *The New Princeton Handbook of Poetic Terms* (Princeton: Princeton University Press, 1994); Roland Chemama, dir., *Dictionnaire de la psychanalyse* (Paris: Larousse, 1993); J. Laplanche and J. B. Pontalis, *Vocabulaire de la psychanalyse* (Paris: PUF, 1967).

16. Sigmund Freud, "Psychoanalysis," *Character and Culture* (New York: Collier Books, 1963), 234.

17. Here we are reminded of Ludwig Wittgenstein's distinction between image and picture. In his *Philosophical Investigations* he points to the difference between the two: the image (*Vorstellung*) is an indirect representation, while the picture (*Bild*) is a direct representation. The contrast between image and picture has no destructive effect on the final relationship that the two propositions may enjoy together. Wittgenstein's support of the correlative link between image and picture becomes apparent when in fragment 301 he remarks: "An image is not a picture, but a picture can correspond to it" (*Philosophical Investigations,* trans. G. E. M. Anscombe (New York: Macmillan, 1968).

18. Jean Cocteau, *Le Testament d'Orphée,* film (Monaco: Ed. du Rocher, 1961).

19. Charles Baudelaire, *The Painter of Modern Life and Other Essays,* trans. Jonathan Mayne (New York: Da Capo, 1964), 12–15.

20. Gotthold Ephraim Lessing, *Laocoön: An Essay on the Limits of Painting and Poetry,* trans. Edward A. McCormick (Indianapolis: Bobbs-Merrill, 1962).

21. Jacques Lacan, "De la jouissance," *Séminaire XX: Encore* (Paris: Seuil, 1975), 9–18.

22. Stanley Cavell, "Baudelaire and the Myths of Film," *The World Viewed: Reflections on the Ontology of Film* (Cambridge, MA: Harvard University Press, 1971), 43.

23. This phrase refers to Steven Spielberg's 1977 film *Close Encounters of the Third Kind,* in which François Truffaut played the role of a French scientist, Claude Lacombe, leading a group of American scientists investigating extraterrestrial sightings.

24. Critics such as Stanley Kaufman have found this expressive quality in Truffaut's cinema an anachronism at a time when the French cinema of the new wave looked ahead to a renewed perception of contemporary culture. See Kaufman, *A World on Film* (New York: Delta Books, 1958).

25. In his recent analysis of the crucial function of the literary intertext in films made by French new wave directors, T. Jefferson Kline sees Truffaut's literary affinities as part of the way in which he constructs his main female character, Catherine, in his 1961 film *Jules and Jim.* In particular he demonstrates the way Merimée's *Vénus d'Ille* and Goethe's *Elective Affinities* become the literary "screen" that delineates Catherine's twofold personality, drawing a clear image for each separate side of her doubleness. See *Screening the Text* (Baltimore: Johns Hopkins University Press, 1992), 7–23.

26. François Truffaut, *Le Plaisir des yeux* (Paris: Cahiers du Cinéma, 1987), 130.

27. We owe this formulation to French poet and critic Michel Deguy, to whom Art, with a capital *A*, is characterized as simultaneously diverse and singular—diverse because it presents several artistic forms and singular because these forms are linked together to create something "comme-un," which in English may be translated as "like-one" and "comm-on(e)." In *La Poésie n'est pas seule. Court traité de poétique* (Paris: Seuil, 1987) he writes: "The arts are several, numerous, diversified. Something links them, make them *like-one/comm-on(e)*, and this affinity is marked by the use of the singular form, the capital A, the collective-Art. In addition, something disjoins them, engages them individually to the specific matter isolating them" (142). According to this formulation, in becoming *like-one/comm-on(e)*, different art forms live in a mimetic relationship, as indicated by the adverbial conjunction *like*, while keeping their own sense of individuality inscribed in the numeral adjective *one*, to become "comm-on(e)," which then implies the alliance between the arts and Art.

28. Sigmund Freud, "Femininity," *New Introductory Lectures on Psychoanalysis* (New York: Norton, 1965).

29. Jean Laplanche and J. B. Pontalis, *Fantasme originaire, fantasme des origines, origines du fantasme* (Paris: Hachette, 1985).

Chapter 1

1. Baudelaire, *Paris Spleen,* trans. Louise Varèse (New York: New Directions Paperbook, 1970), ix–x.

2. According to Schor (*Reading in Detail. Aesthetics and the Feminine* [New York: Methuen, 1987], 4), the detail has traditionally been associated with the feminine, which it devalorized in the process. Schor sets out to take such an association apart; beyond her effort to release the detail from the feminine sphere, however, she still wonders "whether or not the 'feminine' is a male construct," whether or not feminine specificity can emerge unscathed from "the deadly asperities of male violence and destruction" (97).

3. "Approaching the Lyric," *Lyric Poetry,* ed. Chaviva Hošek and Patricia Parker (Ithaca: Cornell University Press, 1985), 33.

4. These operations contribute to the dismembered female body on display throughout Baudelaire's lyrical poems. They also contribute to the composition of poems like "The Beautiful Ship" in which female body parts are carefully disposed within the rhythmical spaces separated by an array of poetic cuts.

Baudelaire's action of cutting the body has also become part of a critical practice developed by the structuralist school. In his celebrated reading of Baudelaire's poem "The Cats" Roman Jakobson applies a methodology of cutting, or "detailing," as I have referred to it previously, to poetry as an innovative and effective way of analyzing textual enterprises in all literary genres. For Jakobson the poem is a dissectible object par excellence, and in his incisive analysis the poem stands in a reflexive position vis-à-vis the dissected bodies of the poetic cats. Structuralist linguistics treats the bodies in the poem (cats, Sphinxes, women) as main providers of grammatical and lyrical tools that, when applied to the versified body of the poem, reenact problematics of gender differences. Roman Jakobson, "'Les Chats' de Charles Baudelaire," *Questions de poétique* (Paris: Seuil, 1973), 401–19.

5. Christian Metz, *Le Signifiant imaginaire* (Paris: Christian Bourgois, 1984).

6. See chapter 3 for an analysis of this fetishistic motif.

7. The same question is also put forth by many other male characters in Truffaut's films.

8. Truffaut, *Le Plaisir des yeux* (Paris: Cahiers du Cinema, 1987).

9. Isabelle Adjani made her debut in Truffaut's film *The Story of Adèle H.* (1975), in which she plays the compelling role of nineteenth-century French writer Victor Hugo's daughter, who relentlessly pursues the soldier she loves in all his faraway military outposts.

10. Charles Baudelaire, "Woman," *The Painter of Modern Life and Other Essays,* trans. Jonathan Mayne (New York: Da Capo, 1964).

11. Nicolas Boileau, *Oeuvres complètes* (Paris: Editions de la Pléiade, 1966), 546.

12. Immanuel Kant, *The Critique of Judgment,* trans. James Creed Meredith (Oxford: Oxford University Press, 1952); *The Philosophy of Kant,* ed. Carl Friedrich (New York: Random House, 1952).

13. Louis Marin, "On the Sublime, Infinity, Je ne Sais Quoi," in *A New History of French Literature,* ed. Denis Hollier (Cambridge, MA: Harvard University Press, 1989), 340–45.

14. Immanuel Kant, "The Sense of the Beautiful and of the Sublime," *The Philosophy of Kant,* ed. Carl Friedrich (New York: Random House, 1952), 4.

15. *Séminaire 11,* 53.

Chapter 2

1. Petrarch, *Lyric Poems: The Rime Sparse and Other Lyrics,* ed. and trans. Robert Durling (Cambridge, MA: Harvard University Press, 1976).

2. Théodore de Banville, *Petit traité de poésie française* (Paris: G Charpentier et Cie, 1988), 4–5.

3. Robert Durling, *Petrarch's Lyric Poems: The Rime Sparse and Other Lyrics* (Cambridge, MA: Harvard University Press, 1976), 26.

4. Georg Hegel, *Aesthetics: Lectures on Fine Arts,* trans. T. M. Knox (Oxford: Clarendon Press, 1975), 981.

5. Giuseppe Mazzotta, "The Canzoniere and the Language of the Self," *Studies in Philology* 75 (1978): 271–96, 294–95.

6. Teresa De Lauretis, *Alice Doesn't: Feminism, Semiotics, Cinema* (Bloomington: Indiana University Press, 1984), 13.

7. Nancy J. Vickers, "Diana Described: Scattered Woman and Scattered Rhyme," *Critical Inquiry* 8, no. 2 (Winter 1981): 266.

8. Yves Bonnefoy, *L'Improbable et autres essais* (Paris: Gallimard, 1980), 36.

9. Michel Foucault, "Qu'est-ce que les lumières?" *Le Magazine Littéraire* 309 (Apr. 1993): 67.

10. Blaise Pascal, *Pensées* (Paris: Librairie Générale Française, 1972), 32.

11. Michel Deguy, "Le Corps de Jeanne," *Poétique* 3 (1970): 334–47.

12. Annette Insdorf chooses to give the fourth chapter of her classic book on Truffaut the title "Are Women Magic?" See *François Truffaut* (1978; rpt., Cambridge: Cambridge University Press, 1994).

13. Anne Gillain, *François Truffaut. Le secret perdu* (Paris: Hatier, 1991).

14. More specifically, it is the "rotor," "a large wooden cylindrical drum in which people flattened against the side walls, are suspended in mid-air by the centrifugal force as the drum whirls around at top speed" (*Adventures of Antoine Doinel*, 23), which attracts Antoine at the amusement park. Truffaut, following the cinematic tradition established by Hitchcock, actually makes a cameo appearance in the rotor scene; he physically enters the rotor with Antoine.

15. Naomi Schor, *Reading in Detail: Aesthetics and the Feminine* (New York: Methuen, 1987), 84.

16. Roland Barthes, *Mythologies* (Paris: Seuil, 1957), 70.

17. In 1960 Truffaut produced Cocteau's novel *Le Testament d'Orphée.*

18. *The New Wave: Truffaut, Godard, Chabrol, Rhomer, Rivette* (New York: Oxford University Press, 1976).

19. I do not intend to offer a limiting version of the cinematic apparatus but simply wish to recall that the human voice was not part of the filmic experience in the first decades in the development of cinema. Cinema was primarily a visual experience sometimes supplemented by musical arrangement but always without vocal dialogues. For Truffaut voice always occupies a distinctive place in relation to the image it narrates. Indeed, Truffaut often uses the narrative voice-over to comment on his images, or, as in the case of *Jules and Jim,* voice stands by itself against the absence of images. Truffaut's desire is less to blend sound and image than to dramatize one in contrast with the other.

20. In the *Acoustic Mirror* Silverman lays out some of the different theories and practices informing her discussion on the maternal voice in the course of two lengthy chapters (72–140). These chapters are valuable accounts on the different perspectives shaping the question of the influence of the maternal voice in the infant's life and its practical translation into the filmic creation. The first chapter convincingly applies the opposing views of Michel Chion and Guy Rosolato, respectively, to Litvak's *Sorry, Wrong Number* (1948) and to Beinneix's *Diva* (1981). Although the actual readings of both films cover a minimal number of Silverman's arguments, she nonetheless creates propitious discursive conditions for the dialectical nature of Chion's and Rosolato's theories, which will be further discussed in this section. In the following chapter Silverman focuses on Julia Kristeva's various writings on motherhood, and she uses *Riddles of the Sphinx,* a 1977 film directed by Laura Mulvey and Peter Wollen, to deconstruct Kristeva's limited view on the spiritualized mother-infant dyad.

21. See Guy Rosolato, "La Voix. Entre corps et langage," *Revue Française de Psychanalyse* 37, no. 1 (1974): 79.

22. Jacques Lacan, "Le Stade du miroir," *Ecrits* (Paris: Seuil, 1966), 93–100.

23. In *The Child before Birth* (Ithaca: Cornell University Press, 1978) Linda Ferrill Annis offers a clear account of fetal sensory development. Her research has led her to confirm the poor visual power of the newborn in sharp contrast with his or her almost fully developed auditive perception. A few hours after birth the child is able to distinguish sounds clearly, while his or her eyesight remains weak until the fourth month. In fact, the child's ability to focus on details continues to improve until the sixth birthday (52–58).

24. Michel Chion, *La Voix au cinéma* (Paris: Editions de l'Etoile, 1982).

25. Translation mine.

26. As I have examined it in chapter 1, Lacan gives sporadic theoretical glimpses of the Real throughout his (published) writings. In *Séminaire 2,* as he rereads Freud's prototypical dream about Irma, one of his hysterical female patients, he locates the possible emergence of the Real inside her mouth. According to him, the subject loses itself under the horrifying vision presented by the interiority of Irma's mouth. Confronted with the horror generated by "the abyss of the female organ," which may be seen as the abyss of the female genitalia, the subject cannot produce any signifying system of communication and representation to speak of the spectacle offered by femininity, by the "real" apparition of woman's body (196).

The Real cannot speak, however; it reveals itself unexpectedly, unsettling the subject and threatening its existence. Similarly, the spectator/subject under construction in *Jules and Jim* is threatened to lose its visual identification power when the female voice leaps out of the dark screen several times to unsettle its specular integrity.

27. *Le Cinéma selon Hitchcock* (Paris: Robert Laffont, 1966).

28. Leo Bersani, *Baudelaire and Freud* (Berkeley and Los Angeles: University of California Press, 1977), 86.

29. "Diana Described: Scattered Woman and Scattered Rhyme," *Critical Inquiry* 8, no. 2 (Winter 1981): 265–79.

Chapter 3

1. Jacques Lacan, *Séminaire 11* (Paris: Seuil, 1973), 181.

2. Serge André, *Que veut une femme?* (Paris: Navarin, 1986), 221.

3. Roland Barthes, *S/Z* (Paris: Seuil, 1970), 120.

4. Translation mine.

5. Sigmund Freud, "Female Sexuality," *Sexuality and the Psychology of Love* (New York: Collier, 1963), 198.

6. Michel Foucault, "What Is an Author?," *Language, Counter-Memory, Practice* (Ithaca: Cornell University Press), 113–38.

7. Jacques Lacan, *Ecrits* (Paris: Seuil, 1966), 285.

8. Jane Gallop, *Reading Lacan* (Ithaca: Cornell University Press, 1985), 148.

9. Freud, *New Introductory Lectures on Psychoanalysis,* 135.

10. Freud, "Some Psychological Consequences of the Anatomical Distinction

between the Sexes," *Sexuality and the Psychology of Love* (New York: Collier, 1963), 187.

11. J. B. Hubert, *L'Esthétique des "Fleurs du mal"* (Genève: Cailler, 1953), 228–33.

12. Freud, *Beyond the Pleasure Principle* (New York: Norton, 1961), 7.

13. In order to demonstrate the private character of pain and its impossibility ever to denote a single object, Wittgenstein, in sections 293–94 of his *Philosophical Investigations* (trans. G. E. M. Anscombe [New York: Macmillan, 1953]), gives the example of "the beetle in the box," in which everyone knows what a beetle is, after looking at their own beetle locked in their own box.

14. See Georges Blin, *Le Sadisme de Baudelaire* (Paris: Corti, 1948); Léo Bersani, *Baudelaire and Freud* (Berkeley and Los Angeles: University of California Press, 1977).

15. Freud, "The Economic Problem of Masochism," *General Psychological Theory* (New York: Collier, 1963), 288.

16. Robert Smadja, *Poétique du corps. L'image du corps chez Baudelaire et Henri Michaux* (New York: Peter Lang, 1988), 13.

17. Acrisius is informed by the oracle that, if his daughter, Danae, were to give birth to a male child, the latter would later in life kill his grandfather. Acrisius locks his daughter up in a bedroom built beneath the castle; however, she is secretly visited by Zeus, who appears in the form of a golden shower. From their amorous encounter a male child named Perseus is born. Fearing for his life but incapable of killing his own daughter, Acrisius locks Danae and Perseus in a coffinlike ark that he throws into the sea. Danae and Perseus are later rescued by a fisherman off the island of Seriphos, where they are both welcomed to stay. Polydectes, the ruler and tyrant of Seriphos, falls in love with Danae, who is protected by her now grown son. Like all the youth on the island, Perseus has to present Polydectes with a wedding gift when the latter pretends that he will marry Hippodameia. Overjoyed by the prospective wedding of Polydectes with someone other than his mother, Perseus suggests giving Polydectes the "impossible" gift: the head of the Gorgon Medusa. Polydectes accepts. Perseus sets forth on his dangerous adventure, which will eventually lead him to the cave where the frightful monster lives. Made invisible by Hades' helmet and using a shield to catch the reflection of Medusa indirectly, he finally beheads her and continues to use her decapitated head to kill/petrify his enemies when he returns to Seriphos. It is only later in the Perseus story that he accidentally kills his grandfather, Acrisius. Robert Graves, *Greek Myths* (Baltimore: Penguin Books, 1957).

18. She asks: "What being with only one voice, has sometimes two feet, sometimes three, sometimes four, and is weakest when it has the most?" Graves, *Greek Myths,* 2:10.

19. Jean-Pierre Vernant, *La Mort dans les yeux* (Paris: Hachette, 1986), 80.

20. Notes, and footnotes, hold a particular fascination for critical readers of Freudian psychoanalysis, who also derive analytical pleasure in reading private texts. It may be because of their implicit yet essential nature that notes and footnotes—as they form a sort of subtextual network of ideas not yet fully formed—have attracted a number of critical readers. Among them Shoshana Felman has offered a

compelling analysis of an intriguing and valuable footnote from Freud's *Interpretation of Dreams* ("Postal Survival, or the Question of the Navel," *Yale French Studies* 69 [1985]: 49–70). The footnote in question reveals an analogy between the navel and the point of unplumbability in the dream. Felman argues that the navel figures a knot of women tying Freud's tongue on the subject of femininity, hence tying the psychoanalytical dialogue to the (re)production of a feminine resistance to Freud's theory. I will return to this idea in chapter 4, when dealing with Freud's womb fantasies.

21. Neil Hertz, *The End of the Line: Essays on Psychoanalysis and the Sublime* (New York: Columbia University Press, 1985).

22. Freud, "Medusa's Head," *Sexuality and the Psychology of Love* (New York: Collier, 1963), 212.

23. Hélène Cixous, "The Laugh of the Medusa," *New French Feminism*, ed. Elaine Marks and Isabelle de Courtivron (New York: Schocken Books, 1981).

24. Marks and de Courtivron, *New French Feminism*, 255.

25. Cixous, "Castration or Decapitation?" *Signs* 7, no. 1 (1981): 49.

26. Translations are mine, from Roland Barthes, *La Chambre claire. Note sur la photographie* (Paris: Cahiers du Cinéma, Gallimard, Seuil, 1980).

27. All translations from Barthes, *La Chambre claire*, are mine.

28. See chapter 2.

29. Jacques Derrida, *La Vérité en peinture* (Paris: Flammarion, 1978).

30. Anne Gillain, *Le Cinéma selon Truffaut* (Paris: Flammarion, 1988), 248.

31. Derrida, *La Vérité en peinture*, 93.

32. Georges Blin, *Le Sadisme de Baudelaire* (Paris: Corti, 1948), 31.

33. In French the word *coupable* means both "guilty" and "cuttable." The pleasures evoked in the poem may be intimately linked to the expression of guilt felt by the voyeuristic subject observing the total erotic abandonment of the female body, and it may also be referring to the subject's realization that her decapitation satisfies his own sadistic desire to cut her body.

34. Freud, "The Infantile Genital Organization of the Libido," *Sexuality and the Psychology of Love* (New York: Collier, 1963), 173.

35. Guy Rosolato, *Le Désir et la perversion* (Paris: Seuil, 1967), 17.

36. Metz, *Le Signifiant imaginaire*, 71.

37. The translation of *feston* by the word *furbelow* (*fur/below*) is a pun intended by the translator sensitized to the fetishistic implications of this trimming on the woman's gown. In fact, Freud accounts for the fetishistic qualities of furs with regard to the little boy's first encounter with the mother's genitals: "Velvet and fur reproduce the sight of the pubic hair which ought to have revealed the longed-for penis." "Fetishism," *Sexuality and the Psychology of Love*, 217.

38. His desire is a real desire in Lacanian terms, an unsatisfied desire; it is a desire to desire, according to Lacan, a desire without any other object than itself. See "Direction of Treatment and Principles of Its Power," *Ecrits*, 256–77.

39. Scarry, *Body in Pain*, 162.

40. With the low-angle shot the subject looks up toward its object, a visual angle that allows him to peep from underneath between the woman's legs. The study later

addresses the question of the low-angle shot as a perverse shot, easily transportable into Freud's scenario on fetishism. What the low-angle technically reenacts is the spatial relationship of the body of the young child when he looks up at his mother's body to discover the shocking reality of her "mutilated" genitals. In *Lettre ouverte à François Truffaut* (Paris: Albin Michel, 1987) Eric Neuhoff notes the infantile quality of the low-angle shot used by Truffaut each time he directs his camera on women's legs: "From an early age, boys grow up amidst a forest of knees. Similarly, your heroes peek at women's legs from underneath, as if they were still children. You were just like them, you only saw women in low-angle shots" (59).

41. Truffaut, *Jules et Jim* (Paris: Seuil, 1971), 9.

42. Tom Conley, "Vigo Van Gogh," *New York Literary Forum* 5 (1983): 154.

43. Roland Barthes, *Barthes by Barthes* (New York: Hill and Wang, 1977), 68.

44. Freud, "Fetishism," *Sexuality and the Psychology of Love*, 217.

Chapter 4

1. The film was adapted in 1987 by American director Leonard Nimoy under the title *Three Men and a Baby*.

2. Among other films revolving around the theme of male pregnancy let me mention two popular farces, a French one: *L'Evénement le plus important depuis que l'homme a marché sur la lune*, by Jacques Demy (1973), and a recent American one, *Junior*, by Ivan Reitman (1994).

3. For Freud the expression *dream woman* must be taken quite literally as we see him develop his scientific method of exploring the human unconscious starting with the analysis of his own "specimen" dream, which offers a scene from his private oneiric theater involving him and one of his female patients, Irma. In *The Interpretation of Dreams* Irma is Freud's "dream woman."

4. Tania Modleski, *Feminism without Women: Culture and Criticism in a "Postfeminist" Age* (New York: Routledge, 1991), 78.

5. For a pertinent reading of the Madonna figure in Western art and in psychoanalysis, see Mary Jacobus, *Reading Woman* (New York: Columbia University Press, 1986), 137–93.

6. Cynthia is the name given to the moon by a number of English poets, among them Shakespeare, Keats, Byron, and Shelley.

7. The speaker in "The Moon Offended" intrudes on Cynthia's privacy by questioning her love relationship with Endymion: "Do you yet steal with clandestine embraces / To clasp Endymion's pale, millennial charm?" In Greek mythology Cynthia—Diana, the moon—fell passionately in love with a handsome shepherd called Endymion. After putting him to sleep, she visited him every night and kissed him in his sleep. She also obtained from Jupiter that Endymion be endowed with eternal beauty. Endymion is associated with Cynthia's secret love affair, and for Cynthia, characterized as a cold and insensitive divinity, the poet's question about her relationship with Endymion represents as much an intrusion into her buried secret as her offensive words represent an intrusion into the poet's secret love for his mother.

Beyond the personal offense Cynthia's chafing words could be interpreted as a jealous reaction directed against the poet—himself an Endymionic figure in the poem—whose love for his mother seems to compete and clash with Cynthia's legendary demand for the exclusivity of his passion.

8. The silence of the poet after he is confronted with the unexpected and offensive image of his mother has been interpreted by Jacques Crépet (Baudelaire 1:1111–14) in relationship to Baudelaire's life. "The Offended Moon" is a very early piece that Baudelaire chose not to publish in the two editions of *Flowers of Evil,* as if, according to Crépet, he felt that the second tercet would hurt his mother's feelings. Finally, in 1862 Baudelaire published "The Offended Moon" in the journal *L'Artiste,* but it was only after his death, and at Asselineau's request, that Baudelaire's mother saw the copy of *L'Artiste* in which the poem first appeared. The late decision to publish this early poem may be interpreted as years of silence on the part of Baudelaire, whose complete financial and emotional dependency on his mother made him reluctant to publish verses so directly related to his alienation from her, an alienation that Baudelaire could not fully accept even at times when a stormy argument between mother and son would momentarily break off their relationship.

9. Freud, *Sexual Enlightenment of Children,* 34.

10. Freud, "Anxiety and Instinctual Life," 100.

11. Ferrand's dream of feminine beauty surpasses the woman herself. Before the swimming pool scene we witness Ferrand's exasperation at Stacey, who refuses to appear in her bathing suit. For Ferrand, Stacey is only a beautiful woman on the set when she performs in the dream he has created for her. Outside the set she is the hysteric idiot who refuses to show her body, as his comment to Joëlle about Stacey indicates: "Listen, Joëlle, find me another scene to shoot in place of this one; that will give this idiot time to calm down."

12. Ferrand eventually comes to terms with the reality of Stacey's pregnancy, arranging for her to finish her work on the set before it becomes too visible. She also returns to the set at the end of her pregnancy and helps Ferrand understand Julie's sudden psychological crisis. It is as if Ferrand/Truffaut not only accepted her maternity but also placed upon it the value of female intelligence—only a mother-to-be can understand the vagaries of femininity.

13. Lacan, *Le Séminaire 2,* 196.

14. In Simone Bécache, *La Maternité et son désir* (Meyzieu: Césura Lyon Edition [Psychanalyse], 1993), 191.

15. Susan Stanford Friedman, "Creativity and the Childbirth Metaphor," *Speaking of Gender* (New York and London: Routledge, 1989), 93.

16. Anne Gillain, *François Truffaut. Le secret perdu* (Paris: Hatier, 1991), 19.

17. Melanie Klein, *Envy and Gratitude* (New York: Free Press, 1975), 142.

18. Jacques Lacan, *Four Concepts,* 214.

19. Danielle Brun, *La Maternité et le féminin* (Paris: Denoël, 1990).

20. Freud admits to his paternal feelings toward Rank in a letter he wrote to Lou Andreas-Salomé in November 1924, at the time when *The Trauma of Birth* was published: "I was very interested to hear that you had personal objections to Rank. For fifteen years he was an irreproachable assistant and a faithful son to me. Now,

since he thinks that he has made a great discovery, he is behaving so refractorily that I can only look forward to his return from America with great apprehension. [. . .] Please do not tell anyone about this for the present; perhaps it can be smoothed over. He would be difficult to replace in his many functions" (*Letters*, 138). One of Rank's "irreplaceable functions" for Freud is that of a son. Because of his filial association with Freud, Rank may be forgiven for turning away from his "father's teaching." For over fifteen years Rank was Freud's favorite disciple. They met in 1905 when Freud was forty-nine and Rank only twenty-one, just a few years older than Mathilde, Freud's oldest daughter. His young age and his enthusiasm for Freud's research made their way into the professor's heart and into his secret psychoanalytical society, The Committee.

21. Freud, *Contributions to the Psychology of Love*, 57.

22. "When the analyst succeeds in overcoming the primal resistance, namely the mother-fixation, with regard to his own person in the transference relation, then a definite term is fixed for the analysis, within which period the patient repeats automatically the new severance from the mother (substitute) figure, in the form of the reproduction of his own birth" (*Trauma of Birth*, 9).

23. Laplanche and Pontalis,*Vocabulaire de la psychanalyse*, 32.

24. Adrienne Rich, *Of Woman Born* (New York: Norton, 1986), 159.

25. Sigmund Freud, *Jokes and Their Relation to the Unconscious* (New York: Norton, 1963), 81.

26. Sarah Kofman, *Pourquoi rit-on?* (Paris: Galilée, 1986), 158.

27. Rich, *Of Woman Born*, 156–85.

28. Emily Martin, *The Woman in the Body* (Boston: Beacon Press, 1987).

29. "The Matrix of War: Mothers and Heroes," *The Female Body in Western Culture* (Cambridge: Harvard University Press, 1986), 119–36.

30. Ludwig Wittgenstein, *Philosophical Investigations*, 101, 302.

31. Melanie Klein and Joan Riviere, *Love, Hate and Reparation* (New York: Norton, 1964), 34.

32. Riviere, "Hate, Greed and Aggression," *Love, Hate and Reparation*, 32.

33. Janine Chasseguet-Smirgel, *Recherches psychanalytiques nouvelles sur la sexualité féminine* (Paris: Payot, 1964), 149.

34. Freud, *Sexuality and the Psychology of Love*, 181.

35. Baudelaire, *Letters to His Mother*, trans. Arthur Symons (New York: Haskell House, 1971), 171.

36. Thomas Szasz, *Pleasure and Pain* (Syracuse: Syracuse University Press, 1988), xxxix.

37. Susan Sontag, ed., *A Barthes Reader* (New York: Hill and Wang, 1983), 48.

38. Marceline Desbordes-Valmore, "A Little Boy's Bedtime," *Poésie* (Paris: Gallimard, 1983), 99–100.

39. Baudelaire, *Correspondance*, 1:338–41.

40. Sima Godfrey, "'Mère des souvenirs': Baudelaire, Memory and Mother," *L'Esprit Créateur* 25, no. 2 (1995): 32–44.

41. Baudelaire, *Correspondance*, 1:153.

42. Baudelaire, *Correspondance*, 1:193–94.

43. Truffaut, *Correspondence, 1945–1984,* 562.

44. Gilles Cahoreau, *François Truffaut, 1932–1984* (Paris: Julliard), 285.

45. Truffaut, *Correspondence,* 384.

46. Jean Collet, *FrançoisTruffaut* (Paris: Lherminier, 1985), 54.

47. Annette Insdorf, *François Truffaut* (1988; rpt., Cambridge: Cambridge University Press, 1994).

48. Freud, "Contributions to the Psychology of Love," 53.

49. Freud, *Inhibitions, Symptoms and Anxiety* (New York: Norton, 1959), 65.

50. Françoise Dolto, *L'Image inconsciente du corps* (Paris: Seuil, 1984).

51. Madelon Sprengnether, *The Spectral Mother: Freud, Feminism and Psychoanalysis* (Ithaca: Cornell University Press, 1990).

52. Freud, *Interpretation of Dreams,* 436.

53. Shoshana Felman, "Postal Survival, or the Question of the Navel," *Yale French Studies* 69 (1985): 49–70.

Conclusion

1. Stephen Heath, *Questions of Cinema* (Bloomington: Indiana University Press, 1981), 184.

2. Sara Ruddick, *Maternal Thinking: Toward a Politics of Peace* (New York: Ballantine Books, 1989); Madelon Sprengnether, *The Spectral Mother: Freud, Feminism, and Psychoanalysis* (Ithaca: Cornell University Press, 1990); Danièle Brun, *La Maternité et le féminin* (Paris: Denoël, 1990); Simone Bécache, *Le Désir et la maternité* (Meyzieu: Césura Lyon Edition, 1993); Elisabeth Badinter, *XY: de l'identité masculine* (Paris: Odile Jacob, 1992); Ann Kaplan, *Motherhood and Representation: The Mother in Popular Culture and Melodrama* (London and New York: Routledge, 1992).

Bibliography

Abraham, Nicolas, and Maria Torok. *L'Ecorce et le noyau*. Paris: Flammarion, 1987.

Allen, Don. *Finally Truffaut*. New York: Beaufort Books, 1985.

André, Serge. *Que veut une femme?* Paris: Navarin Editeur, 1896.

Anzieu, Didier. *Créer, détruire*. Paris: Bordas (Dunod), 1996.

———. *Le Corps de l'oeuvre*. Paris: Gallimard, 1981.

———. *Le Moi-peau*. Paris: Bordas (Dunod) 1985.

———. *Le Penser: du Moi-peau au Moi-pensant*. Paris: Bordas (Dunod), 1994.

Apter, Emily. *Feminizing the Fetish: Psychoanalysis and Narrative Obsession in Turn-of-the-Century France*. Ithaca: Cornell University Press, 1991.

Apter, Emily, and William Pietz, eds. *Fetishism as Cultural Discourse*. Ithaca: Cornell University Press, 1993.

Badinter, Elizabeth. *XY: de l'identité masculine*. Paris: Odile Jacob, 1992.

Banville, Théodore de. *Petit traité de poésie française*. Paris: G Charpentier et Cie, 1988.

Barthes, Roland. *Barthes by Barthes*. Trans. Richard Howard. New York: Hill and Wang, 1977.

———. *La Chambre claire. Note sur la photographie*. Paris: Cahiers du Cinema, Gallimard, Seuil, 1980.

———. *Mythologies*. Paris: Seuil, 1957.

———. *L'Obvie et l'obtus*. Paris: Seuil, 1982.

———. *Le Plaisir du texte*. Paris: Seuil, 1973.

———. *Roland Barthes*. Paris: Seuil (Ecrivains de Toujours), 1975.

———. *S/Z*. Paris: Seuil, 1970.

Bassim, Tamara. *La Femme dans l'oeuvre de Baudelaire*. Neuchatel: La Baconnière, 1974.

Bastide, Bernard, et al. *Etudes cinématographiques: Agnès Varda*. Paris: Minard, 1991.

Baudelaire, Charles. *Correspondance*. 2 vols. (Jan. 1832–Feb. 1860, Mar. 1860–Mar. 1866). Paris: Gallimard (Pléiade), 1973.

———. *Flowers of Evil and Other Poems of Charles Baudelaire*. Trans. Francis Duke. Charlottesville: University of Virginia Press, 1961.

———. *Flowers of Evil: A Selection*. Ed. Marthiel and Jackson Mathews. New York: New Directions, 1955.

———. *Oeuvres complètes.* 2 vols. Paris: Gallimard (Pléiade), 1975–76.

———. *One Hundred Poems from "Les Fleurs du mal."* Trans. C. F. MacIntyre. Berkeley: University of California Press, 1947.

———. *The Letters of Charles Baudelaire to His Mother.* Trans. Arthur Symons. New York: Haskell House, 1971.

———. *The Painter of Modern Life and Other Essays.* Ed. and trans. Jonathan Mayne. New York: Da Capo, 1964.

———. *Paris Spleen 1869.* Translated by Louise Varèse. New York: New Directions, 1970.

Baudry, François. *L'Intime-études sur l'objet.* Montpellier: Editions de l'Eclat, 1988.

Beardsley, Monroe. *Aesthetics from Classical Greece to the Present—A Short History.* Tuscaloosa: University of Alabama Press, 1975.

Bécache, Simone. *La Maternité et son désir.* Meyzieu: Césura Lyon Edition (Psychanalyse), 1993.

Beja, Morris. *Film and Literature: An Introduction.* Longman: Ohio State University, 1979.

Benjamin, Walter. *Charles Baudelaire: A Lyric Poet in the Era of High Capitalism.* Trans. Harry Zohn. London: New Left Books, 1973.

———. *Essais.* 2 vols. Trans. Maurice de Gandillac. Paris: Denoël/Gonthier, 1971–83.

———. *Illuminations: Essays and Reflections.* Ed. Hannah Arendt; trans. Harry Zohn. New York: Schocken Books, 1969.

Bennett, Joseph. *Baudelaire: A Criticism.* Princeton: Princeton University Press, 1946.

Bensmaïa, Reda. "Du Fragment au détail." *Poétique* 47 (Sept. 1981): 355–70.

Berheimer, Charles. *Figures of Ill Repute: Representing Prostitution in Nineteenth-Century France.* Cambridge: Harvard University Press, 1989.

Bernay, Tony, and Dorothy Cantor, eds. *The Psychology of Today's Woman: New Psychoanalytic Visions.* Cambridge: Harvard University Press, 1989.

Bersani, Leo. *Baudelaire and Freud.* Berkeley and Los Angeles: University of California Press, 1977.

Blin, Georges. *Le Sadisme de Baudelaire.* Paris: Corti, 1948.

Boland, Bernard. "L'Image et le corps." *Cahiers du Cinéma* (Aug.–Sept. 1977): 279–80.

Bonnefoy, Yves. *L'Improbable et autres essais.* Paris: Gallimard (Idées), 1980.

Bouchard, Donald, ed. *Language, Counter-Memory, Practice: Selected Essays and Interviews by Michel Foucault.* Ithaca: Cornell University Press, 1977.

Brooks, Peter. *Psychoanalysis and Storytelling.* Cambridge, MA: Blackwell, 1994.

Brun, Danièle. *La Maternité et le féminin.* Paris: Denoël, 1990.

Brunette, Peter, and Davis Wills. *Screen/Play: Derrida and Film Theory.* Princeton: Princeton University Press, 1989.

Burch, Noël. *Praxis du cinéma.* Paris: Gallimard, 1969.

Butor, Michel. *Histoire extraordinaire. Essai sur un rêve de Baudelaire.* Paris: Gallimard, 1961.

Cahoreau, Gilles. *François Truffaut. 1932–1984.* Paris: Julliard, 1989.

Cargo, Robert. *A Concordance to Baudelaire's* Les Fleurs du Mal. Chapel Hill: University of North Carolina Press, 1965.

Cavell, Stanley. *The World Viewed: Reflections on the Ontology of Film.* Cambridge: Harvard University Press, 1971.

Caws, Mary Ann. *A Metapoetics of the Passage: Architextures in Surrealism and After.* Hanover: University Press of New England, 1981.

Chambers, Ross. "Perpetual Adjuration: Baudelaire and the Pain of Modernity." *French Forum* 15, no. 2 (1990): 169–88.

Chasseguet-Smirgel, Janine. *Les Deux arbres du jardin. Essais psychanalytiques sur le rôle du père et de la mère dans la psyché.* Paris: Des Femmes, 1988.

———. *Pour une psychanalyse de l'art et de la créativité.* Paris: Payot, 1971.

———. *Recherches psychanalytiques nouvelles sur la sexualité féminine.* Paris: Payot, 1964.

Chateau, D., A. Gardies, and F. Jost, eds. *Cinémas de la modernité. Films, théories.* Paris: Klincksieck, 1981.

Chérix, Robert-Benoît. *Essai d'une critique intégrale: commentaire des "Fleurs du mal."* Geneva: Pierre Cailler, 1949.

Chion, Michel. *La Voix au cinéma.* Paris: Editions de l'Etoile, 1982.

Cixous, Hélène. "Castration or Decapitation?" *Sign* 7, no. 1 (1981): 41–55.

———. *La Jeune née.* Paris: 10/18, 1975.

———. "Le Rire de Méduse" *L'Arc* (1975). Trans. as "The Laugh of Medusa," in *New French Feminism.* New York: Schocken Books, 1981.

Clair, Jean. *Méduse.* Paris: Gallimard, 1989.

Clément, Catherine. *La Syncope. Philosophie du ravissement.* Paris: Grasset, 1990.

———. *Vies et légendes de Jacques Lacan.* Paris: Grasset, 1981.

Clifton, Roy. *The Figure in Film.* Newark: University of Delaware Press, 1983.

Cocteau, Jean. *Orphée.* Paris: Bordas, 1973.

Collet, Jean. *François Truffaut.* Paris: Pierre Lherminier, 1985.

Colville, Georgiana. "Pères perdus, pères retrouvés dans l'oeuvre de François Truffaut." *French Review* 68, no. 2 (1994): 283–93.

Conley, Tom. *Film Hieroglyphs: Ruptures in Classical Cinema.* Minneapolis: University Press of Minnesota, 1991.

———. "Vigo Van Gogh." *New York Literary Forum* 5 (1983): 153–66.

Le Corps. Analyses et réflexions. 2 vols. Paris: Editions Marketing (Ellipses), 1992.

Coven, Jeffrey, ed. *Baudelaire's Voyages: The Poet and his Painters.* Boston, New York, Toronto, and London: Little, Brown and Company, 1993.

Culler, Jonathan. *On Deconstruction: Theory and Criticism after Structuralism.* Ithaca: Cornell University Press, 1982.

———. *The Pursuit of Signs: Semiotics, Literature, Deconstruction.* Ithaca: Cornell University Press, 1981.

De Baecque, Antoine, and Serge Toubiana. *François Truffaut.* Paris: Gallimard, 1996.

Deguy, Michel. "Le Corps de Jeanne." *Poétique* 3 (1970): 334–47.

———. *La Poésie n'est pas seule. Court traité de poétique.* Paris: Seuil, 1987.

De Lauretis, Teresa. *Alice Doesn't: Feminism, Semiotics, Cinema*. Bloomington: Indiana University Press, 1984.

Deleuze, Gilles. *L'Anti-Oedipe. Capitalisme et schizophrénie*. Paris: Minuit, 1972.

———. *Anti-Oedipus. Capitalism and Schizophrenia*. Trans. Robert Hurley, Mark Seem, and Helen Lane. Minneapolis: University of Minnesota Press, 1983.

———. *Cinéma 1. L'Image-mouvement*. Paris: Editions de Minuit, 1983.

———. *Cinéma 2. L'Image-temps*. Paris: Editions de Minuit,1985.

———. *Pourparlers*. Paris: Editions de Minuit, 1990.

Derrida, Jacques. *La Dissémination*. Paris: Seuil, 1972.

———. "The Parergon." *October* 9 (1979): 3–40.

———. *Positions*. Paris: Minuit, 1972.

———. "Le Sans de la coupure pure." *Digraphe* 3 (1974): 5–31.

———. *La Vérité en peinture*. Paris: Flammarion, 1978.

Desbordes-Valmore, Marceline. *Poésies*. Paris: Gallimard, 1983.

Dixon, Wheeler W. *The Early Film Criticism of François Truffaut*. Bloomington: Indiana University Press, 1993.

Doane, Mary Ann, Patricia Mellencamp, and Linda Williams, eds. *Re-Vision: Essays in Feminist Film Criticism*. Los Angeles: University Publications of America, 1984.

Dolto, Françoise. *La Cause des enfants*. Paris: Robert Laffont, 1985.

———. *L'Image inconsciente du corps*. Paris: Seuil, 1984.

———. *Tout est langage*. Paris: Vertige du Nord / Carrere, 1987.

Ducrot, Oswald, and Tzvetan Todorov. *Dictionnaire encyclopédique des sciences du langage*. Paris: Seuil (Points), 1972.

DuBois, Page. *Sowing the Body: Psychoanalysis and Ancient Representations of Women*. Chicago: University of Chicago Press, 1988.

———. *Torture and Truth*. New York: Routledge, 1991.

Duden, Barbara. *L'Invention du foetus. Le corps féminin comme lieu public*. Paris: Descartes et Cie, 1996.

Durling, Robert, ed. *Petrarch's Lyric Poems: The Rime Sparse and Other Lyrics*. Cambridge, MA: Harvard University Press, 1976.

Eagle, Herbert. *Russian Formalist Film Theory*. Michigan Slavic Materials, no. 19. Ann Arbor: University of Michigan Press, 1981.

Felman, Shoshana. "Postal Survival, or the Question of the Navel." *Yale French Studies* 69 (1985): 49–70.

Ferril-Annis, Linda. *The Child before Birth*. Ithaca: Cornell University Press, 1978.

Flax, Jane. *Thinking Fragments: Psychoanalysis, Feminism, and Postmodernism in the Contemporary West*. Berkeley: University of California Press, 1990.

Flitterman-Lewis, Sandy. *To Desire Differently: Feminism and the French Cinema*. Chicago: University of Illinois Press, 1990.

Fontanier, Pierre. *Les Figures du discours*. Paris: Flammarion, 1968.

Foucault, Michel. *Discipline and Punish*. New York: Vintage Books, 1979.

———. "Qu'est-ce que les lumières?" *Le Magazine Littéraire* 309 (April 1993): 61–74.

Fozza, Jean-Claude, Anne-Marie Garat, and François Parfait. *Petite fabrique de l'image*. Paris: Magnard, 1993.

Freud, Sigmund. *Beyond the Pleasure Principle*. New York: Norton, 1961.

———. *Character and Culture*. New York: Collier Books, 1963.

———. *Cinq psychanalyses*. Paris: PUF, 1985.

———. *Inhibitions, Symptoms and Anxiety*. New York: Norton, 1959.

———. *The Interpretation of Dreams*. New York: Avon Books, 1965.

———. *L'Interprétation des rêves*. Paris: PUF, 1980.

———. *Jokes and Their Relation to the Unconscious*. New York: Norton, 1963.

———. *New Introductory Lectures on Psychoanalysis*. New York: Norton, 1965.

———. *On the History of the Psycho-Analytic Movement*. New York: Norton, 1966.

———. *The Sexual Enlightenment of Children*. New York: Collier Books, 1963.

———. *Sexuality and the Psychology of Love*. New York: Collier Books, 1963.

———. *The Three Essays on the Theory of Sexuality*. New York: Basic Books, 1962.

Friedrich, Carl, ed. *Immanuel Kant's Moral and Political Writings*. New York: Random House, 1949.

Friedrich, Hugo. *The Structures of Modern Poetry from the Mid-Nineteenth to the Mid-Twentieth Century*. Evanston: Northwestern University Press, 1974.

Fuzellier, Etienne. *Cinéma et littérature*. Paris: Editions du Cerf, 1964.

Galand, René. *Baudelaire poétiques et poésie*. Paris: Nizet, 1969.

Gallagher, Catherine, and Thomas Laqueur, eds. *The Making of the Modern Body: Sexuality and Society in the Nineteenth Century*. Berkeley: University of California Press, 1987.

Gallop, Jane. *The Daughter's Seduction: Feminism and Psychoanalysis*. Ithaca: Cornell University Press, 1982.

———. *Reading Lacan*. Ithaca: Cornell University Press, 1985.

———. *Thinking through the Body*. New York: Columbia University Press, 1988.

Gay, Peter. *Freud: A Life for Our Time*. New York: Norton, 1988.

Gillain, Anne. *François Truffaut. Le secret perdu*. Paris: Hatier, 1991.

———. *Le Cinéma selon François Truffaut*. Paris: Flammarion, 1988.

———. *Les 400 coups de François Truffaut*. Paris: Nathan, 1991.

Godfrey, Sima. "'Mère des souvenirs': Baudelaire, Memory and Mother." *L'Esprit Créateur* 25, no. 2 (1995): 32–44.

Goldstein, Laurence. *The American Poet at the Movies*. Ann Arbor: University of Michigan Press, 1994.

Gordon, Colin, ed. *Power/Knowledge: Selected Interviews and Other Writings by Michel Foucault*. New York: Pantheon Books, 1980.

Graves, Robert. *Greek Myths*. 2 vols. Baltimore: Penguin Books, 1957.

Green, André. "Logic of Object (a) and Freudian Theory." *Interpreting Lacan*. New Haven: Yale University Press, 1983.

Harrington, John. *Film and/as Literature*. Englewood Cliffs: Prentice-Hall, 1977.

Hayward, Susan, and Ginette Vincendeau, eds. *French Film, Texts and Contexts*. New York: Routledge, 1990.

Harter, Deborah. *Bodies in Pieces: Fantastic Narrative and the Poetics of the Fragment.* Stanford: Stanford University Press, 1996.

Heath, Stephen. *Questions of Cinema.* Bloomington: Indiana University Press, 1981.

Hegel, G. W. F. *Aesthetics: Lectures on Fine Arts.* Trans. T. M. Knox. Oxford: Clarendon Press, 1975.

———. *Esthétique. Textes choisis.* Paris: PUF, 1953.

Heidegger, Martin. *Poetry, Language, Thought.* Trans. and intro. Albert Hofstadter. New York: Harper and Row, 1971.

Hertz, Neil. *The End of the Line. Essays on Psychoanalysis and the Sublime.* New York: Columbia University Press, 1985.

Hollier, Denis, ed. *A New History of French Literature.* Cambridge, MA: Harvard University Press, 1989.

Hosek, Chaviva, and Patricia Parker, eds. *Lyric Poetry beyond New Criticism.* Ithaca: Cornell University Press, 1985.

Hubert, J. B. *L'Esthétique des "Fleurs du mal."* Genève: Cailler, 1953.

Huet, Marie-Hélène. *Monstrous Imagination.* Cambridge: Harvard University Press, 1993.

Hugo, Victor. *Choses vues.* Paris: Calmann Levy, 1900.

Insdorf, Annette. *François Truffaut.* Rev. ed. Cambridge: Cambridge University Press, 1994.

Irigaray, Luce. *Ce sexe qui n'en est pas un.* Paris: Minuit, 1977.

———. *Speculum de l'autre femme.* Paris: Minuit, 1974.

Jacobus, Mary. *Reading Woman—Essays in Feminist Criticism.* New York: Columbia University Press, 1986.

Jakobson, Roman. "'Les Chats' de Charles Baudelaire." *Questions de poétique,* 401–19. Paris: Seuil, 1973.

Johnson, Barbara. "Apostrophe, Animation, and Abortion." *Diacritics* (Spring 1986): 29–47.

———. *The Critical Difference.* Baltimore: Johns Hopkins University Press, 1980.

———. *Défiguration du langage poétique.* Paris: Flammarion, 1979.

———. "Gender and Poetry: Charles Baudelaire and Marceline Desbordes-Valmore." In *Understanding French Poetry: Essays for a New Millennium,* ed. Stamos Metzidakis. New York: Garland Publishing, 1994.

———. *A World of Difference.* Baltimore: Johns Hopkins University Press, 1987.

Jolly, Martine. *Introduction à l'analyse de l'image.* Paris: Nathan, 1994.

Kaës, R., D. Anzieu, and L. V. Thomas. *Fantasme et Formation.* Paris: Bordas (Dunod), 1984.

Kant, Immanuel. *The Critique of Judgement.* Trans. James Creed Meredith. Oxford: Oxford University Press, 1961.

Kaplan, E. Ann. *Motherhood and Representation: The Mother in Popular Culture and Melodrama.* London and New York: Routledge, 1992.

Karpf, Fay. *The Psychology and the Psychotherapy of Otto Rank.* Westport, CT: Greenwood Press, 1970.

Kaufman, Stanley. *A World on Film.* New York: Delta Books, 1958.

Klein, Melanie. *Envie et gratitude, et autres essais.* Paris: Gallimard, 1968.

————. *Envy and Gratitude and Other Works: 1946–1963*. New York: Free Press, 1975.

Klein, Melanie, and Joan Riviere. *Love, Hate and Reparation*. New York: Norton, 1964.

Klein, Richard. *Cigarettes Are Sublime*. Durham: Duke University Press, 1993.

Kline, T. Jefferson. *Screening the Text*. Baltimore: Johns Hopkins University Press, 1992.

Knibielher, Yvonne, and Catherine Fouquet. *Histoires des mères*. Paris: Montalba, 1977.

Kofman, Sarah. *L'Enigme de la femme. La Femme dans les textes de Freud*. Paris: Galilée, 1980.

————. *Pourquoi rit-on? Freud et le mot d'esprit*. Paris: Galilée, 1986.

Konisberg, Ira. *The Complete Film Dictionary*. New York: Meridian, 1987.

Kristeva, Julia. *Histoires d'amour*. Paris: Denoël, 1983.

————. *Pouvoirs de l'horreur*. Paris: Seuil, 1980.

————. *La Révolution du langage poétique*. Paris: Seuil (Points), 1974.

Lacan, Jacques. *Book 2: The Ego in Freud's Theory and in the Technique of Psychoanalysis*. Trans. Sylvana Tomaselli. New York and London: Norton, 1988.

————. "De la psychanalyse dans ses rapports avec la réalité." *Scilicet 1*. Paris: Seuil, 1968.

————. *Ecrits*. Paris: Seuil, 1966.

————. *Ecrits: A Selection*. Trans. Alan Sheridan. New York and London: Norton, 1977.

————. *Le Séminaire 2*. Paris: Seuil, 1978.

————. *Le Séminaire 4*. Paris: Seuil, 1994.

————. *Le Séminaire 7*. Paris: Seuil, 1986.

————. *Le Séminaire 11*. Paris: Seuil, 1973.

————. *Le Séminaire 20*. Paris: Seuil, 1975.

Lacoue-Labarthe, Philippe, and Jean-Luc Nancy. *The Literary Absolute*. Albany: SUNY Press, 1988.

Laplanche, Jean. *Nouveaux fondements pour la psychanalyse*. Paris: PUF, 1987.

————. *Vie et mort en psychanalyse*. Paris: Flammarion, 1970.

Laplanche, Jean, and J. B. Pontalis. *Fantasme originaire, fantasme des origines, origines du fantasme*. Paris: Hachette, 1985.

————. *Vocabulaire de la psychanalyse*. Paris: PUF, 1967.

Le Berre, Carole. *François Truffaut*. Paris: Etoile / Cahiers du Cinéma, 1993.

Lebovici, Serge, and Serge Stoléru. *Le Nourrisson, la mère et le psychanalyste*. Paris: Editions Bayard, 1994.

Lemoine-Luccioni, Eugénie. *Partage des femmes*. Paris: Seuil, 1976.

————. *La Robe. Essai psychanalytique sur le vêtement*. Paris: Seuil, 1983.

Lessing, Gotthold Ephraim. *Laocoön: An Essay on the Limits of Painting and Poetry*. Trans. Edward A. McCormick. Indianapolis: Bobbs-Merrill, 1962.

Leutrat, Jean-Louis. *Le Cinéma en perspective. Une histoire*. Paris: Nathan, 1992.

Lieberman, E. James. *Acts of Will: The Life and Work of Otto Rank*. New York: Free Press, 1985.

Loncke, Joycelynne. *Baudelaire et la musique*. Paris: Nizet, 1975.

Lussier, André. "Les Déviations du désir. Etude sur le fétichisme." *Revue Française de Psychanalyse* 47 (1983): 43–59.

Lyotard, Jean-François. *The Inhuman*. Stanford, CA: Stanford University Press, 1991.

Mannoni, Octave. *Clefs pour l'imaginaire ou l'autre scène*. Paris: Seuil, 1969.

Marini, Marcelle. *Lacan*. Paris: Pierre Belfond, 1986.

Marks, Elaine, and Isabelle de Courtivron, eds. *New French Feminism*. New York: Schocken Books, 1981.

Martin, Emily. *The Woman in the Body: A Cultural Analysis of Reproduction*. Boston: Beacon Press, 1987.

Mazzotta, Giuseppe. "The Canzoniere and the Language of the Self." *Studies in Philology* 75 (1978): 271–96.

Mehlman, Jeffrey. "Trimethylamin: Notes on Freud's Specimen Dream." *Diacritics* (Spring 1976): 42–45.

Menaker, Esther. *Otto Rank: A Rediscovered Legacy*. New York: Columbia University Press, 1982.

Metz, Christian. *Le Signifiant imaginaire*. Paris: Christian Bourgois, 1984.

Michelson, Annette, et al. *October: The First Decade, 1976–1986*. Cambridge, MA: MIT Press, 1987.

Miller, Jacques-Alain. "Suture (elements of the logic of the signifier)." *Screen* 13, no. 4 (1977–78): 24–34.

Mitry, Jean. *La Sémiologie en question. Langage et cinéma*. Paris: Editions du Cerf, 1987.

Modleski, Tania. *Feminism without Women: Culture and Criticism in a "Postfeminist" Age*. New York: Routledge, 1991.

Monaco, James. *The New Wave: Truffaut, Godard, Chabrol, Rohmer, Rivette*. New York: Oxford University Press, 1976.

Monk, Ray. *Ludwig Wittgenstein: The Duty of Genius*. New York: Penguin, 1991.

Morier, Henri. *Dictionnaire de poétique et de rhétorique*. Paris: PUF, 1961.

Mulvey, Laura. *Visual and Other Pleasures*. Bloomington: Indiana University Press, 1989.

———. "Visual Pleasure and the Narrative Cinema." *A Film Theory Reader*. New York: Columbia University Press, 1986.

Murray, Timothy. *Like a Film: Ideological Fantasy on Screen, Camera and Canvas*. London and New York: Routledge, 1993.

———. *Theatre Legitimation: Allegories of Genius in Seventeenth Century England and France*. New York: Oxford University Press, 1987.

Neuhoff, Eric. *Lettre ouverte à François Truffaut*. Paris: Albin Michel, 1987.

Nochlin, Linda. *The Body in Pieces: The Fragment as a Metaphor of Modernity*. New York: Thames and Huston, 1994.

O'Brien, Mary. *The Politics of Reproduction*. Boston: Routledge and Kegan Paul, 1981.

Olender, Maurice, "Aspects de Baubô." In *Revue de l'Histoire des Religions* 1 (Jan.–Mar. 1985): 3–55.

Olivier, Christiane. *Les Enfants de Jocaste. L'empreinte de la mère*. Paris: Denoël/Gonthier, 1980.

Ovide. *Les Métamorphoses*. Paris: Garnier Frères, Flammarion, 1966.

Paglia, Camille. *Sexual Personae: Art and Decadence from Nefertiti to Emily Dickinson*. New York: Vintage Books, 1991.

Pascal. *Pensées*. Paris: Librairie Générale Française, 1972.

Pétrarque. *Canzoniere*. Paris: Gallimard, 1983.

Pfeiffer, Ernst, ed. *Sigmund Freud and Andreas-Salomé: Letters*. Trans. William and Elaine Robson-Scott. New York: Norton, 1972.

Pichois, Claude, ed. *Baudelaire: Oeuvres complètes*. Paris: Gallimard (Bibliothèque de la Pléiade), 1975, 1976.

Pitcher, George. *The Philosophy of Wittgenstein*. Englewood Cliffs, NJ: Prentice-Hall, 1964.

Pontalis, J.-B. *Entre le rêve et la douleur*. Paris: Gallimard, 1977.

——, dir. "L'Enfant." *Nouvelle Revue de Psychanalyse 19*. Paris: Gallimard, 1979.

Pontalis, J.-B., and Jean Laplanche. *Fantasme originaire, fantasme des origines, origines du fantasme*. Paris: Hachette, 1985.

——. *Vocabulaire de la psychanalyse*. Paris: PUF, 1967.

Poulet, Georges. *La Poésie éclatée. Baudelaire/Rimbaud*. Paris: PUF, 1980.

Prouteau, Michel. *Les Miroirs de la perversité*. Paris: Albin Michel, 1984.

Rank, Otto. *Art and Artist: Creative Urge and Personality Development*. Trans. Charles Francis Atkinson. New York: Norton, 1989.

——. *The Trauma of Birth*. New York: Harcourt, Brace and Company, 1929.

——. *Le Traumatisme de la naissance*. Trans. S. Jankélévitch. Paris: Payot, 1976.

——. *Truth and Reality*. Trans. Jessie Taft. New York: Norton, 1978.

Raymond, Marcel. *De Baudelaire au surréalisme*. Paris: Corti, 1952.

Rentschler, Eric. "Terms of Dismemberment: The Body in/and/of Fassbinder's Berlin Alexanderplatz (1980)." *German Film and Literature.* New York: Methuen, 1986.

Rich, Adrienne. *Of Woman Born*. New York: Norton, 1986.

Riffaterre, Michael. *Sémiotique de la poésie*. Trans. Jean-Jacques Thomas. Paris: Seuil, 1983.

Ropars-Wuilleumier, Marie-Claire. *Le Texte divisé*. Paris: PUF, 1981.

Rosen, Philip, ed. *Narrative, Apparatus, Ideology: A Film Theory Reader*. New York: Columbia University Press, 1986.

Rosolato, Guy. "Le Fétichisme." *Le Désir et la perversion*. Paris: Seuil (Points 124), 1967.

——. "La Voix entre corps et langage." *Revue Française de Psychanalyse 37*, no. 1 (1974): 75–94.

Ross, John M. *What Men Want: Mothers, Fathers, and Manhood*. Cambridge, MA: Harvard University Press, 1994.

Ross, Kristin. *Fast Cars, Clean Bodies: Decolonization and the Reordering of French Culture*. Cambridge, MA: MIT Press, 1995.

Roubaud, Jacques. *La Vieillesse d'Alexandre. Essai sur quelques états récents du vers français*. Paris: Ramsay, 1988.

Ruddick, Sara. *Maternal Thinking: Towards a Politics of Peace*. New York: Ballantine Books, 1989.

Scarry, Elaine. *The Body in Pain*. Oxford: Oxford University Press, 1985.

Schor, Naomi. *Reading in Detail—Aesthetics and the Feminine*. New York: Methuen, 1987.

Scilicet 2/3. "Le Clivage du sujet et de son identification. Compte rendu du Séminaire 4: L'identification." Paris: Seuil, 1970.

Scilicet 6/7. "Jouissance et division." Paris: Seuil, 1976.

Seltzer, Mark. *Bodies and Machines*. New York and London: Routledge, 1992.

Showalter, Elaine, ed. *Speaking of Gender*. New York: Routledge, 1989.

Silverman, Kaja. "The Acoustic Mirror." *The Female Voice in Psychoanalysis and Cinema*. Bloomington: Indiana University Press, 1988.

———. *The Subject of Semiotics*. Oxford: Oxford University Press, 1983.

Sitney, Adams P. *Visionary Film: The American Avant-Garde*. New York: Oxford University Press, 1979.

Smadja, Robert. *Poétique du corps. L'image du corps chez Baudelaire et Henri Michaux*. New York: Peter Lang (Publications Universitaires Européennes), 1988.

Sontag, Susan, ed. *A Barthes Reader*. New York: Hill and Wang, 1983.

Sprengnether, Madelon. *The Spectral Mother: Freud, Feminism and Psychoanalysis*. Ithaca: Cornell University Press, 1990.

Stanton, Domna C. *Discourses of Sexuality: From Aristotle to Aids*. Ann Arbor: University of Michigan Press, 1992.

Suleiman Rubin, Susan ed. *The Female Body in Western Culture*. Cambridge, MA: Harvard University Press, 1986.

Suter, Ronald. *Interpreting Wittgenstein: A Cloud of Philosophy, a Drop of Grammar*. Philadelphia: Temple University Press, 1989.

Szasz, Thomas. *Pain and Pleasure: A Study of Bodily Feelings*. Syracuse: Syracuse University Press, 1988.

Sztulman, H., A. Barbier, and J. Caïn, eds. *Les Fantasmes originaires*. Toulouse: Privat, 1986.

Taylor, Richard, ed. *The Poetics of Cinema: Russian Poetics in Translation 9*. Oxford: RPT Publications, 1982.

This, Bernard. *Le Père. Acte de naissance*. Paris: Seuil, 1980.

Thompson, William, ed. *Understanding Baudelaire: A Collection of Readings*. Nashville: Vanderbilt University Press, 1997.

Todorov, Tzvetan. *Les Genres du discours*. Paris: Seuil, 1978.

Trebilcot, Joyce. *Mothering: Essays in Feminist Theory*. Totowa, NJ: Rowman and Allanheld, 1983.

Truffaut, François. "L'Amour en fuite." *L'Avant-scène du cinéma* 254 (1980).

———. *L'Argent de poche*. Paris: Flammarion, 1976.

———. *The Adventures of Antoine Doinel*. New York: Simon and Schuster, 1971.

———. *Les Aventures d'Antoine Doinel*. Paris: Mercure de France, 1970.

———. *Le Cinéma selon Hitchcock*. Paris: Lafont, 1966.

———. *Correspondance*. Paris: Hatier, 1988.

———. *Correspondence: 1945–1984*. Trans. Gilbert Adair. New York: Farrar, Straus and Giroux, 1990.

———. "L'Enfant Sauvage." *L'Avant-Scène Cinéma*, 1970.

———. *Les Films de ma vie*. Paris: Flammarion, 1975.

———. *The Films of My Life*. Trans. Leonard Mayhew. New York: Da Capo, 1994.

———. *L'Homme qui aimait les femmes*. Paris: Flammarion, 1977.

———. *Jules et Jim*. Paris: Seuil, 1971.

———. *La Nuit américaine*. Paris: Seghers, 1974.

———. *Le Plaisir des yeux*. Paris: Cahiers du Cinema, 1987.

———. *Les 400 coups*. Paris: Seghers, 1969.

———. *The Story of Adèle H*. New York: Grove Press, 1976.

———. *Truffaut par Truffaut*. Paris: Chêne, 1985.

Vallet, François. *L'Image de l'enfant au cinéma*. Paris: Cerf, 1991.

Vanoye, Francis, and Anne Goliot-Lété. *Récit d'analyse filmique*. Paris: Nathan, 1992.

Vernant, Jean-Pierre. *La Mort dans les yeux*. Paris: Hachette, 1986.

Vickers, Nancy J. "Diana Described: Scattered Woman and Scattered Rhyme." *Critical Inquiry* 8, no. 2 (Winter 1981): 265–79.

Weber, Samuel. *The Legend of Freud*. Minneapolis: University of Minnesota Press, 1982.

Wittgenstein, Ludwig. *Philosophical Investigations*. Trans. G. E. M. Anscombe. New York: Macmillan, 1953.

Wollen, Peter. *Signs and Meanings in Cinema*. Bloomington: Indiana University Press, 1969.

Young-Bruehl, Elisabeth, ed. *Freud on Women: A Reader*. New York: Norton, 1990.

Index